REASON, TRADITION,
AND THE GOOD

REASON, TRADITION, AND THE GOOD

MacIntyre's Tradition-Constituted
Reason and Frankfurt School
Critical Theory

JEFFERY L. NICHOLAS

University of Notre Dame Press

Notre Dame, Indiana

Copyright © 2012 by University of Notre Dame Press
Notre Dame, Indiana 46556
www.undpress.nd.edu
All Rights Reserved

Manufactured in the United States of America

Library of Congress Cataloging-in-Publication Data

Nicholas, Jeffery, 1969–
Reason, tradition, and the good : MacIntyre's tradition-constituted
reason and Frankfurt School critical theory / Jeffery L. Nicholas.
    p.   cm.
Includes bibliographical references and index.
ISBN-13: 978-0-268-03664-5 (pbk. : alk. paper)
ISBN-10: 0-268-03664-0 (pbk. : alk. paper)
E-ISBN: 978-0-268-08764-7
1. Political science—Philosophy. 2. Reason. 3. Critical theory.
4. Political sociology. 5. Frankfurt school of sociology. 6. MacIntyre,
Alasdair C. 7. Habermas, Jürgen.   I. Title.
JA71.N53   2012
320.01—dc23

                                                                2012014925

∞ *The paper in this book meets the guidelines for permanence and
durability of the Committee on Production Guidelines for Book Longevity
of the Council on Library Resources.*

To

JANET

I do not feel obliged to believe that the same God who has endowed us with sense, reason, and intellect has intended us to forgo their use.

—Galileo Galilei

When valour preys on reason, it eats the sword it fights with.

—William Shakespeare

Reason has always existed, but not always in a reasonable form.

—Karl Marx

Contents

Preface

We are rational animals, creatures endowed with reason. Yet our lives often seem irrational. We live lives of superstition, of faith, of fear, of nationalism, and reason often seems to be something we leave to those we think of as having more time or more education than we do. I grew up in two worlds: a world in which people had little time or money for formal education, where street smarts were more important than book smarts, and where you had to be careful not to let a black cat cross the street in front of you, and another world of books, imagination, and college-preparatory education with the idea that I would become a priest, one of those who, at least in my neck of the woods, were the smart ones.

When I discovered Voltaire and the Enlightenment in high school, I found a world of promise, of hope for humanity based in the full development of human reason for everyone. Voltaire's cry of *Écrasez l'infâme* stirred me, though not against the Church. A friend of mine in graduate school said he wanted a bumper sticker that read, "I'll let prayer in school when you let thinking in your church." I learned how to think in and through the Church, always challenged by priests and nuns, always challenged by the educators in my Catholic high school to think through things. Yet every day that I walked to school or to church, I witnessed the idiocy of our world: the poor and homeless, the hungry, people needing jobs in an era of cutting. We still lived under the imminent threat of nuclear war in the 1980s—not that we drilled for nuclear bombs, but we perceived the threat in the movies and stories we had. The infamy Voltaire warned against consisted in the prejudice and superstition and fear that I saw so much in the everyday world.

The present work has its roots deep in that experience of confronting an irrational world while being educated to believe that reason should direct our lives, that reason is the higher faculty of the human person. It arises from the fear found in Voltaire's "The Story of a Good Brahmin," in which a Brahmin, passing a poor woman doing her laundry, notices that she seems happier than he is, and wonders if it is because he is overeducated. Does reason lead, in the end, to happiness or to misery?

Through the years of studying philosophy, of being awakened to the satire of Monty Python, of learning politics and then learning about social justice and about the challenges of those like Herbert Marcuse and Michel Foucault to the twentieth-century world, the question of reason and happiness stayed with me. It took the form of the question of "enlightenment": does reason lead to a better, more just world?

This book says little of happiness, but it does address the failure of reason in modernity to bring about a just society, a society in which people can attain fulfillment. I argue that we rely too heavily on a conception of rationality that is divorced from tradition and, therefore, incapable of judging ends. Without the ability to judge ends, we cannot debate about the good life or the proper goods we as individuals and we as a society should pursue. I argue, in short, that the project of enlightenment failed because it was based on a deformed notion of reason as mere rationality, and that a critical theory of society aimed at human emancipation must turn to substantive reason, a reason constituted by and constitutive of tradition. Substantive reason comprises thinking about and acting on the set of standards and beliefs within a particular tradition. "Reason" names a set of social practices that involve the asking for and giving of reasons, the evaluation of those reasons and the asking for and giving of such, and, importantly, the evaluation of the good. It is the complete inability of enlightenment rationality to evaluate ends and the ability of substantive reason to evaluate ends that make the one unsuitable and the other suitable for a critical theory of society. The argument remains committed to the promise of reason to help individuals achieve a good and just society and a good life. It requires, however, a complete revolution in the way we approach social life at every level. It ends with some suggestions of what work is required to begin that revolution.

I could never have undertaken this work without the support of numerous people. The current book is a revision of a dissertation written under the direction of Theodor Schatzki at the University of Kentucky. He gave me free rein and encouragement to pursue the questions that drove me in an endeavor that really should have been and would have been beyond me had it not been for his careful reading, guidance, and challenges of my earlier work. I also owe thanks to Dan Breazeale, Wolfgang Natter, Ernie Yanarella, and Christopher Zurn. Wolfgang taught me, not the first, but the best course on early Frankfurt School critical theory, and he was always available to talk about the work of the Frankfurt School and encouraged me in other endeavors. Special thanks are due, also, to David Ingram, who came in at the last minute from a different university as an outside reader for the dissertation. The questions of all of these helped me to reframe the research and craft a better argument.

I also thank Gerald Twaddell, Kelvin Knight, and two anonymous readers provided by the University of Notre Dame Press who wrote detailed comments on an earlier draft of this book and encouraged its publication. Kelvin Knight, whom I first contacted about a different project on Alasdair MacIntyre, generously took time to read the full draft, pointed out ways I had misunderstood MacIntyre, and challenged me in how I addressed certain issues in the work, especially that of the human constants mentioned in the final chapter. He showed me, rightly, that I had more in common with MacIntyre than I originally understood. He has become a good colleague and friend since that time as we have worked together to build the International Society for MacIntyrean Enquiry (www.macintyreanenquiry.org). I also thank Chuck Van Hof, who guided me and the project through the review process at the University of Notre Dame Press.

To my great delight, I also owe thanks to Alasdair MacIntyre, who read and commented on chapter 4. He highlighted how I had originally missed the importance of the concept of truth in his work. Moreover, he has been a constant encouragement to me to publish this work when I was sure it did not deserve to be published.

Writing, of course, whether it's philosophy or fiction, does not occur in a vacuum, and I am indebted to my family and friends who supported me over the years, encouraging me, discussing my ideas with me, and challenging me: Christopher Ciocchetti, Brandon Clay-comb, and Ben Cordry. Brandon has spent many hours debating the issues at the heart of this work with me.

My greatest gratitude goes to my family. My children, Ana, Kyra, and Tesa, have spent many afternoons and nights keeping silent while I worked and sometimes even making dinner for themselves. My partner and wife, Janet, has been more than supportive, forcing me to march on when I wanted to have nothing more to do with this project or with philosophy, taking the children away for the weekend by herself, supporting my crazy career choice in philosophy, and just being there for me. *Amo te.*

Jeffery L. Nicholas
Good Friday/Earth Day
22 April 2011

Abbreviations of Frequently Cited Works

DOE	*Dialectic of Enlightenment.* Max Horkheimer and Theodor Adorno.
EC	"Epistemological Crises, Dramatic Narrative, and the Philosophy of Science." Alasdair MacIntyre.
Eclipse	*Eclipse of Reason.* Max Horkheimer.
Modernity	"Modernity: An Unfinished Project." Jürgen Habermas.
PMT	*Postmetaphysical Thinking.* Jürgen Habermas.
TCA1	*The Theory of Communicative Action,* vol. 1. Jürgen Habermas.
TCA2	*The Theory of Communicative Action,* vol. 2. Jürgen Habermas.
AV	*After Virtue.* Alasdair MacIntyre.
RPP	"Relativism, Power, and Philosophy." Alasdair MacIntyre.
3RV	*Three Rival Versions of Moral Enquiry.* Alasdair MacIntyre.
WJWR	*Whose Justice? Which Rationality?* Alasdair MacIntyre.

Introduction

The Question of Reason

"I want to be like Mike!" So went one advertisement for Nike. The Mike the character wanted to be like was Michael Jordan, former famed basketball player for the Chicago Bulls. Michael Jordan has been a spokesperson for Nike for many years, earning as much as $20 million per year. Nike, of course, is one of many multinational corporations that manufacture their products overseas. Allegedly Nike manufactures much of its apparel in sweatshops in Indochina. Such sweatshops pay their employees pennies a day; someone might earn 25¢ to churn out several pairs of Nike shoes that sell for over $100.00 a pair in the United States. In 1996, a *Time* magazine reporter confronted Michael Jordan about his endorsement of a company that uses sweatshop labor. Jordan replied, "My job with Nike is to endorse the product. Their job is to be up on that."[1]

"My own view is that science ought to be unfettered and that every possible alternative ought to be explored."[2] So stated former senator Arlen Specter concerning the continuing embryonic stem cell debate. Specter voices a common view among many people of modern Western democracies: science should proceed according to its own dictates. They allow no discussion of the ends of science, even with respect to how medical and biological science serve human beings. Rather, science occupies its own domain apart from ethics, and politics and government had best stay out of it.

1

| In 1998, Dolly was born. Dolly, a sheep, is (allegedly) the first mammal clone to be born alive. Since the announcement of that successful clone, the news media has been awash with reports of possible clonings of other animals, real clonings of other animals, and the march toward the first cloning of a human being. Former President Clinton created a committee to investigate the ethics of cloning, and cloning of human beings has been banned in the United States and other countries. Italy remains one country that has not banned cloning. There, Severino Antinori and Panayitie Zavos have established a clinic to research human cloning. Their interest lies in helping infertile couples, particularly since cloning represents the only chance that infertile males have to father genetic offspring. In discussing the ethics of their project, Antinori says, "Some people say we are going to clone the world, but this isn't true. . . . I'm asking all of us in the scientific community to be prudent and calm. . . . We're talking science, we're not here to create a fuss."[3]

| In the late 1990s, gambling got a big boost in the United States. Many gambling casinos were established throughout the country, including along the Ohio River and in Indiana. These casinos draw in large amounts of money from the surrounding states, which lacked (at the time) such gambling establishments. Access to casino gambling has, reportedly, hurt Kentucky horse racing. People have more opportunity to gamble at casinos, where they have more chances to win than at the racetrack. Thus, in 2002, the Kentucky state legislature passed a bill that allowed slot gambling in Kentucky at racetracks. Various Kentucky legislators and Kentucky newspapers debated the ethics and benefits of slot gambling in Kentucky. On Sunday, February 24, however, the editorial board of the Kentucky *Herald-Leader*, the main newspaper for central Kentucky, claimed that slot gambling was not an ethics issue because gambling already existed in the form of the racetrack and state lottery.

| In Cincinnati, Ohio, in 1990, the city council attempted to close the Contemporary Arts Center. They closed the museum because of a particular exhibit it was hosting—a series of photographs by Rob-

ert Mapplethorpe. Some of these photographs were of children in sexual situations, of men with objects inserted in their anuses, and of other sexually explicit material. In an interview about his work, Mapplethorpe explained that he identified with the Warhol movement. "I'm not talking so much about the product as the statement—I mean the fact that Warhol says 'anything can be art,' and then I make pornography art."[4]

   | What unites these five events? Not that they all involve morality or politics, though in fact they do. Nor is it a matter of clear-cut cases of what is right or wrong in these situations. Rather, the link between these five stories is the attitudes that their central figures have to questions about morality. Michael Jordan denies any responsibility for the morality of the situation with Nike; Senator Specter cried out to let science be, and Severino Antinori claims that he is just doing science and not creating a fuss, by which he means, a moral fuss; the editors of the *Herald-Leader* are not concerned about questioning the established moral practices in the state but about how to increase revenue; and Mapplethorpe is just making art. The question of morality does not arise for these actors. Morality is, instead, a matter for philosophers and theologians. The actors in the above stories simply consider the activities and means of achieving their individual goals in particular situations. They have emphatically embraced the differentiation of rationality spheres that marks modernity.

According to Jürgen Habermas (following Max Weber), cultural modernity is marked by the increasing differentiation of three rationality spheres: science, art, and morality and law. Whereas in premodernity issues and modes of justification were closely united across these three spheres, in modernity debates within each sphere go at their own pace without reference to debates in the others. Habermas claims that this differentiation of rationality spheres is progress. If the above scenarios are any indications, however, it is not clear that humanity can survive such progress. In the general American culture, many divorce issues of the good life from the discussion of right and wrong actions. Some separate questions of science and the role of technology and questions of business and profits from questions of the good life and notions of moral right and wrong. The notions of right and wrong have been eviscerated of any force of critique. They are no longer considered in the practical affairs of life, whether those be business (and welfare), science (and fertility), politics (and right), or art (and the good life).

International affairs highlight these issues even further. On September 11, 2001, two jetliners crashed into the twin towers of the World Trade Center in New York City, while another jetliner crashed into the Pentagon, and a fourth went down in Pennsylvania. These crashes were not accidents but intentional acts of destruction against the people of the United States. A group of Middle Eastern terrorists known as al Qaeda, spearheaded by Osama bin Laden and associated with the Taliban sect of Islam, which controlled Afghanistan, perpetrated these acts. President George W. Bush vowed revenge and immediately prepared a campaign to wipe evil from the face of the earth. To this end (among others), he ordered increased spending for the military in the United States.

The documentary *Why We Fight*, by Eugene Jarecki, discusses this particular war in the context of the political culture of the United States. Jarecki interviews a number of people, from Senator John McCain, Republican of Arizona, to former CIA analysts, to the grandson of President Dwight D. Eisenhower. The CIA use a term "blowback." This term names not an expected or foreseen reaction to some military action but an unexpected, unforeseen reaction to US military action that appears mysterious to the American public. It appears mysterious because the American public remains ignorant of many of the reasons and of the actions of the U.S. military in foreign countries. While examining this concept of blowback, Jarecki interviews the two stealth fighter pilots who dropped the first bunker-buster bombs on Baghdad at the beginning of the Iraq War on March 19, 2003. Reflecting on whether they regretted their actions since we later discovered that Saddam Hussein had no weapons of mass destruction, both pilots reported that they were soldiers who followed orders and could not question their commander.

When we combine the notion of blowback with the attitude of professional soldiers, we begin to see, again, an unwillingness to address the ethical issues of actions. At the individual level, the pilots make a seemingly obvious move and contend that soldiers cannot question the actions of their commanding officer. I am not worried here about whether their actions prove right or wrong. Rather, I highlight simply the fact that they have removed themselves as soldiers from ethical deliberation. Likewise, when the CIA is aware of possible blowback and yet continues to act, we have to recognize that policy trumps ethics. The issue, again, consists in a refusal to address ethical issues when appropriate. What Jarecki's movie points out is something that we can contemplate eight years later as President Obama orders the U.S. military to participate in the bombing of Libya. The question concerns not the justice of the war or motive but the lack of moral discussion before the engagement for "national interests."

The failure to question, to raise ethical issues, or to examine one's own way of life is common in modernity and in Western industrialized countries. These problems arise, I shall argue, from a certain lack. Modernity has stripped reason of its ability to evaluate and critique. Sure enough, many people do criticize and do evaluate the practices and political activities of their own countries and other nations. Yet these critiques lack both substance and force. They lack substance because they do not arise from a shared vision of right and wrong or a shared sense of community and justice, and they lack force because they cannot appeal to shared standards of reason that might motivate change. Rather, they arise from a reason that has fettered itself by reducing all value to self-preservation. Modernity is infected; it is infected by a reason that refuses to evaluate and question.

Proponents of the project of enlightenment during the historical Enlightenment period (see chapter 1) believed that critique would free humanity from constraints of irrational beliefs—from ignorance, religion, and myth. They sought to create a new human being—a rationally autonomous member of a scientifically based society (*DOE* 3). The philosophers of the Enlightenment sought an unchaining of humanity from the barbarisms that resulted from its subjection to the irrational forces of nature and the irrational forces of human society. Through enlightenment, or the "emergence from one's self-imposed immaturity"[5] or unwillingness to use one's reason, human beings were to take control of nature and society for the sake of freedom. When they established the control of society and nature as the ends of reason, thinkers, from Francis Bacon explicitly (through the direct mastery of nature) to Immanuel Kant implicitly (through the mastery of the will regardless of phenomenal circumstances), established a form of self-preservation as the goal of enlightenment. They did so by establishing subjective rationality, that is, instrumental rationality and formal rationality, as the dominant form of reason in modernity.

Subjective rationality consists of both instrumental rationality and formal rationality. I call them together subjective because they share a common, important trait: both instrumental rationality and formal rationality lack the ability to evaluate ends. Instrumentalists and formalists may argue against each other, just as siblings do, but they belong to a common rationality: subjective rationality. Subjective rationality, in its instrumentalist form, undergirds market capitalism as the most efficient means for satisfying pregiven ends in modernity. One only need consider Thomas Hobbes' conception of "reason," so characteristic of modernity, to understand the relationship between market capitalism and subjective rationality. For Hobbes, reason was mere reckoning and had nothing to do with selecting or evaluating goals already given to one by one's desires. If goals or desires cannot be evaluated because reason abandons the traditional beliefs that ground such evaluations, then the primary task facing individuals lies in satisfying those desires in the most efficient way possible. Market capitalism, as everyone knows, distributes resources for the satisfaction of desires most efficiently.

Subjective rationality in its formal aspect undergirds capitalism as the formal means of distributing scarce resources for the satisfaction of pregiven desires. In this case, Kant's formal principle of practical reason, the categorical imperative, supports capitalism because capitalism formalizes all relations by equalizing everything through the construct of money. Money or currency is purely formal and has no substantive content. People use money to purchase what goods they desire on the understanding that all others will do the same and bargain from formally equal positions.

Market capitalism embodies the perfected form of subjective rationality, which is aimed at satisfying individual desires and creating formal methods of transaction. It proves "true" because it is efficient, and efficiency must be made universal, because truth is universal. Its sole goal is the satisfaction of pregiven ends. It has come to encompass the globe, creating a fast-food, quick-entertainment culture by the process of industrialization Marx describes in *Capital* and making culture a product to sell in movies (*Seven Years in Tibet, Mulan*), food (Taco Bell, Olive Garden), and other cash products (The Bavarian Santa, Clinton Nesting Dolls). In so doing, capitalism extinguished more traditional ways of life.

While subjective rationality supports the capitalistic economic form, it lacks the ability to adjudicate ends or alternative ways of life. This lack means that it cannot evaluate different ethics that propose alternative ways of life and conceptions of the good. It can only show how people should act in order to satisfy their ends and support their ways of life. Subjective rationality, then, makes ethical values subjective and, thus, abets ethical relativism. These two movements of market capitalism and ethical relativism produce the paradoxical situation that humankind faces the loss of its variety of cultural living while cultures claim rights to exist in a pluralistic society. We gain meaningless cultural artifacts at the expense of traditional forms of life.

The argument presented here sets out to undermine not the only, but the *dominant* form of reason in modernity—subjective rationality. It locates itself in the critique of modernity so well formulated by the members of the early Frankfurt School, particularly Max Horkheimer. Horkheimer called for a renewed interest in reason and an investigation into the very roots of reason. Although I do not delve into those roots, I do propose a theory of reason to counter the modern form of subjective rationality. The argument continues the tradition of critical theory by analyzing the failure of modern, subjective rationality. It revises that tradition by proposing a merger with Alasdair MacIntyre's tradition-constitutive reason that, I will show, does not end in relativism.

I argue that an alternative to subjective rationality exists in its opposite—substantive reason. Substantive reason contrasts with subjective rationality in both its forms. That is, whereas subjective rationality as instrumental and/or formal lacks the ability to evaluate ends, substantive reason empowers its users to evaluate their ends and their very forms of reasoning. Even though Kant's categorical imperative means to critique "substantively" the utilitarian instrumentalist reason, it cannot be considered a form of substantive reason. Kant's formal (practical) rationality remains subjective because it remains formal— that is, unable to evaluate ends. The distinguishing characteristic of substantive reason consists in the ability to evaluate ends.

Such a substantive reason can only be found within traditions, however.[6] Thus, contrary to the Enlightenment penchant for opposing reason to tradition, the very power of reason depends on tradition. I reject, as a result, Jürgen Habermas's conception of communicative rationality, which searches for universal characteristics of practical rationality. I argue, instead, that a critical theory of society must turn to a tradition-constitutive and tradition-constituted conception of practical reason such as that developed by Alasdair MacIntyre. Using MacIntyre's theory, I develop a theory of substantive reason. Substantive reason is informed by a tradition's conception of the good and thereby able to sustain not only reason giving but also evaluation. Because reason is part of a tradition, the conception of the good within a tradition informs the very standards of reason. Its tradition-constituted nature means that people can not only make progress within their own tradition but also morally evaluate and learn from rival traditions. (I will discuss this point more in chapter 5.) A central function of reason, then, is justification or critique.

The rest of this introduction will provide a brief etymology of the term "reason" and offer a synopsis of the argument as a whole.

Etymology of "Reason"

The reader might find all of this discussion a little overbearing: Don't we know what reason is? Do we really need a three-hundred-page book to tell us? In fact, though reason is the central concept of philosophy from Parmenides on, agreement on its use remains elusive. Whereas the 1967 edition of the *Encyclopedia of Philosophy* states that "there is, then, no universally agreed or uniquely correct sense of 'reason,'"[7] the 1997 version omits an entry on reason altogether. Lest one think this omission indicates that a correct sense of reason has been found or that philosophers in their infinite wisdom have reached agreement about how to use this lofty term, the literature suggests otherwise. In 1995, Kurt Baier wrote, "It seems clear that there is no single such conception [of the faculty of reason and its powers] accepted in all the disciplines and contexts in which reason is invoked."[8] In short, what reason is remains unclear in the philosophical realm.

Given the fact of the disagreement about the proper understanding of reason in philosophy, the reader might find it useful to note the etymological roots of the term "reason." The *Oxford English Dictionary* lists "monetary reckoning" as an outdated sense of the term.[9] The dictionary also defines the idioms "*to give, yield* or *render (a) reason*" (italics original) as "to give an account (of one's acts or conduct)," designating these idioms, too, as archaic (although, of course, Habermas seizes upon this understanding of the term for his theory of communicative rationality). Other understandable and perhaps forgotten uses of the term are worth mentioning: a saying or observation, statement, or speech; a ground or cause for something; an intellectual power or faculty; the methods of science; and, in math, ratio.

The mathematical use calls to mind the Latin root of the words "reason" and "rationality": *ratio.* "Reason" itself derives from the French *raison,* which in turn derives from the Latin *ratio.* In Latin the word has meanings similar to those of English "rationality," though more mathematical and economic: "a reckoning, numbering, casting up, account, calculation, computation."[10] The third definition under *ratio* is "a reckoning, account, settlement, computation, explanation," with the qualifier "after full deliberation." Only in the final definition does one find such understandings as reasonableness, propriety, and law. The Greek *logos,* whose primary sense is "word" or "speech," is also sometimes translated "reason" and can refer to a computation or a reckoning of an amount of money, an account of the relation between objects, or an explanation, particularly a plea or case in law or argument.[11] The history of the term "reason," then, shows it to refer at once to formal calculation and to what is sometimes taken today to be its primary referent: a reason for or explanation of something (a belief, action, etc.).

What is it one asks for when one requests a reason or an explanation? What is it one offers when one proffers an explanation or reason?

A reason is not merely an excuse for a belief or action; if it were, we would never accuse anyone of just making excuses. The deeper meaning of providing a reason, then, is providing a justification. Justification depends on something passing muster, or certifies that it does so—that it has been evaluated. The argument of this book will demonstrate that reason is a practice of evaluation, that human beings can evaluate their ends and goals, and that they can do so because reason is constituted by tradition. This evaluation means, at least, giving reasons for; but reason giving seems too limited a concept to capture all of what substantive reason does as both constituted by and constituting tradition.

Reason, then, is not rationality, though we often use the words interchangeably. Following Max Horkheimer and the general tradition of continental philosophy, I use the term "rationality" to refer to instrumental and means-ends forms of reasoning, of which logical procedures and categorization are examples. The term "reason" is broader, encompassing not only means-ends reasoning but also the broader categories of giving and asking for reasons, evaluating ends, and deciding whether something is worthy. Rationality, consequently, is a subspecies of reason.

I shall defend the following conception of reason, to which I will refer often throughout the book:

> Reason names a set of social practices that involve the asking for and giving of reasons, the evaluation of those reasons and the asking for and giving of such evaluation, and, importantly, the evaluation of the good. It comprises thinking about and acting on the set of standards and beliefs of a particular social order.

Synopsis

The first chapter lays out the need for a concept of substantive reason. The early Frankfurt School of critical theory criticizes modernity for its failure to bring about freedom because of a reliance on subjective rationality. Horkheimer and his associates relied on a Marxism developed by Gyorgy Lukács that combined Karl Marx's notion of reification with

Max Weber's notion of rationalization. The union of Marx and Weber allowed Horkheimer and his associates to examine how, throughout history, reason has led to the reification of social life. Reification, in turn, inevitably led to domination. Interestingly, Horkheimer and company connect the domination of nature with the domination of human beings; both forms of domination result from reification, of nature and of humanity. This reification, moreover, results from the dominance of a particular form of reason—subjective rationality.

The problem with subjective rationality, according to Horkheimer, is that it proves incapable of evaluating ends: as the dominant form of reason in modernity, subjective rationality systematically prevents the evaluation of ends on an individual and social level. At times, however, Horkheimer suggests that subjective rationality does have content, namely, the promotion of self-preservation. Later, I shall show that subjective rationality is, indeed, not devoid of content. Its failure lies, instead, in its reduction of all evaluation to instrumental evaluation. This fact, however, does not undermine Horkheimer's analysis, for the problem of modernity still lies in the domination of subjective rationality, which results in the reification of human beings and nature. The solution called for by Horkheimer is the development of a substantive reason—a reason capable of evaluating ends.

Chapter 2 examines one response to this problem, the notion of communicative rationality as developed by Jürgen Habermas, the prominent contemporary heir to the Frankfurt School. Habermas importantly shows where Horkheimer's analysis of modernity fails and provides an initial step toward a conception of substantive reason. According to Habermas, the analysis of modernity developed by Horkheimer and his colleagues remained tied to a philosophy of consciousness. More adequate analyses and responses require moving to a philosophy of language. Habermas bases his philosophy of language on the idea that human beings through communicative language come to an understanding with their interlocutors. This conception of language as oriented toward understanding informs his notion of communicative action, in whose terms the notions of freedom and equality can be spelled out and given some grounding as values for social organization. Communicative rationality lies in the willingness and ability of actors to make and defend validity claims. Therefore, it is procedural and situated. That is, communicative rationality is a formal procedure that recognizes its historical and social origin and use.

Habermas's communicative rationality moves beyond a philosophy of individual consciousness and recognizes that reason is located in and rests upon social interaction. In calling communicative rationality "postfoundational," Habermas rejects the idea that rationality proves capable of resolving all issues. Moreover, because language is used to reach understanding, interlocutors can question each other in order to reach that understanding. Such questioning may involve discovering not only the reasons for a given belief, request, or action but also whether the reasons given are appropriate. Hence, Habermas's communicative rationality is a move in the right direction. Communicative rationality, however, fails to amount to a substantive notion of reason. Relying on Charles Taylor's criticisms of Habermas, I argue that, as a procedural—or "formal," as Habermas calls it—rationality, communicative rationality fails to recognize its own underlying substantive values. In other words, Habermas draws from the notion of a formal conception of rationality substantive values for interaction with others. Without prior commitment to those values, however, communicative language lacks moral force: it remains a reason incapable of evaluating ends.

The rest of the book develops a substantive reason capable of evaluating ends. I begin, in chapter 3, with Alasdair MacIntyre's theory of tradition-constituted reason. The move to MacIntyre's work as a resource for critical theory might surprise many; it ought not to. I begin by showing that MacIntyre's critique of modernity resembles Horkheimer's: both place the failure of modernity in the inability of individuals and society to evaluate ends, and both see that failure as a result of the dominance of a faulty conception of reason. MacIntyre develops a conception of reason to combat this failure, by arguing that reason is constituted by and constitutes tradition: what is reasonable from the point of view of one tradition may be unreasonable from that of another. The very standards of reason found within a tradition vary because those standards are constituted by the tradition. I examine MacIntyre's notion of tradition-constituted and -constitutive reason by reviewing his arguments from the history of moral philosophy and from his analysis of cosmology-laden languages. Thomas Kuhn's conception of a disciplinary matrix proves a useful way of thinking about MacIntyre's ideas on tradition and reason.

While MacIntyre provides a convincing argument for understanding reason as constituted by tradition, his analysis requires elaboration to show that reason is capable of judging ends because, as constituted by tradition, it is informed by a conception of the good in its tradition. In chapter 4, therefore, I suggest that MacIntyre cannot account for the ability of a tradition-constituted reason to judge ends because he does not fully spell out the relationship between the standards of reason and the conception of the good found in a tradition. Moreover, MacIntyre deals solely with what he calls traditions of enquiry. Such philosophical traditions are rarefied phenomena and do not give much guidance to comprehending reason in concrete, cultural traditions.

I demonstrate, further, exactly how the conception of the substantive good in a tradition constitutes and is constituted by the standards (exemplars and paradigms) of reason in the tradition. That is, I examine the interrelated concepts of tradition, the good, and reason in order to show that the standards of reason found in a tradition are informed by that tradition's conception of the good. This examination proves thick: I look at three cultural traditions to bring out this interrelationship.

Following MacIntyre, I define "tradition" as a socially and historically embedded set of arguments about the good with insiders and outsiders. A tradition embraces a cosmology, a conception of the good, values and symbolic generalizations, ways of life, and exemplars of reason. All conceptions of the good that are held by traditions defined in this way can be defined as the best that is achievable by human beings conceived of as such and such a kind of creature. These conceptions, that is, rely on or are informed by a conception of human nature. What a tradition conceives as the best possible condition of a human being is what that tradition defines as the good. These conceptions of the good, in turn, determine, in part, the standards of reason in a tradition: what is reasonable in a tradition is determined by what is considered worthy or good. These standards of reason then allow human beings and traditions in general to evaluate their ends, their conceptions of the good, and their very standards of reason in light of a conception of the good. A substantive reason has been found! The hermeneutic circle here is nonvicious, as chapter 5 will show.

My discussions and comparisons center on various concrete traditions. Philosophical traditions include more rarefied theorizing, whereas cultural traditions are lived daily by groups of people. I examine such philosophical traditions as Aristotelianism, Thomism, Humeanism, Kantianism, and Utilitarianism. I also look at three cultural traditions: Roman Catholicism, Zande magic, and Lakota conceptions of landownership. This analysis highlights some of the important relationships between the conception of the good and the conception of human nature in a tradition.

Further, each of these three cultural traditions brings something unique to the analysis. Roman Catholicism, for instance, is a tradition with a natural bridge to more philosophical ones (though I consider only Thomism in this chapter, one could also make links to Augustinianism, Franciscanism, Liberation Theology, etc.). Furthermore, the Roman Catholic tradition is both historically rich and highly intellectual. Finally, because it is a tradition that the author lives (or attempts to), examining Roman Catholicism provides the opportunity for the special insight that comes from being a member of that tradition. Studying the Zande magic tradition, on the other hand, offers different benefits. Foremost among these is the significant amount of secondary literature about the Azande. Indeed, many of the debates about the intercultural comparisons of reason have centered on the Azande. The examination of the Lakota tradition, finally, provides yet a third benefit. It is both a non-Western tradition and a tradition with which many are not familiar (to their detriment). These two factors make the Lakota tradition concerning landownership ideal for discussing different conceptions of the good, ideals of the human person, and standards of reason. Together, these three cultural traditions provide ample resources for discussing various issues concerning substantive reason as it is actualized in nonphilosophical traditions.

Having developed a substantive reason that sees the standards of reason constituting and constituted by the substantive good of a tradition, I must address two criticisms: incoherence and relativism. Might the holy grail of a substantive reason be the result of the fitful throes of a demonic dream? Donald Davidson has argued that the idea of a conceptual scheme is incoherent. The notion of a substantive reason constituted by tradition as developed in this book gainsays that thesis. Davidson's error lies in his equating the issue of conceptual schemes with the issue of translating languages. By contrast, I argue that traditions, though embodied in language, cannot be understood simply as mere languages. Davidson and critics of MacIntyre have misunderstood MacIntyre's position.

Other readers will argue that a theory that situates reason in traditions leads to a relativism that allows all sorts of atrocities. If reason is bound by tradition, so many will argue, then reason cannot adjudicate disputes between different traditions: such an understanding of reason denies a universal reason and, therefore, a universal justice. In reply to this argument, I affirm Richard Bernstein's rejection of the objectivism/relativism dichotomy. Objectivism and relativism arise only on the premise that reason must be foundational or arise from sure foundations. Rejecting such a foundational premise undercuts the charge of relativism. Moreover, the notion of truth is fundamental both to MacIntyre's tradition-constituted reason and to my substantive reason. As MacIntyre shows, members of traditions make truth claims that are claims about adequacy to the world. Such adequacy is judged according to historical experience in the world.

My final argument, in chapter 5, begins with MacIntyre's discussion of reasonable progress within traditions. Traditions can undergo an epistemological crisis, in the face of which they must evolve if they are to cope. Such evolution is reasonable if it meets the standards of reason within the tradition; it is not the case that anything counts as reasonable or unreasonable. Of course, a tradition may not be able to cope with its crisis. In the face of failure a tradition might, using its own standards of reason, come to recognize another tradition to be more reasonable than itself and adopt that other tradition. Change between traditions can, then, also be reasonable.

MacIntyre's arguments deal only with epistemological crises. To address the more pressing cases of moral crises, I turn, in chapter 5, to the work of Charles Taylor. Developing the notion of ad hominem arguments, Taylor incorporates MacIntyre's notion of reasonable progress within traditions into his discussion of practical reason. He goes beyond MacIntyre in defending further forms of ad hominem reasoning and in utilizing Hans-Georg Gadamer's notion of a fusion of horizons. Unlike MacIntyre, consequently, Taylor sees traditions not as atomistic islands in a sea but as fluid entities capable of expanding their horizons to include alien notions from rival traditions. Members of traditions/cultures encounter empirical constants that serve as correctives to beliefs in those traditions and provide a foothold for intercultural and intertraditional dialogue. That is, they provide opportunities for and encourage "learning from" other cultures. In sum, rather than succumbing to a false dichotomy between objectivism and relativism, a substantive reason provides the very opportunities for inter- and cross-cultural comparisons and for growth in wisdom. It does so by allowing what subjective rationality cannot permit—the evaluation of ends and of reason itself.

If I defend a conception of substantive reason as tradition-constituted and tradition-constitutive, then my argument itself must belong to and extend a tradition. It should be obvious from the discussion that my argument attempts to merge the work of Frankfurt School critical theorists like Horkheimer and Marcuse with the work of Alasdair MacIntyre and Charles Taylor. That is, I attempt a marriage of (a version of) Marxism and a (version of) Thomistic-Aristotelianism. Of these figures, Horkheimer and Marcuse establish the primary research question, while Taylor and, most significantly, MacIntyre establish the answer that I then develop. MacIntyre is, I think, a premier philosopher with many insights into human social life and the life of reason. He has contributed significantly to several prominent debates, including the rationality debates in the philosophy of social science during the 1970s and the renewal of virtue theory in the 1980s. His work provides a unique vantage point, which all discussions of tradition and reason must consider.

Though my concept of substantive reason arises from MacIntyre's theory of a tradition-constituted reason, the concept of substantive reason I develop goes beyond his. It does so, first, in grasping the relationship between substantive reason and the conception of the good in a tradition. Second, my theory more substantively grapples with cultural traditions, like that of the Azande and the Lakota. Finally, where MacIntyre provides a starting point for social analysis with a theory of tradition-constituted reason, I bring that starting point into discussion with the (so-far) failure of another tradition: Frankfurt School critical theory. MacIntyre's philosophy, especially his discussion of practices, proves revolutionary.[12] My theory attempts to expand that revolutionary potential by discussing substantive reason as a foothold for a critical theory of society (more of which will be spelled out in my concluding reflections). Because it allows reasonable comparisons with other societies, substantive reason establishes a foothold for undermining practices of power and domination by showing alternative conceptions of good and evil found within traditions. In so doing, it gains greater power of evaluation. MacIntyre is a hero, but one who stands alongside Horkheimer and Marcuse.

1 | The Frankfurt School Critique of Reason

Denunciation of what is currently called reason is the greatest service reason can render.

—*Eclipse* 187

Over sixty years ago, Max Horkheimer and Theodor Adorno penned their *Dialectic of Enlightenment*. They would be the first to admit that all texts have their own historicity—texts are defined by their history and their social milieu. Yet the *DOE* still speaks to us today. This chapter addresses in a fundamental way the question, how does what Horkheimer and Adorno wrote in those pages pertain to contemporary American society?

This analysis will adopt Horkheimer and Adorno's underlying principle, namely that social freedom is inseparable from enlightened thought. What they add to that starting point, however, makes their analysis useful for today. I will address five theses:

1. the Enlightenment has failed, and everywhere humanity is in chains;
2. these chains are not simply associated with capitalism;
3. rather, a whole system of domination underlies capitalism, a domination of human beings and of nature;
4. this domination involves the reification or objectification of human persons and of nature;
5. finally, this objectification results from a particular conception and use of reason as subjective rationality.

In short, one could state the central theme of the *DOE* as follows: subjective rationality "reduces truth to success and, in the process, robs reason of all substantive content."[1] The *DOE* shows that modernity emphasizes a form of reason, subjective rationality, incapable of evaluating ends. In modernity, reason lacks all content because it does not reference some higher order outside of the subjective end of the self-preservation of individual human beings. The analysis of what Horkheimer and Adorno offer is apropos of contemporary social and political theory exactly where they point to the domination of subjective rationality in modernity and to its results. The dialectic of the Enlightenment rests simply in the fact that, at the same time that the Enlightenment aimed to free humanity from the tyranny of nature and tradition (particularly, religion), it removed all possibility of such freedom by gutting reason. Once we understand this failure of reason, this gutting by Enlightenment philosophy, we will be able to pursue a more substantive conception of reason in the following chapters.

The Term "Enlightenment"

Before one can understand the dialectic of enlightenment as discussed by Horkheimer and Adorno, one must first understand the term "Enlightenment," the name both of a time period and an idea. The Enlightenment refers to that period in history from about 1650 to 1800 CE in Europe during which leading thinkers focused on freedom and social progress. The term "the Enlightenment" refers foremost to a period in time marked off from others by what is referred to as its project. This project, which can be called enlightenment, involved the promotion of autonomous reason and science as a privileged form of knowledge—or what was called enlightenment.[2]

The term "enlightenment" refers generally to the idea that human beings can find freedom or a better life through the use of their reason. Plato's allegory of the cave provides an excellent statement of the idea of enlightenment. Through the use of reason, humanity can "see" the world as it truly is and find happiness through that insight. The world is lit up for humanity. The idea of enlightenment plays a similar, though not identical, role in Eastern philosophy and religion as well. The Buddhist Noble Eightfold Path is designed to help the individual person achieve enlightenment. Of course, further comparisons and contrasts can be made here, specifically dealing with the role and notion of reason in Platonic philosophy and Buddhism. Platonic philosophy and Buddhism show, however, that the concept of enlightenment can be broader than that conceived in the Enlightenment period and may be defined differently outside of the Enlightenment period. I shall always capitalize the word "enlightenment" when it refers to the time period and leave the term in lower case letters when it refers to the idea.

Understanding the *DOE,* however, requires a more thorough analysis of the concept of enlightenment during the Enlightenment period and in modernity. To begin, one can speak of two different Enlightenment projects. The first involves the rational foundations of a free society; the second, the establishment of morality on neutral reason, or the independent rational justification of morality. This second project is the key target of the criticism of modernity offered by Alasdair MacIntyre. I will deal with that project and his analysis in the third chapter. Horkheimer and Adorno, on the other hand, have as their main target the attempt to provide rational foundations for social freedom.

Still, their analysis of enlightenment can be confusing. Horkheimer and Adorno use the term in two different ways, one positive and one negative, because they want to expose the dialectic of enlightenment. As a dialectical concept, enlightenment has both a positive and a negative side. One part of the concept represents the aim to free humanity from its fear of nature and society, while the other part represents the interests of domination—the domination of nature and of humanity. Horkheimer and Adorno's critique of enlightenment aims to prepare a foundation for a positive notion of enlightenment no longer entangled in blind domination.

Positively, the notion of enlightenment entails that humanity can increase its freedom through the use of reason. During the Enlightenment period, however, enlightenment itself was caught up in a blind domination—the domination of subjective rationality. The dialectic of enlightenment is that at the same time that enlightenment aims at freedom through reason, it also binds human beings to oppressive structures through its alliance with subjective rationality. In the Enlightenment, which embraced finally and fully the movement of freedom, subjective rationality worked to undermine the project of enlightenment and of the Enlightenment. The *DOE,* however, points out that subjective rationality has been with philosophy for a long time, since at least the writing of the *Odyssey* and maybe since the dawn of time. It is now time to reveal the stowaway and, in the process, undermine its hold on us.

The *DOE* picks out, then, the role of reason in the service of both enlightenment and domination. It proves useful to distinguish two notions of (practical) reason: the rational and the reasonable. "Rationality" shall always refer to those more formal aspects of reasoning—logic, classification, instrumental thinking, and so on. "Reason" shall always designate reasoning that in some way references an *ordo* in the universe. One can say of an action that it is rational, in that it satisfies a formal procedure or satisfies the agent's subjective desires; but being rational does not make an action reasonable, nor vice versa. A reasonable action is one that an agent has good reasons for doing or for which the agent can give, on being asked, good reasons. A Zande witch might fail to be rational while being reasonable. As the discussion proceeds, it will both clarify and defend this distinction between the rational and the reasonable.

The Dialectic of Enlightenment

One of the central claims of the *DOE* is that myth becomes enlightenment and that enlightenment becomes myth. This claim highlights the dialectic of enlightenment—that it contains the seeds of its own destruction. The crux of the *DOE* entails understanding that dialectic. For Horkheimer and Adorno, the alliance between enlightenment thought and subjective rationality in the Enlightenment and throughout the history of philosophy brought about the dialectic of enlightenment—that enlightenment contains its own reversal. The use of subjective rationality in modernity is the true cause of the failure of the Enlightenment project, for the philosophers of this time associated enlightened thought with subjective rationality in the form of scientific thinking. Scientific thinking, according to much Enlightenment belief, served as the true key to freedom by releasing humanity from its fear of nature and its submission to the authority of tradition. On Horkheimer and Adorno's account, however, scientific thinking cannot do that. Nor, according to them, is enlightened thought simply a symptom of modernity; it can be traced back through time to the *Odyssey*. Horkheimer and Adorno hope to uncover in their analysis of that work the bourgeois individual—the individual who sacrifices himself for the mastery of nature. Thus, the first essays in the *DOE* combine a critique of science, a critique of enlightenment thought, and a philosophy of history.

I shall focus on two aspects in the *DOE*: the philosophy of history and the critique of enlightenment thought. Part of the critique offered in the *DOE* centers on Kant's epistemology. A discussion of Kant's epistemology, however, would not add to the movement of the argument, and so I shall avoid that discussion.

Accepting Lukács

To understand Horkheimer and Adorno's discussion of the *Odyssey* and of myth and enlightenment, the meaning they ascribe to "domination," and their claim that fascism was an extreme form of capitalism requires understanding their acceptance of the Lukácsian merger of Marx and Weber. While the *DOE* is Marxist in framework, in it Horkheimer and Adorno present a more robust critique of modernity by changing that framework. They do so by accepting Gyorgy Lukács's synthesis of Marxian analysis and Weberian social theory. They use that new synthesis to develop a philosophy of history that looks for the root of the failure of Enlightenment thought in the history of Western philosophy. From its inception, the Institute for Social Research aimed at a Marxist analysis of society. Its founder, its directors, and its members were Marxists of some sort.[3] Generally, Marxists focus on class conflict. Yet the claims of Horkheimer and Adorno in the *DOE* extend beyond a critique of capitalism. In the *DOE* the analysis of class conflict takes secondary position to an analysis of a larger conflict—that between nature and society. Rather than seeing economics as the motor of society, they view the conflict between humanity and nature as the driving force.[4] This change is only one of a number of possible departures from traditional Marxism.[5]

Lukács's seminal *History and Class Consciousness* provides the background for Horkheimer and Adorno. In this work, Lukács combined the conception of reification in Marxism with the concept of rationalization in Max Weber's work.[6] "Capitalist development is for Lukács the source of reification. The core of this development is—and here Lukács aligns himself with Max Weber—a constantly 'increasing rationalization.'"[7] Marx's base-superstructure becomes, then, a form of increasing rationalization which is the true cause of dehumanization. Rationalization is more general than the capitalist mode of production.

Quantification serves as the central motif of the Marxian concept of reification and the Weberian concept of rationalization. The Marxian concept of reification referred to the quantification of labor as time and money relations. The Weberian concept of rationalization meant that calculation allows one to master all things. Quantification, however, leads to ever greater control of human beings. It removes any notion of a subject in itself and replaces it with the notion of an object for manipulation. For Lukács, capitalism is another form of rationalization. It quantifies desires, labor, and human beings for efficiency.

Following Lukács's lead, Horkheimer and Adorno picked up on the central concept of rationalization as control through quantification. For them, quantification becomes the dominant thrust in the historical development of Western society. Thus, Horkheimer and Adorno, unlike Marx, attack not simply the economic structure of society but the whole process of demystification—or rationalization. They saw in Weber's notion of rationalization Marx's concept of reification now construed more broadly.[8] The *DOE* showed that modern culture rested on a history in which humanity established its rule over nature. Horkheimer and Adorno boldly claimed that the continual cultural crisis was a crisis in the fundamental principle of human culture till then. This principle was exactly the tendency toward rationalization. Behind this claim lay the following thesis: the decisive event in human history "was not the development of the modern person and of capitalism, but rather humanity's transition to domination over nature."[9]

From Myth to Enlightenment

To prove this claim Horkheimer and Adorno must step outside of an analysis of the Enlightenment and look at the concept of enlightenment throughout the history of Western civilization. This concept of enlightenment contrasts with the concept of myth. For Horkheimer and Adorno, enlightenment "refers to that mode of 'enlightened' thought which emancipates human beings from the despotism of myth and helps them to control and dominate nature."[10] Yet myth itself has rational elements, that is, attempts to quantify and control nature. Myth and enlightenment, then, turn into each other.

According to Horkheimer and Adorno, myth not only reports and names but also presents, confirms, and explains (*DOE* 8). The rituals associated with myths both described a determined process and also intimated that it could be controlled through magic. Magic embodied the "primitive" human relationship to nature. Magic filled the universe with spirit. As magical, nature was also enchanted. In magic, the spirits of nature could be influenced, but never controlled.

The shaman mimics but never identifies with the objects in nature. Within that mimesis, however, lie the seeds of sovereignty. The invisible power that is worshiped becomes something to which to attain (*DOE* 10). The spirit becomes distinct from nature, laying the road for replacement of representation in magic with universal interchangeability in science. This interchangeability means, for Horkheimer, that all objects in science have no meaning of themselves but only occupy a place within a scientific act. Whereas magic imitates nature, science conceptualizes. In the shaman's magic, an object represents both something other and something which it is like. In scientific practice, the object no longer represents something but is identified as that thing—it is a specimen, something petrified and fixed. In magic, the object has meaning because of its place in an objective system within the world. In science, the object has no meaning outside that given to it by the scientist. All spirit is removed in enlightenment thought. The disenchantment that came with the Enlightenment "is the extirpation of animism" (*DOE* 5).

The antithesis of enlightenment and mythology rests on the principle by which reason "merely" opposes all that is unreasonable (*DOE* 89). On the one hand, myth sees spirit only as immersed in nature. On the other hand, enlightenment replaces spirit with subjectivity. That is, myth finds meaning in nature and natural forces whereas enlightenment seeks meaning in the subject.

In the Enlightenment, according to Horkheimer, subjectivity takes on a particular meaning. The subject stands against nature. The subject appears as ordered and nature as chaotic. Nature is objectified as something outside of the subject. Rationality, as subjective, neutralizes nature, removes all meaning from nature. It must because, no longer tied to an objective hierarchy in the universe, it can reference only the instrumental, formal value of nature outside of humanity. We see this both in Mill's utilitarianism, which reduces every thing to a function of utility, and in Kant's philosophy, which locates meaning in the noumenal realm, inaccessible to the human being except as a demand of practical rationality. Subjectivity, then, becomes a "unique, unrestricted, though vacuous authority" (*DOE* 89–90). Enlightenment sought to remove belief in a transcendent order of nature to which human beings were subject. It did so by characterizing the forces of nature as meaningless resistance to the power of the human subject. The human subject, accordingly, is an authority that is unique in and outside of nature. It becomes unrestricted in its ability to use rationality to master nature; but it also becomes vacuous, for it loses meaningfulness itself. Human subjectivity can no longer refer to an order of nature from which it gains purpose. Subjectivity takes the form of a purposeless purposiveness.

Nor can the subject find meaning within itself. Totalitarian rationality removes all meaning from the world because the subject becomes yet another quantified object. To have meaning, it must have some objective place in the world. Objectivity in terms of values, however, is removed to be replaced by objectivity in terms of quantification, a different sort of value. The moral value of the subject becomes subject to the calculative value of science.

Because subjectivity can master only a de-animated nature, though, imitating its rigidity and ridding itself of spirit, everything becomes identified in a unity in rationality. With rationality, all meaning is re-moved from nature. Nature is reunified under a principle. Enlighten-ment thought systematizes nature. In so doing, it purges nature of spirit, by mimicking nature in thought and scientific practice.

Enlightenment Thought/Scientific Thought

Contemporary science reveals the interest of industrial society as systematization. All that matters within industry is the repeatable manufacturing of material. This whole system determines perception: "The citizen sees the world as the matter from which he himself manu-factures it" (*DOE* 84). In the process of production, judgment adjusts to confirm itself. That is, the processes of production in which human beings partake form their understanding. This formation guarantees that the understanding will only concur with the public judgment of industrial society—everything should aim at production and survival. In modernity, contends Horkheimer, the side of domination wins out.

"In the face of scientific reason moral forces are no less neutral im-pulses and modes of behavior than the immoral forces into which they suddenly change when directed not to that hidden possibility but to reconciliation with power" (*DOE* 86). For the Enlightenment, ratio-nality can only be scientific. It is the faculty of calculation, of planning, and of procedure, remaining neutral with respect to ends. As such, rationality can neither posit nor judge substantive goals—even a goal such as freedom, which is the other side of Enlightenment reason. Rea-son as freedom becomes yet another myth that must be overcome and removed by rationality as calculation, as scientific. The market econ-omy, instantiating rationality as calculation, serves as "the actual form of reason and the power which destroyed reason" (*DOE* 90). The ratio-nality of the free market economy served the only goal that could remain in the inversion of reason as freedom—survival and self-preservation.

Here, though, one must remember the process of rationalization. Rationality links control to calculation. Everything is determined from the start because everything is calculated to reach the particular goal of the owners of the means of production. The relationship between control and calculation makes evident the conflation of thinking with mathematics. Instead of comprehending the goals of the system and evaluating them, instead of examining the system itself, thought can serve the system only as an instrumental tool.

The functioning of reason within industrial society precludes the interests of all. Reason as systematic, as schematism, can only confirm the societal system—it cannot, in other words, point to an end outside the systematization of society for survival. A person reduces to her role within society—she represents only a "geographical, psychological and sociological type" (*DOE* 84). Individuality is lost within the schematism because the particular must be brought under the universal. The individual is individual only insofar as it is one of many of this type. Because of the schematism it cannot be different from everything else.

"In the Enlightenment's interpretation, thinking is the creation of a unified, scientific order and the derivation of factual knowledge from principles" (*DOE* 81–82). According to Horkheimer, the whole concept of reason undergoes transformation during the Enlightenment. Systematization becomes the motif of all thought, modeling itself on the successes of scientific thought. Everything must be brought under one principle.

Science itself, according to Horkheimer, cannot escape its role. It cannot be "conscious of itself: it is only a tool. Enlightenment thought, however, is the philosophy which equates the truth with scientific systematization" (*DOE* 85). Science itself can deal only with concepts that figure into its systematizing operation; terms have no meaning outside of the manipulations of the system. From the system, one predicts facts which confirm it. As parts of practice, the facts determine an individual's interaction with nature as a social object. When thinking fails to harmonize system and perception, thinking conflicts with practice.

Horkheimer and Adorno write, "Enlightenment is totalitarian." The Enlightenment totalizes nature and humanity by impressing it with the stamp of quantifiability. Stated in terms of the theory of rationalization: the Enlightenment tries to control everything through calculation. It reduces everything to something calculable and, thus, controllable. "Whatever does not conform to the rule of utility and computation is suspect. . . . In the process, it treats its own ideas of human rights exactly as it does the older universals. Every spiritual resistance it encounters merely serves to increase its strength" (*DOE* 6).

According to Horkheimer and Adorno, in enlightenment everything is decided from the beginning. The Enlightenment conflates thinking with mathematics. The procedures of mathematics become the paradigm to be followed. Mathematics, moreover, allows no unknowns. Once the unknown becomes part of an equation, it becomes fully known. Equations define all of their elements. Mathematical equations are concerned with discovering the unknown quantity; yet once what is unknown is inserted into an equation, it no longer is unknown. Rather it is known through the equation of which it is a part.

The whole point of knowledge and thought, argues Horkheimer and Adorno, is abandoned in the Enlightenment. The determination of abstract spatiotemporal relations between facts replaces the goal of comprehending the given as such. Reason is reduced to comprehending such spatiotemporal relations because it cannot comprehend anything else. Meaning and essence are removed from the realm of the phenomenal by definition. One knows only one's experience in spacetime. Thus, with the triumph of subjective rationality all goals external to quantification are removed. As formal, or scientific, rationality cannot judge ends. As instrumental, it cares only about reaching the end of self-preservation, only about survival. Once reason becomes formal, however, it loses the ability to suggest ends or to judge them. Science, procedure, technical practice must remain neutral within the Enlightenment. Theory, then, becomes senseless, another superstition. Enlightenment as freedom, tied to the capitalist economic order, becomes myth. It must reject itself as senseless.

The Renunciation of Self

The bourgeoisie, however, had no control over the demon they unleashed in the form of scientific rationality. Scientific rationality turns against the bourgeoisie and against their philosophy. It does not stop at the minimum of belief that the bourgeoisie need to remain established. That minimum of belief would include the belief in freedom as the ultimate goal of society. That belief, however, must disappear under the onslaught of scientific rationality. Scientific rationality rids humanity of all belief as superstition, as yet another metaphysics that posits false entities. Everything must be practical, must be useful for self-preservation.

In saying that the Enlightenment turned against the bourgeoisie, we must be careful to understand what Horkheimer and Adorno have in mind. Throughout the *DOE*, they identify the Enlightenment and enlightenment thought with bourgeois philosophy. The first excursus on the *Odyssey* searches for the bourgeois individual. This search follows from their change in focus from the economy as the dominant factor in Marxism to humanity's relationship with nature. Once one no longer considers the economy as the singular problem, the Marxist can search for the bourgeois individual outside of the confines of the Enlightenment period and modernity. Consequently, one looks for the seeds of the individual, which today are both prevalent in society and a symptom of the forces of domination. We need not think, however, that this individual belongs only to modernity. Indeed, the bourgeois individual can be seen to have always waited on the sidelines for its moment of triumph—when its pursuit of the mastery of nature would proceed uninhibited.

The bourgeois individual represents the Enlightenment and enlightened thought. The bourgeois individual pits himself against nature. In essence, the *Odyssey* recounts the tale of humanity's struggle with nature, according to Horkheimer and Adorno's reading, and in the end humanity, in the figure of Odysseus, wins out through self-sacrifice. At stake in this reading is the identification of enlightenment rationality, understood in Francis Bacon's terms as a mastery of nature, with the bourgeoisie. The bourgeoisie established enlightenment thought in order to rid themselves of the *ordo* of nature and the repression imposed on them by myth.

> The fallen nature of modern [human beings] cannot be separated from social progress. On the one hand the growth of economic productivity furnishes the conditions for a world of greater justice; on the other hand it allows the technical apparatus and the social groups which ad-

minister it a disproportionate superiority to the rest of the population. . . . Even though the individual disappears before the apparatus
which he serves, that apparatus provides for him as never before. In an
unjust state of life, the impotence and pliability of the masses grow with
the quantitative increase in commodities allowed them. (*DOE* xv)

One can easily reply to the claims of Horkheimer and Adorno that
humanity is much better off today than centuries ago. Even the poor
who live on the street can find food and shelter if they try. Furthermore, the workers do not object to their conditions. These sorts of objections, however, miss the point. Indeed, they prove it, for the point of
Horkheimer's criticism is that the masses can no longer think outside
of the system of domination. The starvation of the masses comprises
not the true failing of the Enlightenment but a symptom of that failing.
That is, the masses themselves conflate thought with mathematics.

By conflating thought with mathematics, people abandon the possibility of reflective and free thought. Rather than being able to question the system, their thought only recognizes the instrumental value
of the system. All talk of noninstrumental values becomes suspect as
sales talk, for values do not refer to some objective *ordo* but simply to
the subjective preferences of individual agents. For the subjective rationality of modernity, objectivity rests in numbers alone.

This rationalization allows the sacrifice of humanity for the system. Horkheimer and Adorno link rationality with the denial of nature. Renunciation of the self is the essence of the bourgeois spirit.
Again, this spirit extends beyond the boundaries of the Enlightenment
period. Rather, the bourgeois spirit reveals the emergence of subjective
rationality in the history of humanity. Such subjective rationality aims
only at control through calculation. Because it lays out a spreadsheet
for the execution of this control, all meaning is removed from the very
process of control. According to Enlightenment thought, that meaning
should lie in the fulfillment of human individuality. Such a goal, however, has no meaning because it cannot itself be calculated. Herbert
Marcuse's analysis of the reality principle in Freud shows this clearly.

Using Freudian analysis, Marcuse argues that the opposition of
reason and freedom appears in two principles of the human being: the

reality principle and the pleasure principle. In human beings, the pleasure principle consists in a drive for total and immediate gratification. The environment, however, conflicts with this principle. It is difficult to satisfy desires. Human beings learn "to give up momentary, uncertain, and destructive pleasure for delayed, restrained but 'assured' pleasure" (*Eros* 13). The reality principle enforces a change in both the timing of gratification and the nature of the pleasure. Pleasure turns into something useful rather than harmful to one's society.

Civilization consists in "work for the procurement and augmentation of the necessities of life" (*Eros* 81). As such, it is the grand result of the reality principle. Civilization organizes and delegates the activities of individuals for the common good, for the satisfaction and needs of the whole. This organization creates yet another factor in the reality principle: one must limit one's gratification in light of the needs of others. In the face of the needs and desires of others, one must curtail one's own pleasure principle. All must work for the satisfaction of the whole. The whole, then, takes on a higher status than one's own needs. We work not to gratify ourselves but for the gratification of the whole. Culture utilizes the power of others. Culture and civilization, then, force the sublimation of the pleasure principle. That is, civilization creates domination—the repression of the pleasure principle in most for the gratification of some.

This sublimation of the pleasure principle occurs through the performance principle. Civilization demands that we perform and produce, that we suppress our own pleasure for the creation of products. Civilization, then, embodies and extends the reality principle: it represses gratification in order to achieve more and different kinds of pleasures. In so doing, it puts off gratification until tomorrow in order to meet the needs for today.

According to Marcuse, modernity, in the form of capitalism, and the whole rationalization of history have suppressed human needs. This suppression relies not so much on the creation of a superego but on the structure of society guided toward the suppression of instinct. Control of nature has no other goal than control itself. Human psychology weakened inward and outward nature. Inward nature grows weak as human beings restrict themselves—and as humanity restricts itself—to immediate wish fulfillment. In so doing, humanity renounces many desires. Similarly, outward nature grows weak because it is demystified. The reality principle forces upon human beings the idea that nature "contain[s] immeasurable happiness in addition to its terrors."[11]

The domination of the reality principle lies in the submission of the majority to the rule of computation. This theme finds echoes in Horkheimer's *Eclipse of Reason*. "Although most people never overcome the habit of berating the world for their difficulties, those who are too weak to make a stand against reality have no choice but to obliterate themselves by identifying with it. They are never rationally reconciled to civilization. Instead, they bow to it, secretly accepting the identity of reason and domination" (113).

This submission to the rule of computation finally takes the form of myth itself, which is the reversion of enlightenment to myth. Workers tolerate their reduction to mere objects to be managed in order to maintain the system, which they accept as inevitable. Human beings begin to see the structure of society and the domination of nature as themselves embedded in stone. False consciousness takes hold of the majority of people. Change appears unattainable. Unable to evaluate goals with subjective rationality, humanity loses any prospect of conceiving goals.

"Here in brief is the central theme of the DOE: [Subjective rationality] reduces truth to 'success' and, in the process, robs reason of all substantive content."[12] The preceding analyses point to this conclusion, that the rationalization of society throughout history has exhausted reason of any objective content, of any possibility for emancipation. From the beginnings of myth, rationality has only increased humanity's concern for domination of humanity and of nature. Thus, rationality concerns success and remains formal and instrumental.

Characterizing Subjective Rationality

An extended defense of the arguments from the Frankfurt School lies outside the boundaries of this book, but I shall offer several reasons for accepting what Horkheimer, Adorno, and Marcuse argue.

Deferring part of this argument to chapter 3, we can note, first, that the preponderance in our culture of such statements as I provided at the beginning—from Michael Jordan to Senator Arlen Specter—and the fact that such statements go unchallenged testify to the dominance of subjective rationality in modern cultural and political discourse.

Second, I would suggest that the state of the modern world represents a *reductio ad absurdum*. Let us assume that subjective rationality leads not away from but toward liberation. Today, then, we should be able to find not just examples of enlightenment but overwhelming evidence of it. In what would such enlightenment consist? Would it consist in, for instance in America, a rejection of the theory of evolution for religious grounds? Would, not the domination, but the mere presence of what Dwight D. Eisenhower called the military-industrial complex be explainable in an enlightened age? Would nation-states continue to cut support for education? A better way of raising these same points might be the following: we can genetically engineer crops to feed hungry people, create massive machinery to farm land, or design buildings that tower in the sky. Yet we do not have discussions about the meaning of these accomplishments or to what extent they fit into our everyday lives. The lack of those conversations does not, it seems to me, indicate an enlightened society; just the opposite.

Neither of these is a knock-out argument, but together they can motivate us to discuss a different question. What are the features of modern subjective rationality that underlie the failure of enlightenment? One such feature is the relation in which subjective rationality stands to objective reason. Objective reason references some objective *ordo* in the world, while subjective rationality hides by denying such an *ordo*.

Objective Reason versus Subjective Rationality

Horkheimer characterizes objective reason as follows: "[It] asserted the existence of reason as a force not only in the individual mind but also in the objective world . . . aimed at evolving a comprehensive system or hierarchy, of all beings, including man and his aims. The degree of reasonableness of a man's life could be determined according to its harmony with this totality. Its objective structure, and not just man and his purposes, was to be the measuring rod for individual thoughts and actions" (*Eclipse* 4). Objective reason, then, (1) is outside the individual mind but (2) acts on the mind (in some way). (3) It aims at building an objective order of all existence, (4) which order is used to judge the actions of individuals (5) outside of the individuals' ends.

The primary characterization of objective reason is that it is a reason that accesses a higher realm. This realm lies beyond the subjective interests of human beings to the extent that (a) it finds a particular meaning and good in the universe (b) to which it reconciles the subjective interests of individual human beings. With objective reason human beings can, because of this access, judge their ends as worthy or unworthy. Plato's *Republic* attempts to define and employ such an objective reason. For Plato, reason, in the form of dialectic, accesses a higher realm—the realm of the Forms, particularly the Form of the good. The argument in the *Republic* concludes that if one uses this reason, then one will find happiness. Thus for Plato, the pursuit of objective good with objective reason reconciles one's individual interests with a higher order in the universe.

The notion of an *ordo* sits at the center of objective reason. Objective reason allows access to and presupposes a hierarchical order in the world. It refers both to a structure inherent in reality requiring specific forms of behavior and to acting and thinking which reflects such an objective order (*Eclipse* 11). An example might clarify the issue. For the Lakota, many things exist in the world and require each other for existing. Everything, further, is imbued with *wakan*. The Lakota conceive of all things in the world as equal, and so the model of their universe is that of the circle, or the sacred hoop. This belief requires specific forms of behavior: for example, not claiming property. Further, various acts among the Lakota reflect their view of the world: when they give thanks to the animals they kill, they recognize that all things must exist in harmony and are equal. In contrast, Roman Catholics believe in a hierarchical order in the universe that requires different forms of behavior: for example, humility and trust in God. Roman Catholic acts, further, reflect the objective *ordo* of the universe: prayer might be an example here. In both traditions, we find an *ordo* in the beliefs people have about the structure of the world and an *ordo* reflected in the acts that define a tradition.

In contrast to objective reason, subjective rationality has two basic components: a formal component and an instrumental component. As formal, subjective rationality consists in a set of functions devoid of meaning. As instrumental, it comprises a function of finding the most efficient means to a given end. The examples of a spreadsheet and a child help elucidate the distinction here.

As formal, subjective rationality can be compared to a spreadsheet. The spreadsheet contains functions without any content. The functions themselves have no meaning; they only serve to process the data that is put into the spreadsheet by the user. The same spreadsheet can be used for different purposes, according to what the user of the spreadsheet intends. In short, the spreadsheet contains blanket operations that have no meaning but perform some "function" on a given content. It organizes and processes the entering data. Kant's categorical imperative operates as such a function.

As instrumental, subjective rationality can be compared to a young child. The child is unable to evaluate its ends. The child sees a lollipop. The child then determines the best way to get the lollipop. It considers asking politely, crying, throwing a tantrum, and simply reaching for the lollipop. The child then decides between those activities. In so deciding, the child finds the best means to the given end—eating the lollipop. It does not consider its end, except insofar as it considers its own self-preservation. (This should not be underestimated at this point. When the child is old enough to consider whether it will be spanked or punished for reaching for the lollipop, or what have you, it considers its self-preservation, that is, its happiness.)

According to Horkheimer, "the force that ultimately makes reasonable actions possible is the faculty of classification, inference, and deduction, no matter what the specific content—the abstract functioning of the thinking mechanism. This type of reason may be called subjective rationality" (*Eclipse* 3). Subjective rationality, then, (1) is a faculty (2) concerned with logical analysis (3) devoid of content, concerned either with (4) judging whether the means fits the end—that is, is instrumental—or with (5) satisfying a formal function. Insofar as it considers ends, subjective rationality views them in relation to self-preservation. Subjective rationality, then, (6) refers primarily to the subject and not to something outside of the subject. Here the term "subject" can refer either to an individual or to a community insofar as the community considers only the end of self-preservation either of itself or of the individual. Utterly alien to subjective rationality is the idea that an end might be reasonable for its own sake.

The notion of self-preservation needs some clarification here that Horkheimer does not provide. While the notion of self-preservation proves important for how Horkheimer views subjective rationality— that is, as something that can only obey the dictates of self-preservation— I do not think he has clarified what place self-preservation holds conceptually. Marcuse's discussion of self-preservation under the aspect of the reality principle, while theoretically rich, does not of itself clarify the role of self-preservation in the concept of subjective rationality.

At issue here is the conflict between claiming that subjective rationality cannot evaluate ends and Horkheimer's insistence that subjective rationality elevates self-preservation to the primary goal. Instrumentally, subjective rationality pursues self-preservation at all costs. No other goal can be pursued but that of self-preservation, in part, because no other goals exist. When Horkheimer holds that subjective rationality is devoid of content, what he means is that, unlike objective reason, subjective rationality cannot access some *ordo,* some higher realm with a hierarchy of goods. For subjective rationality, ends cannot be reasonable in themselves outside of their function for some subjective interest. This claim is perfectly compatible with the claim that rationality can and does judge ends in terms of their relation to self-preservation. Thus, the singular pursuit of self-preservation constitutes a primary characteristic of subjective rationality and, in fact, brings the instrumental and formal aspects of subjective rationality together under one rubric.

This understanding of subjective rationality proves conceptually strong because it maintains the critique of subjective rationality while recognizing the role that the pursuit of self-preservation has had in undermining the Enlightenment project. When Francis Bacon elevated the domination of nature to the highest goal of science, he, at one and the same time, announced the victory of the bourgeois individual and sabotaged enlightenment in the modern period. Only a renunciation of subjective rationality can correct this fault.

Table 1.1 analyzes the differences between objective reason and subjective rationality by way of introduction to a more thorough analysis of subjective rationality as formal and instrumental.

Table 1.1: Subjective Rationality vs. Objective Reason

Subjective Rationality	Objective Reason
Faculty of the mind	Acts on mind
Devoid of content	Discovers an objective *ordo*
Instrumental	Reconciles subjective ends with *ordo*
Ends pregiven	ends outside Individual
Singular pursuit of self-preservation	Orders self-preservation under general values in the *ordo*

Subjective Rationality as Formal and Instrumental

According to Horkheimer, both the formal and the instrumental component of subjective rationality fail to bring about freedom, each in a different way. Formalization strips rationality of the ability to judge goals as worthwhile in themselves apart from subjective interests—that is, the interest in self-preservation; instrumentalization harnesses rationality to any given goal and promotes the principle of self-preservation above all other ends. An analysis of each aspect in turn shows that Horkheimer's discussion remains unclear. In particular, he does not draw out clearly the relationship between the principle of self-preservation and subjective rationality. This further creates confusion concerning the fact that Horkheimer holds that at one and the same time subjective rationality lacks content and yet promotes self-preservation.

Subjective Rationality as Formal

On the one hand, reason has been formalized in modernity. As formal, it is incapable of judging ends. Horkheimer rejects subjective rationality because of this incapacity. The "present crisis of reason consists fundamentally in the fact that at a certain point thinking became either incapable of conceiving . . . objectivity at all or began to negate it as a delusion" (*Eclipse* 7).

To hold that reason has been formalized entails two points: first, reason has lost any reference to a higher *ordo* in modernity, and second, reason cannot judge ends as reasonable in themselves. Let's return to the examples of the Lakota and Roman Catholicism above. If reason among either group is formalized, then no reference can be made to an objective worldview by which one knows values and the importance of things in the world. Thus, the Lakota would not know that all things are equal, and the Roman Catholic would not know that God is the highest being. When it came time to judge some end as worthy of pursuit—say the preservation of the tribe for the Lakota or the honoring of saints for the Roman Catholic—then neither would be able to judge these ends as worthy or unworthy of pursuit. Rather the pursuit of an end must satisfy a formal procedure. It would need to be entered into a function on a spreadsheet to determine what results. Nothing is intrinsically good or bad. In some sense, reason is reduced to the satisfaction of a logical word game.[13]

Formalization has several implications both theoretically and practically. First, if the subjective conception of rationality is the reigning conception of reason, then rationality cannot help a person choose any goal as desirable in itself—that is, as "reasonable" (*Eclipse* 7). Goals can be rational; they can serve the subjective interests (i.e., self-preservation) of the agent. They cannot, however, be justified with reference to some order innate in the world. An agent can pursue a goal X that satisfies some subjective interest; but the agent is unable, does not have the appropriate materials, to judge the worthiness of the subjective interest for which the agent pursues X.

According to Horkheimer, the formalization of reason arose out of its changing relationship to religion. Importantly, as religion weakened, so did objective reason. Horkheimer targets the Enlightenment project to replace religion as a foundation for ethics and society with an independent rationality. Religion provided an objective view to reality that allowed the evaluation of ends. Thus, religion and objective reason were linked together.

The reformation and decline of the medieval Catholic Church brought an end to this way of life and objective view of reality. The division within Christianity both removed the possibility of having a unified conception of the universe and the good and resulted in wars and the torture of nonbelievers. One of the main objects of criticism in the Enlightenment, particularly by *philosophes* like Voltaire, was the intolerance of other religions. Reason was seen as opposed to fanaticism and civil war. Rather, reason aimed at the well-being of people. In the process, it became formalized. It took on a conciliatory attitude, according to Horkheimer (*Eclipse* 13). In the promotion of tolerance, creeds and beliefs lost their status as something worth defending with one's life.

Christian ethics were secularized. The Enlightenment period saw an attempt to ground the goals of a well-ordered society not upon the basis of some religion or faith but on the basis of reason alone. Philosophers attempted to find self-evident truths that could ground what they saw as the best society. (More on this in the third chapter, where I discuss Alasdair MacIntyre's critique of modernity.) Individual and social aims were derived from these self-evident truths and innate ideas, which were linked by reason to objective truth. In the Enlightenment's (rightful) attack on religion, it undermined objective reason as well.

The objective truth provided by religion was no longer guaranteed by any dogma extraneous to reason or humanity itself. In the end, this unity of fundamental human beliefs was shattered. Philosophy, however, did not mean to abolish objective truth; it meant only to provide a new rational foundation for such truth. It debated not only the nature of the world with religion, but the role of philosophy and religion for the world. The central question is not the nature of the absolute, but whether "objective truths should derive from theology or philosophy" (*Eclipse* 16).

Eventually, according to Horkheimer, this debate between religion and philosophy reached a stalemate. Each was relegated to a separate and distinct sphere of culture. Thus religion was neutralized; its claim to an objective status was contradicted by the fact that it was only one sphere of culture. Philosophy was neutralized as well. When philosophy is seen as one aspect of culture, its claim to objectivity is contradicted by its compartmentalization. Horkheimer claims that the neutralization of religion led not only to its elimination as a medium for spiritual objectivity but also to the denial of objectivity (*Eclipse* 17). The idea of an objective reality loses any plausibility.[14]

According to Horkheimer, then, a central result of the Enlightenment period, specifically of the Enlightenment's separation of objective truth from religion and religious belief, is the disempowerment of reason. Formalization, Horkheimer claims, entails that such concepts as justice, equality, happiness, and tolerance have lost their intellectual roots. Though they are still ends, no rational agent can link these ends to an objective reality (*Eclipse* 23). Without that authorized agency, the ends appear as simply another subjective preference of individual agents. They lose their motivating power and their force as world-transforming concepts.

Subjective Rationality as Instrumental

The formal aspect of subjective rationality consists in the loss of all content related to an objective order. The instrumental aspect of reason consists in its reduction to a mere tool. It neither justifies nor condemns but, rather, allows for the efficient pursuit of given desires and ends, no matter what the content of those desires and ends.

As instrumental, rationality loses all content, only to be put to the service of any goal brought forth by an agent. Goals themselves cannot be judged by rationality, but rationality can serve any end—this defines its instrumentality. More importantly, though, from the view of a critical theory of society, this instrumentality can be put to the service of domination just as easily as it can be put to the service of freedom. The formal aspect points to its inability to judge any goals. That is, rationality is formal to the extent that it has lost any referent in an objective order. The instrumental aspect points to its ability to service any pre-given goal. That ability tends to lead to greater oppression and domination in society.

For an example, Horkheimer considers what it is to have a hobby. When rationality becomes instrumental, all activities derive their meaning through their connections to other ends. A person who, as a hobbyist, walks in the woods daily views the hobby differently when he sees it as purely subjective and outside of any meaningful order. The walk can no longer be understood as part of that meaningful order but must be tied to some other end of the walker—health, habit, and so on. Eventually, all of these ends become linked to self-preservation as the only goal to pursue.

As a hobby, an activity references no objective reason. It lacks an inherent sense. "The person who indulges in a hobby does not even make believe that it has any relation to ultimate truth" (*Eclipse* 38). The hobby remains irrational outside of its relations to other ends that the hobbyist has, particularly that of self-preservation.[15]

In the modern period, according to Horkheimer, the notion of self-interest becomes dominant in society. At one time self-interest was seen as part of the objective order. During the liberalistic period, however, self-interest subdues all other motives considered fundamental to the functioning of society (*Eclipse* 19–20). The imperialism of the principle of self-interest deprives reasons for social cohesion of persuasiveness. Society exists only insofar as it serves the interests of the individual. The cohesion of society proves necessary only in service to the self-interest of the individual.

Horkheimer claims that liberalism tends toward fascism because the principle of self-interest underlies modern society. Further, the defenders of intellectual and political liberalism make peace with its opposite—fascism—on the grounds of self-interest. Fascism names, primarily, government that dominates individuals through appeals to self-preservation. Horkheimer, an emigrant from Germany and writing during the Second World War, has in mind Hitler's election in the democratic Weimar Republic. People were driven by fear and need. Yet we can find examples of such peacemaking between liberalism and fascism in more contemporary settings.

One such example would be the Persian Gulf War. Interestingly enough, that war spurred little criticism while it was going on, no doubt because of the fear that the United States would repeat its past "mistakes" from the Vietnam War. How were such mistakes viewed in the popular culture? The real mistake of the Vietnam War was the engagement. A subsequent mistake was the rejection of the veterans of the

Vietnam War when they returned home. This denial of the veterans weighed on the collective conscience of Americans as they were confronted with examples of how the veterans were treated after the war as depicted in news and cultural media such as movies and songs. The mistake that Americans feared repeating in the Persian Gulf War, then, was not the actual engagement in such a war but the forgetting of its brave soldiers who went overseas to fight for the American Way. The little yellow ribbons which people tied to their arms and their cars, and which now are so favorably mimicked by groups who want to make sure their members never leave the memory of American minds, attest to the fact that the real concern in the Persian Gulf War was about memory and not about involvement in the war itself.

The involvement in the war, however, exemplifies the tendency of liberalism to make peace with its opposites. The propaganda of the war held that the United States fought over the freedom of various peoples, most particularly the Saudi Arabians and the Kuwaitis. Kuwait, which the Gulf War meant to liberate, however, was and remains a monarchy. Freedom remained just as foreign to them as it did to the enemy Iraqis. The Gulf War was fought not for the freedom of people in the region but over oil. Liberalism aligned itself with the interest of oil because it served the self-interest of the people who constituted the liberal democracies that fought the war. Similar arguments could be made concerning the involvement of United States forces and NATO in the bombing of Bosnia. The given reason for the bombing was to end the ethnic cleansing, which had gone on for years. This reason could only be a cover, for NATO and the United States have not intervened in worse cases of ethnic cleansing in various parts of the world—parts of the world which are not as rich in resources and markets.

Finally, we witness a similar situation in Libya in March 2011. Opposition rose up against decades-long dictators throughout the Middle East and North Africa. While some protests, notably those in Egypt and Tunisia, remained fairly peaceful, in other countries the dictators used the military against opposition protestors. Why was it Libya that the United States and the United Nations decided to intervene in? Why not the Congo before that, which has seen hundreds of thousands of deaths? Or why not Bahrain, which saw the intervention of Saudi

Arabian forces in the interests of the ruling monarchy against opposition protestors?

These examples are not meant to condemn any military commander or president or to suggest that humanitarian reasons did not play some role in the wars, but rather to illustrate that the United States and other Western democracies go to war over and over and not always for consistent reasons or in those situations in which life and liberty are most at stake. Michael Moore's *Capitalism: A Love Story* and Eugene Jarecki's *Why We Fight* show, persuasively, in line with Horkheimer's thesis, that the peoples of Western democracies have allied with fascist elements to maintain a certain way of life aimed simply at the instrumental satisfaction of pregiven ends. An alliance formed between the military-industrial complex and citizens of these nation-states that, according to Dwight D. Eisenhower, threatens the very democracies people depend on. At the same time, the taxes that go to the war machine mean that people go without health insurance, go without food, or lose houses. They demonstrate, then, Horkheimer's meaning and highlight that this same tendency—the tendency of liberalism to acquiesce to its opposites—continues today.

According to Horkheimer, this tendency testifies to the fact that rationality loses any value outside of its instrumental tendencies. In modernity, instrumental rationality became "completely harnessed to the social process. Its operational value, its role in the domination of men and nature, had been made the sole criterion" (*Eclipse* 21). As a tool, instrumental reason can be used in the service both of freedom and domination. Yet its very instrumental nature more easily aligns it to domination. Concepts are stripped and rationalized to serve a function. They denote similarities, enumerate qualities, and function only in a classificatory and logical way. Words and concepts are seen no longer as having meanings of their own but as reduced to another tool in society. Meaning outside of function becomes suspect. Words and concepts—freedom, equality—sell things rather than reveal truth. Thus, we all understand the latest politician's appeal to freedom, to "change we can believe in," as a ploy to get us to vote for him and not as some meaningful commitment on his part. Lacking any meaning, such words belong more to an inhumane than to a humane world.

As instrumental, rationality loses its power of critique. According to Horkheimer, faced with the worst evil, enlightened people could name neither it nor its threat to humanity. To do so exposes one to questions of motive. Why did Bill Clinton bomb Libya at the time of the Monica Lewinsky affair? Why did Bill Clinton bomb Iraq almost daily for eight years? Did we go into Iraq so that George junior could finish his father's business? Yet Horkheimer is saying more. He is holding that, as instrumental, rationality cannot look at the world as filled with any meaning outside that of the subjective preferences of individual agents and that of their self-preservation. With the removal of an objective order in its formalization, rationality in its instrumentalization remains impotent in the face of evil.

In the end, subjective rationality—a formalized and instrumentalized reason—cannot judge ends as worthy in themselves and serves whatever interests are put before it. It no longer has the power to access a higher realm of truth; any talk of such truth is now considered sales talk. Rationality becomes a tool that finds the best means to the given end. These aspects of subjective rationality lead to the failure of the enlightenment.

The Critique of Objective Reason

One might conclude from the foregoing that nothing good can be said of subjective rationality. Horkheimer, however, believes in the dialectic of the enlightenment: that enlightenment had a good and a bad side that contended with each other. Likewise, subjective rationality has a promising side that sits in tension with its negative aspect. This dialectic of subjective rationality has two implications for how he continues to develop the critique in the *Eclipse*. First, Horkheimer believes that the rise of subjective rationality was necessary for humanitarian aims. The problem arises when subjective rationality becomes too all-encompassing; it has become totalitarian in humanity's domination of nature and human beings' domination of each other. Second, as dialectical, subjective rationality is only one side of a coin. Subjective rationality and objective reason dialectically oppose each other, which means that they form a whole. "The two concepts of reason do not represent two separate and independent ways of the mind although their opposition expresses a real antinomy" (*Eclipse* 174).

The *Eclipse*, then, discusses how to put reason, in both its subjective and objective forms, at the service of humanitarian aims. Mostly this project demands a critique of subjective rationality as the dominant, but not only, form of reason in the modern era. Subjective rationality triumphs everywhere, leading to fatal results. Objective reason, in Horkheimer's analysis, must be favored to counter that triumph. It must question the objective and romantic form of myth that subjective rationality has taken.

Indeed, the *Eclipse* at times reads like a call to go back to objective reason.[16] The careful reader must search high and low for the few criticisms Horkheimer offers of objective reason. Many times these criticisms explicitly engage neo-Thomism. Only in the last chapter of the *Eclipse*, "On the Concept of Philosophy," does Horkheimer reveal his whole program, in three parts.

First, it points to the subjectivization of reason in its instrumental and formal aspects. This project Horkheimer began with Adorno in the *DOE*, but he continues it in the *Eclipse* with a clearer and more philosophical analysis. In contrast with the *DOE*, the *Eclipse* focuses not so much on literature but on the concept of subjective rationality and its role in contemporary philosophical movements: pragmatism, positivism, and so on. Second, Horkheimer points out the dialectical nature of reason, referring to the subjective and objective antinomies. Horkheimer means to show that one should not simply embrace objective reason against subjective reason but accept them together and work out their humanitarian nature. Third, at the end of the *Eclipse*, Horkheimer points the way toward a more humanitarian or emancipatory conception of reason by emphasizing negation. He points ever so briefly to the cure for the present status of society in its totalitarian form.

Having critiqued subjective rationality, I will now (1) spell out Horkheimer's criticisms of objective reason and his argument that subjective rationality was necessary for true enlightenment, (2) point out the dialectical nature of reason as subjective and objective, and most importantly, (3) analyze his comments concerning the way out of the modern impasse.

Horkheimer notes that several trends revolve around reviving objectivist ontologies. He reacts to these negatively. "If subjective reason in the form of enlightenment has dissolved the philosophical basis of beliefs that have been an essential part of western culture, it has been able to do so because this basis proved to be too weak" (*Eclipse* 62). This appears to be a truism. Of course if A dissolves B, then B did not have enough defenses; that is, it was too weak. The real question for the purposes of a philosophy of emancipation is why the basis of objective ontologies proved too weak to withstand the attack of subjective rationality. Horkheimer continues by arguing that these ontologies themselves become a means to an end rather than an objective reason capable of judging ends. The revival of objectivist ontologies fills the gap left open by instrumental rationality. They are seen as useful to individual groups—religious, enlightened, progressive, and conservative. Objectivity becomes a means for escaping present-day chaos.

According to Horkheimer the revival of objectivist ontologies has the social function of "reconciling individual thinking to modern forms of mass manipulation" (*Eclipse* 65). Contemporary followers of objectivist ontologies streamline their ideas to fit with modern purposes. The question no longer seems to be what are the myths and dogmas of the religion?, but why is religion necessary for the present situation? This approach to religion and other objectivist ontologies is pragmatic. This pragmatism, moreover, affects the concepts of religion and other objectivist ontologies. According to Horkheimer, the central issue in the revival of objectivist ontologies, particularly religion, lies not in belief in the traditional objects of adoration but in belief itself. Belief transforms into a panacea for social and psychological problems.

Further, the modern forms of objectivist ontologies, for instance neo-Thomism, tend to inhibit thinking at the point of ultimate questions—for example, whether there is a supreme being. This charge certainly applies to contemporary forms of objectivist ontology. The recent rise of the conservative right—or Christian right—attests to it. The Christian right attempts to establish their own politics, embodying their values and beliefs within the modern legal system, because they have God on their side. To ask anyone of this group why one should adopt policy X, the questioner will hear only about the truth of the Bible—for example in regards to abortion, homosexuality, stem-cell research, and so on. The Bible becomes the federal game preserve for privileged dogma—no questions beyond this point please, including questions about the Christian right's interpretation of Scripture. The same can be said for the forefathers of these objectivist ontologies; they stopped thought.

Horkheimer contrasts neo-Thomism with positivism throughout the *Eclipse*. He finds that positivism establishes its own unquestioned dogma. Positivism sells the idea that science can test all values by their causes and effects.[17] At one point, science functioned to denounce the censorial power of objective ontology in a revolutionary past; now it plays censor, rejecting anything nonscientific or which questions science and the scientific method.

According to Horkheimer, the lack of self-reflection makes positivism a poor philosophy because of "its incapacity to understand its own philosophical implications in ethics as well as in epistemology" (*Eclipse* 84). Modern positivists reject the assumptions of other philosophies as metaphysical, but they fail to realize their own assumptions. Their objectivist philosophy, therefore, is just like others—it prevents questioning and enforces the acceptance of a particular view of the world.

Here, Horkheimer seems close to making a point I wanted to push on him, namely, that subjective rationality has itself become an objective ontology. Subjective rationality attempts to exclude anything outside itself, becoming not only totalitarian but yet another form of objective reason. At a certain point positivism blocks "critical thinking by authoritarian statements . . . about science as the surrogate of supreme intelligence" (*Eclipse* 80).

Even though Horkheimer contrasts neo-Thomism with positivism, his argument also demonstrates the ways neo-Thomism and positivism mirror each other. He faults neo-Thomism from the start, not only in its modern form. The problem is that neo-Thomism makes truth and goodness identical to reality. Positivism, however, shares this fault. Both positivists and neo-Thomists appear to believe that fitting human beings to reality would lead them out of current troubles. They accept that failure or success plays an integral part in behavior. Horkheimer contends, in contrast, that the attempt results in intellectual decay because it amounts to conformism.

Conformism proves a primary failure of thought in its objectivist forms. By attempting to reconcile humanity with theory, objective reason stops critical thought of society and of theory. It tends to force people into the same mold, to construct their lives as part of an unquestionable whole. The job of critical thought, of any emancipatory conception of reason, in part will be to escape this tendency to conformism. Positivism and neo-Thomism fail this critical role. Whereas neo-Thomism forces thought to match the authority of dogma, positivism forces thought to model logical processes.

Horkheimer, while criticizing subjective rationality, notes that subjective rationality proved necessary. He does not want to reverse history and return to a time where objective reason, with its objective ontologies, ruled. Objective ontology is necessary for modern emancipation. Yet we must be wary, Horkheimer warns us, of its tendency to enforce conformity. Objectivist ontologies that referred to an immutable order preclude the hope of progressive emancipation. Emancipation thus required the transition from objective reason to subjective rationality. Mirroring Hegel, Horkheimer requires a dialectical synthesis of reason in its subjective and objective forms.

Yet Horkheimer contends that the notion of progress is itself problematic. As a doctrine, progress "hypostatizes the ideal of the domination of nature and finally itself degenerates into a static, derivative mythology" (*Eclipse* 133). Progress implies progress beyond something—over human fear of nature, which, as has already been argued, includes fear of other human beings. Elevating the idea of progress into an ideal proves contradictory—for it posits change as a changeless value. Both static ontology and the doctrine of progress leave no room for humanity, for they posit unquestioned, immutable values.

The forces of progress spring forth from the concepts of complete fulfillment and unrestrained enjoyment. These concepts fostered a need for toil, research, and invention. Progress became an idol, however, and so did toil, research, and invention. In modernity, toil becomes not a means to an end but an end itself (*Eclipse* 154). Thus, progress forgets its humanistic foundation as the search for fulfillment, and sees progress only in greater means of toil: "The objective mind in our era worships industry, technology, and nationality without a principle that could give sense to these categories; it mirrors the pressure of an economic system that admits of no reprieve or escape" (*Eclipse* 144). The idea of unrestricted progress drives the modern forces of production—progress in the control of nature, which is itself domination of humankind.

According to Horkheimer, any system of ideas laid out in a meaningful way presents a necessary claim to truth. (I shall return to this point in the last chapter, as one that MacIntyre shares with Horkheimer and which grounds the reasonableness of traditions.) This claim of objective ontologies to universal truth causes them to become societal cement. As systems of beliefs claiming universal truth, objective ontologies become part of a social totality in which they reflect current forms of social domination. That is, for Horkheimer, objective ontologies tend to become part and parcel of a system of domination. These claims to truth prove essential for the existence of those forms of domination present in any particular society. They established patterns of hierarchical organization within societies. Outside of these established hierarchies, though, a cleavage existed between culture (that is, this system of ideas) and material life. Some room was left for the expression of individuality—the individual person still held some possibility of use of autonomous reason. In contrast, modern superorganization reduces the individual to functional responses.

What does this observation mean, however, for the search for an emancipatory conception of reason? Again, first and foremost, the answer to the present social crisis is not simply to replace subjective rationality with objective reason. Objective reason itself leads to and supports systems of domination. Yet the point seems to be stronger, for Horkheimer charges in this discussion that all systems of ideas articulated in meaningful language support hierarchical organizations of society. Does this fact mean that the reason sought after must not support any system of ideas? No; rather the aspect which most leads to forms of oppression is the aspect of a claim to universal truth. Thus, autonomous reason must frame claims to possession of universal truth in historicist terms. Understanding reason as substantively constituted by tradition will, I shall argue later, provide the means for doing so.

Whereas Horkheimer argues that subjective rationality and objective reason exist as antinomies and not two separate ways of mind, he makes two overall criticisms of objective reason, which summarize what has been said in the last few pages. First, present-day proponents of objective reason risk falling behind industrial and scientific advances, asserting meaning that turns out illusory, and supporting reactionary ideologies (*Eclipse* 174). Society cannot turn back to older ontologies and forms of life. Objective reason, that is, tends toward romanticism. But, second, as emphasized above, objective reason also tends to support ideologies and lies. Objective reason masks the hierarchical forms of organization in society as truth which all must accept, for it entails that those forms of organization mirror the organization of the universe, that is, that they contain and represent the *ordo*.

Outlines of an Emancipatory Reason

The preceding formative critique of subjective rationality and objective reason motivates a search for a form of reason that supports the goals of a critical theory of society and emancipation. If neither subjective rationality nor objective reason can provide a foundation for a just society, where are we to turn? Horkheimer defines the requirements for a reason capable of critiquing society and leading to fulfillment and enjoyment.

The task of philosophy consists in promoting the critique of objective reason and subjective rationality and preparing "in the intellectual realm the reconciliation of the two in reality" (*Eclipse* 174). At the time of the writing of the *Eclipse,* which occurred more or less concurrently with the *DOE,* Horkheimer still had some hope of attaining an emancipatory conception of reason. This fact nullifies those claims that Frankfurt School critical theory abandoned the Enlightenment project altogether and suggests a less pessimistic reading of the *DOE.* There must be, for Horkheimer, a mutual critique of subjective and objective reason.

The concept of self-preservation, which has been so thoroughly critiqued throughout the writings of the Frankfurt School, is also the saving grace of reason run amok. Horkheimer demands that one combine the aspect of self-preservation contained within subjective rationality with the reference to an objective *ordo* in objective reason to develop a definition of autonomous reason that does not lead to oppression and domination. The objective goals of society must be defined in terms of the self-preservation of the subject.

Yet if the self-preservation of the subject drives the project, why then must objective order enter the picture? Why has not subjective rationality itself led to the emancipation of humankind? For Horkheimer, objective reason enters the picture because subjective rationality proved inadequate for its goal. Subjective rationality must be ordered through social solidarity; otherwise it will dominate individuals and society (*Eclipse* 176). Through self-critique, reason must (a) recognize the impotence of subjective reason with regard to self-preservation and (b) recognize that objective ontologies must include self-preservation as one among the other values of the universe. Thomas Hobbes's *Leviathan* cannot fulfill this task because it makes self-preservation the only value and defines reason as "mere reckoning." Hobbes, however, proved a necessary corrective to past ontologies, which had given no place to self-preservation as a value.

Horkheimer's conclusion comprises prescriptions for future philosophical work; they outline the present tasks of philosophy. In defining an emancipatory conception of reason, one must look to the origin of the disease of reason. Philosophy must analyze the development of the cleavage between subjective rationality and objective reason. This does not mean, however, seeing this cleavage occurring in a historical moment. Rather, one must see that the divide between subjective rationality and objective reason lies in the nature of reason in civilization. Reason failed to emancipate humanity because it formed in the urge to dominate nature. Recovering reason requires understanding its sources.

The project of uncovering an emancipatory conception of reason involves understanding the concrete development of reason in the urges of humanity in relation to its mastery of nature. This goal means looking at reason as natural, an aspect of humanity and nature. Horkheimer obviously intends that philosophy uncover an objective ontology of reason that illuminates how reason is part of nature and involves the pursuit of self-preservation among other values. In separating itself from nature and making nature an object, reason fails to recognize its own naturalness, and is therefore hampered in discovering the truth. (We can say the same thing of human beings: in divorcing themselves from other animals, human beings have distorted their nature and hampered the discovery of truth.) Reason needs to realize its naturalness. "The subjugation of nature will revert to the subjugation of [humanity], and vice versa, as long as [humanity] does not understand his own reason and the basic process by which he has created and maintained the antagonism that is about to destroy him. Reason can be more than nature only though concretely realizing its 'naturalness'—which consists in its trend to domination" (*Eclipse* 177).

Currently, reason is seen as the application of calculative and organizing principles. Rather than think independently, human beings cry out for patterns, systems, and authorities to guide their thinking. Subjective rationality, that is, stifles autonomous thought. In so doing, it further suppresses the principle of self-preservation, which it is to serve. Negative reason must contrast the claims of subjective rationality with the existing social conditions; it must uncover the claim to ultimate truth that subjective rationality asserts for itself as embedded in a historical situation. In so doing, negative reason will denounce the currently accepted conception of reason and lead to greater independent thinking.

| In the Frankfurt School critique of reason, particularly as found in the *DOE*, enlightenment thought is seen to be associated with scientific reason and the desire to control nature. Further, embracing enlightenment thought, because of its inability to judge ends, subverts the true goal of enlightenment—emancipation. Humanity becomes just another object for control. But what lies behind enlightenment thought?

According to Horkheimer, subjective rationality was adopted in the Enlightenment as the form of reason to lead to enlightenment. Yet as formal, subjective rationality cannot judge any ends, and as instrumental, it becomes the slave of any ends set before it. As such, it enslaves human beings. In contrast, objective reason does reference a higher *ordo* in nature, according to which human beings can evaluate their own goals and ways of life. Yet objective reason proves oppressive as well. It lacks the capacity for self-reflection and establishes truth as universal for all peoples at all times. Further, it suppresses the principle of self-preservation. Even in its revised forms, such as neo-Thomism in modernity, objective reason cannot provide the necessary tools for an emancipated society.

A critical theory of society requires a synthesis of subjective rationality—in the form of the principle of self-preservation—with objective reason. Subjective rationality and objective reason can save each other. This synthesis would provide an objective *ordo* by which human beings might evaluate their ends. Such an *ordo* would have as its highest goal the satisfaction of human needs and the freedom of humanity. Such an objective *ordo* must be tempered by the principle of self-preservation, however. This principle would guarantee that natural human needs are satisfied, as opposed to those needs imposed upon humanity by society and particularly by capitalism. Further, it would guarantee that individuals would not be sacrificed needlessly for the whole. That is, each individual would count equally in an emancipated society based on such a merger of objective reason and subjective rationality.

I will now consider a proposal of a conception of reason meant to provide a basis for an emancipatory society, a proposal from Jürgen Habermas called communicative rationality. I will argue that his proposal fails to meet the needs of an emancipatory society and will show where it diverges from Horkheimer's prescription. This rejection will allow the discussion to move to a positive construction of a concept of substantive reason. Substantive reason is the merger of objective reason and subjective rationality. Based in traditions as a response to the natural needs of human beings, substantive reason both references a higher *ordo* and respects the principle of self-preservation.

2 | Habermas's Communicative Rationality

The critique of enlightenment reason from the perspective of the Frankfurt School of Social Research, particularly as formulated by Max Horkheimer, focused on subjective rationality as both devoid of content (formal) and subservient to any pregiven end (instrumental). The earliest accounts of Western history and mythology, on this critique, foreshadowed the elevation of self-preservation to the telos of humanity in modernity. In short, Horkheimer challenged subjective rationality for failing to bring about enlightenment as promised.

Is there a way out of this failure? If not, is there another conception of reason which will allow humanity a chance at enlightenment?

Jürgen Habermas, a second-generation critical theorist, developed a notion that promised to give humanity that chance: the notion of reason as communicative rationality. The idea proves important for two reasons: first, it stands as one of the predominant conceptions of reason in contemporary philosophy. If one wants to talk about reason in political philosophy, one must know Habermas. Second, it points the way to a proper conception of reason without quite getting there. Habermas wants to move from a paradigm of consciousness, as found in modern philosophy, to a paradigm of intersubjectivity based in a philosophy of language. Habermas does not go far enough, however. When examining the concept of reason, we must move from a paradigm of consciousness past a paradigm of intersubjectivity to a paradigm of tradition.

Habermas rejects the Frankfurt School critique of reason. He argues that Horkheimer and colleagues became mired in a philosophy of consciousness and proposes that critical theorists turn to a philosophy of language or intersubjectivity as a way out of Frankfurt School pessimism. This turn to a philosophy of language will allow him to provide a better account of the concepts of freedom and reconciliation. Habermas develops his theory of communicative action as a social theory grounded on the formal pragmatics of language, from which he defends a notion of reason he calls communicative rationality. While Habermas's communicative rationality proves a step in the right direction, I contend that he does not go far enough. Instead of stopping at a philosophy of language, we must move to a philosophy of tradition. I will argue for this position using both Charles Taylor's critique of communicative rationality as too formal and an argument from Plato's *Republic*. In short, though Plato's guardians might accept the value of rationality, they could not settle for a communicative rationality and a social theory based on a formal pragmatics of language.

Toward a Philosophy of Language: Habermas's Critique of the *DOE*

Habermas's Characterization of the *DOE*

As we saw in the Frankfurt School critique of reason, Horkheimer and Adorno condemn the Enlightenment because it failed to bring about the emancipation of humankind as it promised. Following Lukács, they held that the rationalization of society, which involved the demystification of culture and the increasing differentiation of rationality spheres characteristic of modernity, is an essentially reifying process. Rationalization reifies both society and nature such that both seem to exert control over helpless individuals. Moreover, this reifying process became embedded in society to such an extent that it was viewed as absolute. Employing instrumental rationality managed not to disillusion humanity but rather to ensorcel humanity even more, albeit under a different spell. Habermas characterizes Horkheimer and Adorno of the *DOE* as black writers of modernity.[1] Although they no longer believed that the Enlightenment could lead to greater freedom and less suffering, following Walter Benjamin they wanted to maintain some sort of hope that greater freedom and less suffering were possible.

For Habermas, the core of Horkheimer and Adorno's claim in the *DOE* is that the differentiation of rationality spheres and "the collapse of the substantive reason still incorporated in religion and metaphysics" dis-empowers reason until it is mere instrumental rationality in the service of self-preservation.[2] To make this claim, they utilize Lukács's theory of reification in sociopsychic terms. They want to accomplish two things by using Lukács's theory: first, explain the resiliency of capitalism in the face of predictions of its immanent downfall from Marx to Lukács; second, revitalize the critique of commodity fetishism so central to Marxist analysis (*TCA*1, 322). Lukács maintained that rationalization had a limit determined immanently by the nature of rationality. Horkheimer and Adorno want to reject such a claim. Yet, they also want to radicalize and to use his critique of reification.

According to Habermas, Horkheimer and Adorno generalize Lukács's theory of reification in three steps. First, rather than taking wage labor as the model for the objectivity characteristic of capitalism (as Lukács did), Horkheimer and Adorno take as fundamental the structure of consciousness found in the methods of modern science and Kantian philosophy. Second, "Horkheimer and Adorno give such an abstract interpretation of the structure of reified consciousness that it covers not only the theoretical form of identifying thought but even the confrontation of goal-oriented acting subjects with external nature" (*TCA*1, 378). At stake for Horkheimer and Adorno is humanity's relationship to nature and human beings' relationships with each other. Their analysis of the structures of consciousness that permit a reifying attitude allows them to examine those relationships. Third, they understand instrumental rationality to include domination over things and over human beings.

Thus, in Horkheimer and Adorno's hands, according to Habermas, the theory of reification is no longer limited to a discussion of capitalist society. Rather, their theory of reification yields an analysis of all of modern society, from its beginnings and in its whole outlook. Thus they move from a focus on the specific historical rise of capitalism to the development and rise of subjectivity and the self-formative process of ego-identity (*TCA*1, 379–80). They shift the analysis of society both temporally (to include all of Western civilization, not just the modern historical moment) and substantively (so that what is at stake is not simply capitalist relations of production but the drive for self-preservation and the repression of instinctual nature). Thus, their critique expands beyond the specific modern period.

Habermas frames their insights in terms of the ego. The ego forms in the individual's attempts to coordinate the desires of her inner nature with the forces of outer nature. The ego results from "the accomplishments of instrumental reason" in two respects (*TCA*1, 380). First, the ego is that which takes control of outer nature, subjugating it, developing it, and disenchanting it. Such control is seen as enlightenment. Second, the ego is also that which must learn to master itself, repressing its own nature (drives) and objectifying itself. Every victory of outer nature entails a defeat of inner nature. The story of Odysseus illustrates this dialectic. This dialectic, in turn, occurs because reason becomes rationality to serve self-preservation, the new absolute end.

According to Habermas, Horkheimer and Adorno's thesis concerning the dialectic of enlightenment and the domination immanent in instrumental rationality shows that the relation between nature and spirit has been distorted beyond recognition and become catastrophic. This relationship between spirit and nature, however, can be seen as distorted only if one conceives of truth as tied to a universal reconciliation (*TCA*1, 380–81). This reconciliation occurs between human beings and nature, that is, spirit and nature. Habermas writes, "If spirit is the principle that brings external nature under control only at the price of suppressing internal nature, if it is the principle of self-preservation that is at the same time self-destruction, then subjective [rationality], which presupposed the dialectic of spirit and nature, is as much entangled in error as objective reason, which maintains the original unity of the two" (*TCA*1, 381). Instrumental rationality opposes spirit to nature, or subject to object, whereas objective reason sees nature filled with spirit—with subjectivity. Both forms of reason are in error, according to Horkheimer, because both misconceive the actual relationship between spirit and nature, subjectivity and objectivity: objective reason totalizes and subjective rationality nullifies the relationship.

The point Habermas makes here is that, for Horkheimer and Adorno, both subjective rationality and objective reason contain an untruth. Yet the nature of those untruths remains muddled. For Habermas, however, a different problem emerges in their analysis: the *DOE* does not direct the reader to the correct mediation of the two concepts of reason, which he finds in the differentiation of rationality spheres, universal features of validation, and an underlying unity of rationality.

Rather, according to Habermas, Horkheimer and Adorno trace the path of instrumental rationality back to its origins, which Habermas interprets as the very beginning of reason. From its very beginnings, according to Horkheimer and Adorno, so Habermas reports, reason has been unable to discover the truth. For Habermas, this reflection suggests that a concept of truth must be tied to the "guiding idea of a universal reconciliation" (*TCA*1, 382). Yet Horkheimer and Adorno are unable to do more than suggest this concept of truth, for the concept points to a "reason that is before reason." The placeholder for this primordial reason is mimesis, a concept they neither can nor do fill out. They cannot explicate or propose a theory of mimesis because such an activity would result in a type of universal theory that they condemn throughout the *DOE*. Thus, the *DOE* becomes ironic because, at one and the same time, it points the way to truth and denies the possibility of truth.

(Note that the discussion of truth will be central to the defense of a tradition-constituted reason in the last chapter. I shall argue for a conception of truth, however, that does not posit some reconciliation of spirit and nature in the way Habermas proposes here. The approach to truth provides a useful distinction between Habermas's communicative rationality and MacIntyre's (and my) tradition-constituted reason.)

Habermas's Solution: A Philosophy of Language

For Habermas, the program of early critical theory foundered because it relied on an exhausted paradigm of the philosophy of consciousness. He thinks the program can be renewed by turning to a philosophy of language (*TCA*1, 386). According to Habermas, the fear of a fallback into metaphysics, which Horkheimer and Adorno shared, occurs only within the horizon of a modern philosophy of consciousness. The idea of a reconciliation of nature and subject finds no room in the philosophy of consciousness from Descartes to Kant and is only extravagantly formulated in objective idealism from Spinoza to Hegel (*TCA*1, 387). In empiricism and rationalism, the concept of the subject, as theoretically grasping objects, absorbed the concept of self-preservation. In objective ontologies, self-preservation consists in realizing an end that derived from a being's essence, which essence, in turn, came from a natural world order. In contrast, modern thought detaches self-preservation from a system of highest ends. Thus, self-preservation takes the forms of knowing and of acting, two modes of being by which the subject relates to the object. Under a metaphysical worldview, knowing and acting occur within a system of being which orders all of nature, including knowing and acting. Under the modern worldview, however, no such system exists; self-maintenance, that is, self-preservation of subjects, encapsulates all that matters.

According to Habermas, in this modern worldview the relation of the social subject to nature mirrors the relation of the individual subject to the object: reproducing the life of society demands exploiting nature. This exploitation becomes the central way persons relate to each other in society and the subject relates to her internal nature. The very nature of instrumental rationality prevents expression of the objectified viewpoint; yet instrumental rationality comprises all that is available to people in modernity. Thus, for instance, the appeal to solidarity to highlight that the instrumentalization of society and its members destroys something cannot open up a way to articulate what is destroyed.

Bound to the philosophy of consciousness, Horkheimer and Adorno's critique of subjective rationality denounces an effect whose character it cannot explain because it lacks a conceptual framework flexible enough "to capture the integrity of what is destroyed" through subjective rationality (*TCA*1, 389). Horkheimer and Adorno do call what is destroyed "mimesis" and call forth various aspects of it. Habermas contends, however, that one must abandon a philosophy of consciousness if one wants to lay bare the rational core of mimesis. One must embrace instead a philosophy of language. This philosophy of language focuses on how people understand communication intersubjectively. Under such a paradigm, cognitive-instrumental rationality falls within the general concept of a comprehensive communicative rationality.

Adorno, according to Habermas, suggests this change in paradigm in several passages. Adorno lacks the means to clarify mimesis, however, in reference to an abstract instrumental rationality opposed to it. The ideas of reconciliation and freedom that Habermas finds in Adorno must be understood through a specific understanding of intersubjectivity. Intersubjectivity makes "possible a mutual and constraint-free understanding among individuals in their dealings with one another, as well as the identity of individuals who come to a compulsion-free understanding with themselves" (*TCA*1, 390). This idea of intersubjectivity can be spelled out only in a new paradigm—the paradigm of the philosophy of language or communication. Habermas holds that we should think not of individual subjects who represent and manipulate an objective world but of the intersubjective relations found when acting subjects reach understanding.

Reaching understanding implies communicating in order to achieve a valid agreement, that is, one reached without coercion. Habermas additionally sees unconstrained communication as central to any conception of reason. Because the nature of coming to an understanding refers to uncoerced communication, Habermas hopes that a conception of reason might be found in a philosophy of language. This conception of reason will arise out of the "formal properties of action oriented to reaching understanding" (*TCA*1, 392). Furthermore, Habermas believes that a new conception of reason will express how the different spheres of rationality in modernity interconnect. For Habermas, then, communicative rationality must be formal and must maintain the differentiation of rationality spheres.

Clearly, Habermas's analysis of Horkheimer and Adorno's critique of enlightenment focuses exclusively on instrumental rationality. Habermas refers repeatedly in his analysis to the failings of instrumental rationality but writes nothing of the failings of formal rationality. He does not seem to recognize that subjective rationality includes both instrumental rationality and formal rationality. Rather, in Kantian character, he has set himself up to critique instrumental rationality from the perspective of formal rationality. This reliance on formal rationality will prove the downfall of communicative rationality as a solution to the problem that Horkheimer and Adorno point to.

Habermas's Communicative Rationality

Habermas's conception of communicative rationality is developed within the context of his general theory of society, which he lays out thoroughly in the two-volume work *The Theory of Communicative Action*. This work is not primarily a philosophical work but a socio-theoretical one. Thus, as Maeve Cooke notes, the development of the concept of communicative rationality must be seen within the context of Habermas's larger project.[3] His theory of communicative rationality remains important because of that larger project and also because of its contemporary standing within the philosophical and social theoretical communities.

The Larger Context: Theory of Society

Habermas wants to defend the insights of the Frankfurt School of Social Research while correcting its diagnosis of society. He begins by accepting a two-level distinction in society along Marxian lines. Whereas Marx thought society could be analyzed in terms of (economic) base and superstructure, Habermas devises the two concepts of lifeworld and systems. Habermas explains that deformations form in the lifeworld when systems inflict violence upon it. This two-level distinction in society allows Habermas to develop his theory of communicative action on the level of the lifeworld.

The theory of communicative action is a formal-pragmatic theory of language as oriented to reaching understanding. The term "formal-pragmatic," or "universal-pragmatic," points to two aspects of the theory of communicative action. The theory is universal and formal, in the sense that Habermas searches for universal features of language as such. That is, Habermas seeks to discover those universal presuppositions that underlie "everyday communication in modern societies."[4] The theory is pragmatic in that it looks for these universal presuppositions in the use of language.

In general, for Habermas, all communicative use of language has a telos of reaching understanding. Taking up Austin's distinction between locutionary, illocutionary, and perlocutionary acts, Habermas attempts to show that every use of language, in order to succeed, must rely on the supposition that the language user is attempting to reach an understanding with another language user. The theory proves important in the present context because of how development of the theory of communicative action leads to and informs a conception of reason as communicative rationality. "The concept of communicative rationality is based on the thesis that the basic units of everyday linguistic activity raise various kinds of intersubjectively criticizable validity claims."[5] That is, in the everyday use of language, people raise claims that they are prepared to defend as valid through open communication with others. Habermas locates rationality within this raising and defending of validity claims.

The phrase "communicative action" names that interaction "in which *all* participants harmonize their individual plans of action with one another and thus pursue their illocutionary aims *without reservation*" (*TCA*1, 294). The coordination of the actions of agents in society is due not to the egocentric calculations of success but to acts of reaching understanding. More particularly, plans of action are harmonized by way of people raising a validity claim that others either accept or reject based on grounds or reasons. Through the raising and acceptance or rejection of validity claims, members of society coordinate their activities. The idea that communicatively achieved agreement has a rational basis proves most important for a discussion of the critical power of practical reasoning. Agreement rests, for Habermas, on common convictions. Two communicators base their acceptance or rejection of a validity claim on potential grounds or reasons that support or undermine that claim (*TCA*1, 287). Such communication, furthermore, rests on unquestioned background knowledge: a knowledge that participants normally consider an obvious truth. The knowledge is implicit, historically structured, and not at the disposal of speakers. Following Wittgenstein, Habermas holds that this background knowledge is something about which "we normally know nothing" explicitly (*TCA*1, 337).

Communicative Rationality and Postmetaphysical Thinking

Maeve Cooke, an interpreter of Habermas, contends that

communicative rationality is the mode of dealing with validity claims that is practiced by participants (primarily) in *postconventional* forms

of communicative action. Participants necessarily suppose not only
[1] that all taking part are using the same linguistic expressions in the
same way, [2] that no relevant opinions have been suppressed or excluded, [3] that no force is exerted except that of the better argument,
and [4] that everyone is motivated only by the desire for truth but also
[5] that no validity claim is in principle exempt from the critical evaluation of the participants.[6]

A postconventional form of communicative action is one whose practice presumes that no claim lies beyond question. The parameters established by this understanding of communication set the standards of
rationality. These parameters involve the open-endedness of the communication, the identity of expressions, the general equality of participants in being able to participate, and the goal of finding truth without
resort to something outside of the force of the better argument. In these
parameters, Habermas finds a postmetaphysical, situated conception
of reason.

Cooke lists five aspects of postmetaphysical thinking: first, rationality is seen as procedural; second, philosophy is seen as fallible and
not foundational; third, rationality is situated within a historical context and is not abstract; fourth, the focus is not on consciousness but
on the pragmatics of language; and fifth, language is recognized as
being concerned not only with theoretical truth and representation but
also with moral-practical and expressive dimensions. In short, postmetaphysical thinking recognizes three validity dimensions of reason:
"propositional truth, normative rightness, and subjective truthfulness
or authenticity."[7] Through reliance on these five aspects of postmetaphysical thinking, Habermas aims to save a conception of reason from
the nihilism that threatens it from postmodern, antimodern, and pre-
modern corners. Two of those aspects of postmetaphysical thinking—
proceduralness and situatedness—merit attention here.

Procedural Rationality

For objectivist ontologies, either reason is found in the structure of
the world or the world is given structure by reason itself. Thus reason
constitutes a part of the whole and the parts—that is, reason can be

found in the parts of the universe and also in the universe as a whole. In contrast, for Habermas, procedural rationality is found only within the approach and procedure of a given rationality sphere. It is procedural because it rests within formally defined processes of argumentation.[8] Rationality lies in the procedures of argumentation. Content disappears from rationality; what counts as rational "is solving problems successfully through procedurally suitable dealings with reality" (*PMT* 34). Two restricted domains provide examples: for modern empirical science rationality lies in the method of scientific knowledge, while for autonomous morality rationality lies in the abstract point of view "from which moral insights are possible."

On a procedural approach to rationality, philosophy can no longer claim a privileged access to truth. In contrast to the foundational knowledge of *prima philosophia,* modern science proceeds by way of hypothesis. Hypotheses are justified through empirical testing or their fit with the rest of an already accepted theory. Philosophy, as a result, takes on a different role. Lacking a privileged access to truth, to a unique method, or to a unique field of investigation, philosophy turns to pose universal questions within each and to reconstruct the intuitive, pretheoretical knowledge of speaking and acting subjects in terms of the subject matter of each rationality sphere. Finally, philosophy may also act as mediator between expert cultures—those of (1) science, (2) morality and law, and (3) art—and the everyday communicative practice of individuals.

Situated Reason

> From the possibility of reaching understanding linguistically, we can read off a concept of situated reason that is given voice in validity claims that are both context-dependent and transcendent. . . . The validity claimed for propositions and norms transcends spaces and times, but in each actual case the claim is raised here and now, in a specific context, and accepted or rejected with real implications for social interactions. (*PMT* 139)

Habermas wants to reject the claims of a transcendent metaphysical reason while retaining the power of reason to make claims that are context transcendent. In objectivist ontologies, reason provided an objective point from which to ascertain truth or rightness. Habermas associates this sort of thinking with Kant and Hegel. Reason and its claims transcended the here and now. In postmetaphysical thinking, however, reason is seen as contextualized within space and time. Stronger, reason is part of a historical context that limits its ability to make "objective" claims outside of space and time. The claims of reason are justified within a specific historical context.

The idea here is the following: every linguistic community shares certain concepts, such as truth, rationality, and justification. It might be true that in each different linguistic community these concepts are interpreted differently and even applied according to different criteria. Regardless of those semantic divergences, they each play the same syntactic role: they act as normative limit concepts that determine the validity of a speech act. For example, according to Habermas, every language community has a notion of truth. Furthermore, they distinguish between what is true and what the members of the community hold to be true. Whereas one language community might understand truth as "X" and another language community understands truth as "Y," both communities distinguish between that to which they assign the quality X or Y and that which actually has the quality X or Y.

These claims about X or Y arise within specific historical and social contexts. Rationality does not operate from some extramundane standpoint, nor is the subject making truth claims understood to stand at some extramundane location. Rather, communicative rationality constitutes a conception of rationality that is "already operative in the everyday communicative practices of modern societies."[9] Communicative rationality is not something available only to a few or only in certain circumstances, but something everyone already uses in daily life.

Even so, rationality must be able to make transcendent claims. According to Habermas, Hilary Putnam "establishes the unavoidability of an idealizing conceptual construction" (*PMT* 137). Putnam claims that we are able to improve our standards of rationality. This improvement is possible because of a distinction found in everyday communicative practices between what we hold to be true here and now and what we hold to be true in all places and times. Because one can distinguish between the true-for-us and the true simpliciter, one makes claims that are supposed to transcend space and time, but which are made in the here and now and can be challenged in the here and now.

I have been focusing on the notion of truth. For Habermas, though, the same things can be said about rationality or justification. These terms, though interpreted differently, play the same role in each linguistic community. Thus, whenever issues of rationality and justification arise in local contexts, they tend to transcend those contexts. "Even in the most difficult processes of reaching understanding, all parties appeal to the common reference point of a possible consensus, even if this reference point is projected in each case from within their own context. For although they may be interpreted in various ways and applied according to different criteria, concepts like truth, rationality, or justification play the *same* grammatical role in *every* linguistic community" (*PMT* 138; emphasis original). This claim relies on the procedural nature of Habermas's formal pragmatics. This formal pragmatics claims that procedural rationality relies no longer on the rationality of the content but only on the rationality of suitable methods for dealing with the world. The content of the concept of rationality in each language is of no consequence; rather, one should focus on the role it plays in those languages. Because that concept plays the same role in every language, it lends itself to a universal rationality.

Three Rationality Spheres: Antifoundationalism

Given that rationality is procedural and situated, Habermas claims that philosophy should no longer seek to use reason to establish a foundation for knowledge or society. Just as Newton and his followers did not need philosophy to provide a foundation for "modern" science, neither does modern culture need philosophy to provide a foundation for it. Following Max Weber, Habermas holds that, in modernity, three rationality spheres have been differentiated: scientific, legal and moral, and aesthetic. Modern culture gave rise to these spheres of rationality without the help of philosophy: "With modern science, with positive law and principled secular ethics, with autonomous art and institutionalized art criticism, three moments of reason crystallized without help from philosophy. . . . The sons and daughters of modernity learned how to divide up and develop further the cultural tradition under these different aspects of rationality—as questions of truth, justice, or taste." Science, therefore, puts aside questions of worldviews and proceeds without interpreting nature or history "as a whole"; cognitive ethics sheds problems of the good life and concentrates on deontological, universalizable aspects of law; and autonomous art chases a pure articulation of the basic aesthetic experience of subjectivity that transcends "spatio-temporal structures of everyday life" (*TCA2*, 397).

The shedding of these superfluous aspects by each rationality sphere is the signature of modernity, according to Habermas. Further, no rationality sphere rests on a transcendental foundation of justification. Two questions remain to be answered: Can rationality retain its unity even with the differentiation of these rationality spheres? and, What mediates between these spheres and everyday practice? These questions can be answered by a formal pragmatics together with the theories of science, of law and morality, and of aesthetics, through the reconstruction of the history of their differentiation under different aspects of validity. This knowledge would constitute the self-understanding of the rationality spheres.

Habermas attempts to answer the first question, namely, what provides for the unity between the three rationality spheres? "In each of these spheres, differentiation processes are accompanied by counter-movements that, under the primacy of one dominant aspect of validity, bring back in again the two aspects that were first excluded." Thus, the boundary of each sphere is delimited by the processes unique to it. These differentiating processes themselves, however, are joined by countermovements so that the other two spheres are brought back into the first. They come back only under the domination of the primary sphere. According to Habermas, only through this mediation in the human sciences is a "critical social theory made possible" (*TCA2*, 398). In each sphere, while issues that arise in the other two spheres might enter in, the procedures of the home sphere remain dominant. For example, questions of moral and aesthetic viewpoints may be raised in the sphere of science without undermining the pursuit of truth. Again, these debates occur not in everyday communication but in the differentiated cultural spheres of rationality—that is, specialized topic-specific discourse.[10]

Saving Modernity

At this point discussing several themes from earlier in this chapter will prove helpful: Habermas's critique of the first-generation Frankfurt School, his proposed change in paradigm from a philosophy of the subject to a philosophy of language, and the conception of communicative rationality which emerges from his theory of communicative action. Habermas's critique of the Frankfurt School involved the claim that the project begun by Horkheimer ended in ruins. Critique became total when it focused on reason and on critique itself. Unable to escape a philosophy of the subject, the Frankfurt School could not uncover the power of rationality located in everyday communication.

In line with his larger project of developing a theory of society, Habermas then argues that, for social-theoretical work, the paradigm of the philosophy of the subject must be replaced with the paradigm of the philosophy of language. The concepts of freedom and reconciliation can be spelled out only through a concept of intersubjectivity. Intersubjectivity, in turn, can be explained only from the paradigm of a philosophy of language. Language, as oriented to reaching understanding, presumes that interlocutors can ask for and give reasons for their validity claims. Thus, it presumes a certain equality between and freedom among the participants. Through language use, individuals are recognized as free subjects capable of taking a yes or no stand toward a speech act. Further, the use of language requires (1) that language users are reconciled in their use of linguistic expressions and (2) that through communicative actions they come to an understanding with each other and, thereby, coordinate their actions.

These rationality conditions are spelled out in a postmetaphysical understanding of reason. Communicative actions presume a non-foundational, procedural, historically situated rationality found in the everyday use of language that presupposes the differentiation of rationality spheres. Rationality lies embedded in the processes of everyday communication of individuals; rationality refers no longer to the content of a claim but to the procedure by which communicators arrived at that claim. Finally, a theory of communicative rationality insists that rationality transcends the immediate context while remaining non-metaphysical or foundationalist. This transcendence of reason relies on the pragmatics of language use throughout cultures. All cultures have some similar concepts which function in exactly the same grammatical way, allowing for the possibility of improving the language group's conception of rationality. Linguistic users can, in short, distinguish between the true and the true for us.

With this postmetaphysical conception of communicative rationality, Habermas believes that he continues the project of modernity. "The project of modernity as it was formulated by the philosophers of the Enlightenment in the eighteenth century consists in the relentless development of the objectivating sciences, of the universalistic foundations of morality and law, and of autonomous art, all in accord with their own immanent logic. But at the same time it also results in releasing the cognitive potential accumulated in the process from their esoteric high forms and attempting to apply them in the sphere of praxis, that is, to encourage the rational organization of social relations" (Modernity 45).

Contrary to Horkheimer and Adorno, Habermas claims that the differentiation of rationality spheres does not disempower reason, but instead makes it all that much stronger. Progress is made by allowing each sphere to work out its own questions according to its own logic. Communicative rationality encourages such differentiated activity and finds in it the possibility of true critique. Ideology critique is concerned with separating out and bringing under suspicion those claims that rely on power relationships for their truth. Ideology critique "advances the process of enlightenment by showing that a theory presupposing a demythologized understanding of the world is still ensnared in myth, by pointing out a putatively overcome category mistake." Ideology critique requires that science, morality, and art be "cleansed of all cosmological, theological and cultic dross."[11] Only the differentiation of rationality spheres allows such cleansing. Differentiation removes the foreign issues that invade from separate spheres to distort the particular procedures of the sphere invaded. This differentiation of rationality spheres is steeped in a theory of communicative action.

From a Philosophy of Language to a Philosophy of Tradition

Habermas believes that his approach to rationality—to base it on a philosophy of language—proves superior to Horkheimer's philosophy of consciousness. However, in critiquing instrumental reason from a formal-pragmatics theory of language, that is, with a formal rationality, he misses the whole critique that Horkheimer offers in the *DOE* and the *Eclipse*. He fails to recognize that formal rationality is one with instrumental rationality in its inability to critique ends. He also incorporates hidden ends and values within the theory of communicative rationality, ends and values that undermine the very formality of communicative rationality. An analysis of Charles Taylor's discussion of Habermas's communicative rationality will illustrate both of these failings.

Taylor shows that Habermas's conception of rationality remains a formal conception and, thus, incapable of evaluating ends. An example from Plato's *Republic* will support Taylor's argument while demonstrating the underlying values of communicative rationality. In the end, we must reject Habermas's communicative rationality as an answer to the problem of reason in modernity. However, Habermas's philosophy of language moves in the right direction: it points from a philosophy of consciousness to a philosophy of tradition, an insight that will motivate a consideration of Alasdair MacIntyre's tradition-constituted reason in the rest of the book.

Taylor's Criticism of Habermas

Charles Taylor believes that Habermas's formal ethics mirrors that of Immanuel Kant. He therefore wishes to contrast that formal approach with a substantive morality found in Aristotle. "Kant is the most important representative of formal conceptions, arguing that we should determine the good life not in terms of its contents, namely as a form of life to be realized. Rather, we should determine what is correct on the basis of the procedure we adopt to decide what we should do. It is this procedure that is supposedly rational. It is then rationality as the perfection of the procedure, i.e., procedural rationality, which is the fundamental concept and not, as in Aristotle's work, the good life."[12]

Although a formal morality might be preferred over a substantive one for various reasons, Taylor contends that a formal morality proves inconsistent in the end. A formal morality cannot justify or motivate action. Habermas summarizes Taylor's challenge: "As an actor, I can always ask the question why I should actually proceed according to a particular norm, namely rationally. . . . This is a question which one can only answer, to use my own terminology, with 'strong valuations.'"[13]

This criticism does not hinge on whether one accepts or rejects the norm structurally found in human speech—reaching understanding. Nor is it defeated by Habermas's accusation of performative contradiction. A performative contradiction arises when one uses speech in such a way that the use of it contradicts the underlying logic of the use of language. I cannot, for instance, give a rational argument against rationality per se. Taylor can accept that language is oriented to reaching understanding and that creating solidarity requires rational understanding. Still, he contends he may also already value other things and have other aims and interests. Taylor can ask, consequently, about why the aim of reaching understanding, achieving solidarity, or maintaining an intact intersubjectivity should outweigh any of the other goals a person might have. That is, why should one not violate the logic of discourse if one accepts it as one value among many?

"The fitting answer to this question is to be found only at another level. I must be able to show why it is I attach value to rational understanding so great that it *should* be preferred to all other purposes." If a person can demonstrate that she values rationality above all other values, then she, by default, engages in substantive ethics. She already has a "substantialist concept of human life."[14] Following the logic of discourse makes sense only if one values that logic or if one cannot help but value that logic. Moreover, following the logic of discourse in the way Habermas maps it out makes sense only if one values that course of action above all other courses. Habermas's argument prioritizes the values that flow from communicative action above all other values. Someone else might, however, agree about the logic of discourse and yet have other values that supersede those that come from communicative action. This reference to a code of valuations implies a form of life, or a substantial conception of the good life. Formal ethics can go only so far.

Taylor lays out his criticism in another way. "A fundamental principle of the type comprised by the norm of rational understanding cannot decide all questions of strong valuations."[15] The principle of reaching understanding proves incompatible with authoritarian conditions and exploitation; yet that principle might be indifferent to or agreeable with other values and issues—for example, ecological issues. Answers to these problems require substantial determinations of what constitutes the good life. According to Taylor, Habermas attempts to distinguish questions of justice from questions of the good life. Questions of justice are prior to questions of the good life.

This priority, according to Taylor, proves difficult to defend for three reasons. First, the distinction "starkly contradicts our usual moral consciousness."[16] Defining our form of life as a question of health or beauty as distinct from morality seems bizarre, according to our normal conception. Taylor's first criticism takes aim at the differentiation of rationality spheres in modernity as well as the fragmentation of life. This criticism, however, appears weak given the vignettes from the introduction. If nothing else, those vignettes suggest that contemporary people of Western democracies have in fact separated out questions of form of life from questions of morality. As an ethics instructor, I find this fragmentation to be par for the course for most students, even when strong religious backgrounds are stirred into the mix. Further, as I will discuss in the next chapter, Alasdair MacIntyre's critique of modernity rests just on this fact of fragmentation. As a criticism of Habermas, then, this approach proves only that Habermas has articulated what might be symptomatic of a disordered modernity as though it were ethically superior.

Taylor's second argument against Habermas's communicative rationality has greater merit. Habermas's position entails that reasonableness must be considered a virtue and that reaching rational understanding must be considered an important or guiding ideal. He argues, in short, that both reasonableness and reaching rational understanding are values inherent to the procedures of communicative language. Yet his argument is flawed. A central area of moral problems "focuses on weighing up the often mutually competing claims of different virtues against one another and bringing about a uniform, consistent form of life."[17] Reasonableness and reaching understanding, then, might be important values, but Taylor is suggesting that they must in fact be weighed against other values so that the agents adhering to them develop a "uniform, consistent form of life." Abandoning the need for such consistency, as Habermas seems to do, makes the assertion of the values of reasonableness and reaching rational understanding arbitrary. Just because these values are inherent in or arise from the use of language as oriented to reaching understanding does not entail, by itself, that agents must accept communicative rationality as a highest value or even one value among many others. A question that plagues contemporary moral philosophy, then, also plagues Habermas's discourse ethics: Why be moral?

According to Taylor, for Habermas "two types of virtue are linked to one another. The fact that we should prefer rational understanding to norm-free steering mechanisms is closely bound up with our understanding of human dignity which, in turn, is inseparable from certain concepts of self-development and self-obligation."[18] Our ideas of self-development, which Habermas exiles to the realm of aesthetic rationality, are closely tied to our preference for a form of life which values rational understanding. This claim of Taylor's is the reverse of his previous claim. Not only is rational understanding a value for us, but other values are linked to it. Our preference for a life aimed at rational understanding over one guided by norm-free steering mechanisms relies on conceptions of human dignity.

Habermas does not deny this link. Indeed he affirms it in *Postmetaphysical Thinking*. He links his procedural ethics to a humanist tradition and project that aimed at eradicating all forms of life which do not "endeavor to moderate, abolish or prevent the suffering of vulnerable creatures."[19] He believes that the transition to the modern period is a progressive move to a better understanding of human life. He defends this cultural development through a philosophical account of moral learning. Wilhelm Rehg, in his discussion of the debate between Habermas and Taylor, shows that the difference between the two theo-

rists on this issue cannot be answered without further in-depth empirical studies.[20] Habermas and Taylor present us with different versions of
the rise of modernity, and their accounts rest on empirical studies still
to be conducted. In this regard, however, Habermas has not provided
an unquestioned approach to the question of reason in modernity.
That is, with respect to the designs of a critical theory of society, it remains a viable course of action to develop an alternative conception of
reason, such as the substantive one I develop in this book. Further, the
ambiguity in this second argument pushes us toward the third argument, which proves more difficult for a Habermassian to defeat.

Taylor's third argument against Habermas takes aim at the role of
neutrality in the theory of communicative rationality. The basic premise of a procedural morality, generally tied to a liberal form of justice,
is neutrality concerning the good life. Views of the good life simply
conflict, and no clear way to decide among them exists. Thus, liberals
conclude that what is needed is not a morality based on a conception of
the good life but a formal ethics which outlines a procedure by which
to determine the right course of action. Kant's project lay along those
lines, and the introductory section of *Grounding for the Metaphysics of
Morals* contains several arguments against accepting traditional views
of the good life.

Taylor contends, in contrast, that a theory of the right—whether
Kantian, Rawlsian, or Habermassian—presumes and depends on a theory of the good. As already stated, the norm of rational understanding
is one norm among many—is part of a conception of the good or of the
good life. One can say that language is primarily oriented to reaching
understanding, just as one can say that wool protects against the cold.
Until one grasps or holds dear a fundamental value—that reaching rational understanding is good, that warmth is good—these two factual
statements have no bearing on a person's actions. Only with the presence of strong substantive valuations does the theory of communicative action, as procedural, become a foundation for morality.

Again, this discussion addresses the attempt to draw a sharp line
between questions of the good and questions of justice. Not only is
such a distinction falsely construed, but it "is the unhappy consequence of the underlying decision to opt for a procedural" morality.

The decision for a procedural morality results in not only the distinction between justice and ethics but also the differentiation of spheres of rationality that Habermas "unreservedly incorporates into his own theory."[21] In earlier times, questions of truth, rightness, and authenticity were inextricably bound together. Questions about the normatively right thing to do depended on the truth of the constitution of the cosmos. Questions of authenticity "would have been meaningless to our ancestors." Indeed, Aristotle founds his moral theory on the value of self-realization—which Habermas would treat as an aspect of aesthetic rationality—a value that ultimately relied on claims about the factual constitution of the world.

That these questions of truth, rightness, and authenticity have been relatively differentiated from one another in modernity cannot be doubted. Habermas argues, however, that modernity resolves questions in each rationality sphere based on differing justifying reasons and criteria. Taylor contends that "this thesis rests on two prior assertions: first, that modernity does indeed increasingly treat questions of truth, rightness and authenticity as though each applied in a logically independent sphere of its own; and, second, that this is factually correct, in other words, that modern differentiation constitutes progress by taking into account the logical structure of these questions in their respective particularity more effectively than the traditional interlinking of the different dimensions of validity involved."[22]

For Taylor, both of the assertions prove, if not false, at least open to question. People in general do not begin by ascertaining duties on the basis of procedure. Rather, they "initially recognize differing purposes of life or virtues," then strive to balance them in an appropriate relationship. Deliberations on these matters can be considered neither factual deliberations nor reflective deliberations that only indirectly involve factual deliberation. Rather our thoughts about which purposes "we should accord recognition [to] are inextricably linked to those considerations on what we as human beings *are*."[23] Questions of what should be the case are linked with questions of what is the case. Thus, because they share similar concepts, questions of morals and theories of human motivation are closely tied together. Thus, Taylor rejects Habermas's first assertion, a rejection that means that the second does not even apply.

If the two assertions underlying the theory of the differentiation of validity spheres prove false, then the separation between truth, rightness, and authenticity cannot be maintained. Singling out any of the dimensions distorts the world and human experience. "If this critique holds true, then either rationality as the fundamental ethical principle must be supplemented, or an expanded concept of rationality must be introduced." Such an expanded concept would include substantive criteria, for example, that "one could broach one's own moral situation without distortion thereof." Language, then, would "make it possible to reach understanding only to the extent that it would disclose what our situation was without any distortion."[24]

Taylor finds such a concept of language within part of his reconstruction of Habermas's position—that is, in the discussion of the We-perspectives. To mend tears in the "We" through consensus, people must be able to articulate what content in their form of life "is good and has proved itself in intersubjective terms." Using this observation to summarize his criticism of Habermas, Taylor holds that the enormous benefits a discourse theory of language has for a theory of society are gambled away with the acceptance of a procedural approach to morality and the differentiation of validity spheres. Practical reason becomes distorted in the absence of "the central role language plays as a means of disclosing new terrain."[25] This distortion prevents our understanding of ourselves from contributing to conceptions of normative rightness.

Habermas's Reply

In replying to Taylor, Habermas first characterizes Taylor's criticism. Taylor, Habermas contends, does not deny that rational speech potentially contains communicative rationality; Taylor does hold, however, that Habermas's explanation of rationality is false because it is explained in terms of formalist ethics. Habermas contends, then, that Taylor too quickly "introduce[s] philosophical [morality] into the discussion."[26] Communicative rationality is not limited to the moral-practical sphere of rationality. The everyday practice of communication extends over a wider range of validity claims. Habermas rephrases Taylor's complaint: "Does not *every* concept of rationality have to remain enmeshed with the substantive contents of a particular form of life, with a particular vision of the good?"[27] Taylor can easily accept that communicative rationality is not limited to one aspect or sphere. The real issue lies in the question, to what extent does a form of life underlie every validity claim?

In one sense, Habermas captures part of Taylor's complaint. Taylor does not believe that communicative practice remains limited to one rationality sphere. On the other hand, Taylor's criticism extends beyond that complaint, and so Habermas's reformulation of Taylor's question misses the point. That every concept of rationality must be enmeshed in a vision of the good is not at issue. Rather, Taylor would claim that every concept of rationality, *in order to have moral bearing*, must be enmeshed in a *particular* vision of the good. Right, or morality, or justice cannot be handled separately from questions of the good life. In other words, to raise and answer questions of right, or justice, or morality, one must already embrace a conception of the good life from which one can address those issues.

Missing this essential claim, Habermas attempts to refute Taylor's argument by turning to Humboldt's theory of language, which, Habermas believes, explains how languages entail a formal element on the basis of which one may legitimately institute a formal morality. According to Humboldt's theory, "languages, as the form-giving principles guiding the shape taken by the individual totality of each respectively particular view of the world and way of life, only have an effect to the extent that, by virtue of their universalistic core, they enable translations to be made from each language into every other language and determine the point of convergence towards which all cultural developments are aimed. . . . Thus, nobody may speak to another person in a manner different from that in which the latter, under identical conditions, would have spoken to him."[28]

In *Postmetaphysical Thinking*, Habermas claims that languages serve the function of translating between cultures. In this reply to Taylor, Habermas points to the same function of language to achieve comprehension between different forms of life through language. In *Postmetaphysical Thinking*, this function of translation serves the humanist project. Habermas there holds that the possibility of reaching understanding linguistically laid bare the concept of a situated reason. This concept points to the possibility of adjudicating validity claims which are context dependent and yet transcendent. "The grammatically regulated world views and forms of life . . . correspond to one another in terms of their formal and most general structures. Because all life-worlds have to reproduce themselves through the agency of action oriented towards reaching understanding, so the general character of communicative rationality stands out within the multiplicity of concrete forms of life."[29]

Every language functions in such a way as to reproduce the life-world of the particular people of whom it is a language. Reproducing the lifeworld of a particular people is a general and formal structural function of language that is shared by all languages. Similarly, *Postmetaphysical Thinking* discovered that all languages have the same concepts of truth, rationality, and justification, which—though they may be understood in different ways—play the same roles. These formal characteristics of language comprise the universalistic potential of speech. "If moral philosophy appeals to this [potential] . . . then it can in fact develop a formal or procedural ethics only from it."[30] On Habermas's account, a procedural ethics arises from the very telos of communicative language. On Taylor's account, however, a procedural ethics arises only if a certain condition is met—that the language users already agree to abide by the moral values embedded in such universal characteristics of language. I think that Habermas does not address this point of Taylor's.

The Case of Plato's Guardians

Taylor finds Habermas's morality too formal. To justify his morality, Habermas bases it on a formal conception of rationality that emerges out of the universal characteristics of language and language translation. Because languages share common formal features, Habermas claims that a procedural morality may be developed. Taylor does not deny, however, that a formal morality can emerge from the formal features of language. Rather, he contends that in order for such a procedural morality to have any moral force, people must already subscribe to the strong substantive valuations that underwrite it. In short, that communicative language users presuppose the values of a procedural ethics does not by itself mean that they have already subscribed to the strong substantive valuations that underwrite that procedural ethics. The question is whether they should value these substantive valuations. The following example makes this point.

For members of a modern Western democracy, using language to reach understanding is highly important and valuable. We believe that this means of communication, this way of interacting with other people, is less harmful than other means of interacting and communicating.

Consider Plato's *Republic,* in which he justifies the order of the state on a lie. Plato, of course, believes in the power of reason. He holds that until philosophers become kings or kings become philosophers trained in the use of reason, we will never have a just state. Philosophy by default depends on a commitment to reason. Yet Plato does not believe that most human beings—the many—are capable of following reason most of the time. How could he, when the many killed his beloved master, Socrates? So Plato argues that in order for the state to maintain its harmony, the guardians must lie to the other members of society. They must insist that the common people are made from bronze, that the warriors are made from silver, and that the guardians are made from gold. The guardians are most precious.

In this example from the *Republic,* the commitment to the value of reason takes second place to the value of maintaining the harmony between the different classes in society. Harmony in the state must be maintained in order for the state to be prosperous or happy. This harmony includes, of course, the rule of the wise over those less wise.

Habermas would likely contend that Plato is involved in a performative contradiction. Plato relies on and accepts the conditions of the use of rationality. Yet he undermines those conditions, first, when he denies the reason of the many and, second, when he prioritizes harmony over reason in the lie told about the origins of people. The fact that he prioritizes harmony over rationality in the name of the defense of reason proves his guilt of a performative contradiction only more.

This answer from Habermas cannot succeed, however. First, Habermas's theory of communicative rationality relies on a particular conception of human beings: that human beings are rational beings who use speech to reach understanding. Plato cannot accept this substantive concept of human beings nor this concept of reason. Every moral argument proceeds on the basis of some view of human nature. Habermas's theory of communicative rationality and the formal-pragmatics of morality does not escape this fact, but relies on the possibilities of so escaping it. Second, to contend that Plato violates principles of rationality through his performative contradiction means nothing practically unless Plato believes that performative contradictions are bad per se and must be avoided. That is, the notion of a performative contradiction constitutes a strong substantive valuation. Aside from making a scientific claim, the claim that another engages in a performative contradiction has moral value only if one values not contradicting oneself. Third, and finally, the issue concerns not that one makes a performative contradiction but that Plato values harmony at least as much as he values rationality. Habermas is committed to rationality, and Plato to reason and harmony.

In other words, for Habermas to raise the question of right to Plato, he must already be committed to a form of the good life from which he prioritizes equality over inequality or justice over harmony. In order for communicative rationality to have moral bearing, it must already admit its commitment to a particular vision of the good life. The good is prior to the right; a formal morality depends on a substantive one.

Habermas, admittedly, could argue that Plato does indeed commit himself to a rational approach to justice. What is the force of this commitment, though? Is it a pragmatic force or a moral force? Surely it is a pragmatic force, which Habermas wants to argue works simultaneously as a moral force. The moral force comes, however, from the shared moral insights of people living in modernity. Pragmatically, Plato is committed to reaching justice rationally; morally he is committed to reaching justice by whatever means prove necessary.

I am arguing that questions of justice, the good life, and reality intertwine and depend upon each other for resolution. We cannot effectively pursue the aims of critical theory until we have embraced them in a substantive view of the world and morality—as a form of life that we value as worthwhile for everyone. The point is that a notion of tradition underlies the moral bearing of any conception of reason. Before one can spell out a conception of reason, one must first spell out a conception of tradition and a concept of reason with that conception. The next chapter will explore this claim more fully.

| Habermas rightly contends that Horkheimer and Adorno remain wedded to a philosophy of consciousness. A more fruitful approach to the question of reason and its ability to support a critical theory of society must move away from such a philosophy, and Habermas makes that move. Yet his focus on a philosophy of language falls short of what is needed, a philosophy of tradition. In part, it fails because he focuses only on Horkheimer and Adorno's critique of instrumental rationality as opposed to their critique of subjective rationality—that is, instrumental rationality and formal rationality. In the next chapter I will argue that reason is necessarily embedded in traditions, and that from that embeddedness reason gains content from a conception of the good. That is, the next chapter shows a conception of substantive reason may be developed by linking the concepts of reason, tradition, and the good as mutually constituting each other.

Since a conception of reason is informed by a conception of the good, the definition of reason is much broader than that provided by Habermas. Habermas defines reason as the raising and defending of validity claims, but this definition captures only an aspect of the broader understanding of reason, which is *a set of social practices which involve the asking for and giving of reasons, the evaluation of those reasons and the asking for and giving of such evaluation, and, importantly, the evaluation of the good.* By developing the link between reason and the good within a tradition, I can defend a conception of substantive reason that, in contrast to Habermas's communicative rationality, provides the resources for agents to judge ways of life as fulfilling or inimical to fulfillment.

3 | MacIntyre's Tradition-Constituted Reason

Modernity suffers from a crisis of reason. The Enlightenment project failed because of the dominance of subjective rationality in modernity. Horkheimer and company outlined a program for emancipatory reason, but Habermas showed the Frankfurt School's conception of rationality to be inadequate because of its reliance on a philosophy of consciousness. Yet Habermas's attempt at rescuing modernity founders on the same shoals as did those of other Enlightenment and modern thinkers—the subjectivization of reason—for he proposes a formal rationality that cannot evaluate ends.

Must the pessimism so evident throughout Horkheimer and Adorno's *Dialectic of Enlightenment* be accepted? Or can some other way out of the problem of reason be found? Must one acknowledge Nietzsche's will to power, revitalized by Michel Foucault and other contemporary postmodern philosophers, according to which morality and reason are divergent and morality names only the dictates and practices of the stronger group? Or can we rethink the project of modernity?

Critical theorists need not wallow in pessimism. Rather, a conception of reason can be found in philosophy that will support critical theory in the spirit of the Frankfurt School to pursue emancipation. Reason, however, must be understood not as a universal, ahistorical, or Archimedean phenomenon, but as constituted by and constitutive of tradition. Critical theory à la Horkheimer seeks a reason capable of judging ends. Only with a tradition-constitutive and tradition-constituted reason can ends be critiqued. The basis for this conception lies in Alasdair MacIntyre's account of moral philosophy and traditions of enquiry. For MacIntyre, standards of reason are constituted by tradition. What is reasonable for one tradition may not be reasonable for another. Moreover, argues MacIntyre, a claim of justice can be defended only with the conception of reason inherent in that tradition of justice within which the claim is raised.

MacIntyre's tradition-constituted reason[1] provides a starting point for a substantive conception of reason. MacIntyre discloses the fundamental historicity of reason, but he stops short of a conception of reason useful for a critical theory of society. For it to be useful in that way, a conception of reason must recognize that reason is fundamentally, and essentially, tied to the good and must explain the nature of that tie. Although MacIntyre suggests that an essential tie exists between reason and the good, he does not elucidate that relationship. Because this very relationship between reason and the good secures for reason the ability to judge ends, a critical theory of society must spell out that relationship in order to realize a conception of reason useful for purposes of emancipation.

I begin with a discussion of the need for moving from a communicative rationality to a tradition-constituted reason. This motivation stems from both Horkheimer's diagnosis of reason and the need for unrooting the historical contingencies of reason. I also point out the similarities between Horkheimer and MacIntyre. Both, for instance, reject major parts of modernity because of its failure to provide a means for evaluating ends. Showing the connection between Horkheimer and MacIntyre allows me, then, to examine and expand upon MacIntyre's notion of tradition and his defense of tradition-constituted reason. According to MacIntyre, traditions of enquiry are historically and socially embedded arguments about fundamental agreements; these arguments are shaped both by those who share and by those who do not share those agreements. On MacIntyre's account, reason consists in a set of beliefs and standards found within those arguments. Finally, I address three question for MacIntyre's account: (1) Can a tradition-constituted reason judge ends? (2) Is there a stronger connection between reason and the good than MacIntyre envisions? (3) Are there traditions other than traditions of enquiry, and if so, what is the significance of that fact for a critical theory of society? Question one will be answered in this chapter; questions two and three in the next.

The interpretation of MacIntyre I offer here preferences his treatment of tradition over his treatment of practices. This take differs from that of, for instance, Kelvin Knight in "Revolutionary Aristotelianism" and *Aristotelian Philosophy: Ethics and Politics from Aristotle to MacIntyre*. One cannot understand reason and virtue in MacIntyre's work or, more importantly, at all without looking at how both figure in everyday human practices and tradition. In my opinion, however, tradition serves as the fundamental unifying concept under which to understand reason, because it brings out the relationship not only between reason and practice but also between reason and the other aspects of a tradition: cosmologies, symbolic generalizations, ways of life (practices), and values. In fact, the connection between reason and value serves as the fundamental relationship that defines a substantive reason, which, I am arguing, proves necessary for a critical theory of society.

I seek a conception of reason that can do emancipatory work from the perspective of a critical theory of society. An adequately developed understanding of reason can provide the resources for a theory of society that criticizes society in the hopes of reforming it in the direction of greater freedom. Critique proves immanent in tradition and in practice.

Further, the reference to critique for reforming society in the direction of greater freedom steeps this argument in Frankfurt School Critical Theory as well as in MacIntyre's Thomistic-Aristotelianism. It develops MacIntyre's synthesis of Marxism and Aristotelianism along the same lines that the Frankfurt School Critical Theorists (Horkheimer, Adorno, Benjamin, Marcuse) developed Marxism. Given MacIntyre's relationship to Marx, one might wonder what he has said about the Frankfurt School. Unfortunately, his views as presented in *Marcuse* are ultimately dismissive of Marcuse and of the Frankfurt School in general. In other essays (collected in *Alasdair MacIntyre's Engagement with Marxism*), MacIntyre shows some scant appreciation for Marcuse; in the end, however, he finds Marcuse's approach to society too Hegelian and too pessimistic. More importantly, MacIntyre's "engagement with Marcuse" left the question of reason to the side. Thus, that discussion proves unhelpful in the analysis given here.

Quo Vadimus? From Horkheimer to MacIntyre

Historicizing Reason

In the *Eclipse*, Horkheimer held that "the true critique of reason will necessarily uncover the deepest layers of civilization and explore its earliest history" (*Eclipse* 176). The analysis in the introduction of the etymological roots of the English word "reason" ended with more questions than answers. That etymological analysis points out, however, that neither Horkheimer nor any of his colleagues have given a thorough historical account of reason. Understanding changes in conceptions of reason through the history of Western philosophy should prove fruitful at this juncture. Habermas's efforts to ground a universal, historical rationality do not help. His attempt to understand rationality from the perspective of a philosophy of language, rather than from that of a philosophy of consciousness, while innovative and a movement in the right direction, does not attempt to uncover the "deepest layers of civilization." Such layers appear no more clearly from within a philosophy of language than they do from within a philosophy of consciousness.

Marcuse's discussion of reason in *Eros and Civilization* provides deeper insights into these problems than does Habermas's social theory. Marcuse offers reasons why humanity continues to find itself in the grips of oppressive societies, and he suggests paths out of such oppression. Even here, however, Marcuse does not seem to penetrate deep enough. He certainly delves into the psyche of humanity, using Freudian theory, but he does not look at the historical development of reason or of civilization. The Freudian theory that Marcuse proposes will not be adequate until supplemented by a historical analysis of reason and human civilization. Marcuse's *Eros and Civilization*, like Habermas's *Communication and the Evolution of Society*, remains highly abstract. Both works attempt to establish a theoretical account of the rise of civilization, in terms of either the domination of both the reality principle and instrumental rationality or the evolution of objective structures of morality through the use of language. Neither, however, addresses the actual historical rise of these phenomena.

Marcuse might be excused here to a certain extent. He does not aim to provide an actual historical account of the rise of oppressive societies, but instead to uncover its roots in our collective or societal psyche. Habermas, on the other hand, provides an account which he says must be verified by social science. Such a verification requires the impossible—a glimpse through a time portal at the rise and development of human language. Certainly theorizing about such developments remains valuable for understanding humanity and human social life. Yet Habermas's account fails to understand its own roots and commitments to values.

Indeed, the account of a universal reason within Habermas's social theory appears striking because it seems to undermine his whole project; or, insofar as developing a conception of universal reason comprises his project, Habermas's work seems misguided. As discussed in the previous chapter, Habermas's communicative rationality attempts to find universal features of language that would establish both a universal reason and universal morality. Insofar as these features of language and reason are universal, however, they are also formal. Taylor argues that such formality belies a certain standpoint, which, when denied, undermines the whole project of a universal ethic. Horkheimer, moreover, has pointed out the need to develop a concept of objective reason to balance the dominating aspects of subjective rationality: "By its self-critique, reason must recognize the limitations of the two opposite concepts of reason; it must analyze the development of the cleavage between the two" (*Eclipse* 175).

Habermas's analysis of reason, and his construction of communicative rationality, miss objective (but nonuniversal) reason. In his account of what Horkheimer and Adorno find wrong with reason, he constantly focuses on the instrumental aspect and pays no attention to the formal aspect. Indeed, he must ignore what Horkheimer says about formal reason in order to develop his own conception of communicative rationality. What Habermas finds attractive about his conception of communicative rationality is the very fact that it remains neutral over against competing conceptions of the good—that is, that it is a formal conception of reason. According to Horkheimer, however, its substantive aspect—that is, a conception of the world/cosmos and of the good—renews the concept of reason and provides for its emancipatory power.

I propose the following: If we continually fail to find a solution to the problem of reason in modernity, we must look at the realm of the forsaken—we must seek a solution to the problem of reason in premodernity, upon which the instrumental, Enlightenment critique of objective reason focuses. We must search for an objective reason. This conception can be found in MacIntyre.

Similarities between Horkheimer and MacIntyre

Prima facie, the work of Alasdair MacIntyre seems to contradict that of the Frankfurt School and not to be of any use for a critical theory of society. MacIntyre is often criticized for being conservative, and both his reliance on Aristotle and gradual move to a more Thomistic position have only strengthened that impression, despite Kelvin Knight's persuasive arguments (in "Revolutionary Aristotelianism") to the contrary. Why, then, should a work seeking a critical theory of society look at someone like MacIntyre?

Several reasons can be found. First, if objective reason is needed to balance subjective rationality in modernity, one place to look would be within the philosophies of Aristotle and Thomas Aquinas. Horkheimer addresses neo-Thomism disparagingly in the *Eclipse*, and if the current investigation finds anything of value within Thomistic philosophy, those criticisms will have to be addressed. Yet the task remains to search for a conception of substantive reason, which can be found in MacIntyre's conception of tradition-constituted reason. Second, MacIntyre's criticism of modernity mirrors that of Horkheimer's. Both criticize modernity for its reliance on a subjective rationality incapable of judging ends and argue that modernity needs a substantive reason. MacIntyre, then, is himself a critic of modernity. His criticism begins with a discussion of emotivism.

MacIntyre claims that emotivism has become the dominant moral theory in modernity, whether those who espouse it are aware of making it so or not. Part of the problem with emotivism lies in that it does not allow for the evaluation of ends. Emotivism, like all moral philosophies, presupposes a sociology. Part of the content of that presupposed sociology is an "obliteration of any genuine distinction between manipulative and non-manipulative social relations" (*AV* 23). According to MacIntyre, a key component of pre-twentieth-century moral philosophies is a clear distinction between moral and nonmoral activity; whereas moral activity treats others as ends, nonmoral activity treats them as means. To treat someone as an end means to offer her good reasons for acting one way rather than another, and thereby allow her the possibility of evaluating those reasons. To treat someone as a means entails, in contrast, to use any means necessary to influence or affect that person's actions for one's own purposes. Using someone as a means generally entails that one does not want that person to evaluate one's reasons rationally.

According to MacIntyre, if emotivism is true, the distinction between using people as ends and using them as means becomes illusory (*AV* 24). For according to emotivism, a moral utterance has no value except as the expression of the utterer's feelings or attitudes. The moral utterance, says the emotivist, simply aims to transform the emotions and attitudes of others on an emotional, and not a rational, level. In other words, according to emotivism others are means and not ends; a distinction between manipulative and nonmanipulative social relations disappears. If the point of a moral utterance is simply to work on someone's emotions without regard to that person's reason, the speaker of the moral utterance manipulates rather than convinces with regard to that utterance. The speaker bypasses the possibility that the speaker's utterance undergoes rational evaluation by the hearer. This bypass, however, defines what it means to treat another as a means rather than an end.

Modern organizations and their bureaucratic structures are one arena in which this obliteration affects social relationships. Bureaucratic structures dominate private corporations and government agencies equally. One feature of the organization is its competitive struggle for scarce resources for its predetermined ends. Managers have the responsibility of directing the organization's resources as efficiently and effectively as possible toward those ends (*AV* 25). MacIntyre notes that this understanding of bureaucratic organizations is both familiar from and originates with Max Weber.

MacIntyre's analysis here proves important because of his similarity with Horkheimer. MacIntyre understands bureaucratic rationality to be silent about ends. Likewise, if morality simply expresses feelings, ends cannot be evaluated on a rational basis, but only from the standpoint of how they made one feel. Thus, for MacIntyre, one of the problems with modernity lies in its inability to make real moral judgments or evaluations about ends—that is, judgments and evaluations susceptible to rational scrutiny. Similarly, for Horkheimer, one of the problems with modernity lies in the inability of the individual to make reasonable judgments about ends. They both want to address the inability of individuals in modernity to evaluate ends except insofar as those ends are means to another end that is itself not subject to scrutiny. Horkheimer, that is, while never explicitly saying it, is centrally concerned with the moral evaluation of ends. Such a moral evaluation occurs within the bounds of reason.

MacIntyre expands his discussion of the historical emergence of this problem in *Whose Justice? Which Rationality?* He begins his discussion with the Homeric age. For the purposes of my argument, the salient feature of this discussion is that MacIntyre identifies two forms of reason in Homeric Greece. The Homeric tales contain an understanding of achievement that was important for Homeric Greece and that defined later debates in Athenian Greece about the good life and the good society. In the Homeric poems, "to achieve is to excel, but to achieve is also to win" (*WJWR* 27). One of the reasons MacIntyre identifies understanding of achievement as important is that both sorts of achievement require their own kind of effective practical reasoning. MacIntyre's discussion of achievement in Homer reflects Horkheimer and Adorno's search for modern man in the *Odyssey*. It suggests that what Horkheimer and Adorno had insight to was just that focus on achievement as winning within the *Odyssey*.

According to MacIntyre, post-Homeric discussions, which set the stage for and involved the participation of Socrates, Plato, and Aristotle, center on the question of what kinds of goods exists. The distinction between goods arises out of this Homeric understanding of achievement. Homeric achievement combines the goods of effectiveness with the goods of excellence; being effective and being excellent are the same thing. Post-Homeric Greece faces a different dynamic, however: a reason that aims at the goods of effectiveness and a reason that aims at the goods of excellence.

This distinction between goods of effectiveness and goods of excellence also corresponds to different conceptions of justice and different conceptions of reason. The distinction is made with reference to a hierarchy in, or order of, the universe. On the one conception, the universe should be understood in terms of winning—in terms of a competition in which the most effective persons win (by staying alive or having power, etc.). On the other conception, the universe should be understood in terms of achieving excellence. The goods of effectiveness should not be judged in terms of their rightness or wrongness. Survival and winning in the end define all that matters to someone who accepts and lives with a conception of the world as aimed at competition and winning. It does not matter what specifically one wins at so long as one survives. On the other hand, the goods of excellence will determine what forms of activity are worthy of engagement—that is, which activities are right and which ones wrong regardless of the effectiveness of those goods in terms of winning or surviving. This distinction recalls Horkheimer's criticism that winning and survival constitutes all that is important in modernity.

An immediate question arises: Are there only two world orders—one aimed at effectiveness and one aimed at excellence? The answer to this question proves important in relation to determining how many forms of reason exist: Are there two basic forms of reason—means-ends rationality and (for lack of a better determinant) reason of excellence? Or, are there divisions within reason of excellence, such that two or more hierarchies can be established which either place different values on the same goods or have different lists of goods? Answering these questions requires an understanding of tradition and of tradition-constituted reason in MacIntyre.

This section, though, motivated the move from Horkheimer, through Habermas, to MacIntyre's tradition-constituted reason. The motivation involves (1) the need for insight into the history of reason, which MacIntyre provides, (2) Horkheimer's call for a substantive reason, which Habermas cannot answer and MacIntyre does, and (3) the similarities between the diagnoses of the disease of modernity offered by Horkheimer and MacIntyre. The investigation now turns to the form of substantive reason, a tradition-constituted reason, that is found in MacIntyre's work.

MacIntyre's Tradition-Constituted Reason

Tradition in MacIntyre

In *After Virtue*, MacIntyre provides an initial definition of a tradition or traditional mode of thought: "A living tradition, then, is an historically extended, socially embodied argument, and an argument precisely in part about the goods which constitute that tradition." And again, a tradition is "always partially constituted by an argument about the goods the pursuit of which gives to that tradition its particular point and purpose" (*AV* 222).

MacIntyre defines tradition in *Whose Justice? Which Rationality?* (12) as "an argument extended through time in which certain fundamental agreements are defined and redefined in terms of two conflicts: those with critics and enemies external to the tradition who reject all or at least key parts of those fundamental agreements, and those internal, interpretive debates through which the meaning and rationale of the fundamental agreements come to be expressed and by whose progress a tradition is constituted." A tradition includes several features, then: (1) a historically and socially situated (2) argument (3) over fundamental agreements with (4) outsiders and (5) insiders, the latter of which can (6) define rational progress within the tradition. Chapter 5 will focus on the progress within a tradition in order to quell accusations of relativism aimed at a notion of substantive reason. This chapter and the next will demonstrate the historically and socially situated nature of a tradition by focusing on the fundamental agreements of said tradition.

Those fundamental agreements include "shared attitudes, beliefs, and presuppositions, developed in very different ways within each particular tradition" (*WJWR* 401). Central for the purpose of my argument is the inclusion of a notion of the good among these fundamental agreements, highlighted by MacIntyre in the definition of tradition in his earlier *After Virtue*, cited above. This pursuit of the good defines in part a good life.

MacIntyre conceives the good life as including the virtues a person should have, given the roles she occupies in the practices she engages in in her society. That is, the notion of virtue proves fundamental for MacIntyre's notion of the good life. Fundamental to the notion of virtue, in turn, is the notion of practice. The exercise of the virtues in practices allows one to attain the goods that are both external to and internal to the practices. The distinction between external and internal goods is similar to the distinction between accidental and essential goods. The good is external to the practice if it can be achieved without the exercise of the practice through some social custom or by some accident. For example, money is the primary external good to many practices in contemporary society. An internal good is a good that is attained only through the exercise of the practice. Wisdom, presumably, is an internal good attached to the practice of philosophy. Virtues, on MacIntyre's understanding, include the right attitudes. Thus, for MacIntyre living the good life involves having the right attitudes—the shared attitudes of one's tradition. So for MacIntyre, every tradition must have a particular point or purpose—a conception of the good.

Thus we see that a tradition is a socially and historically embedded, extended argument concerning fundamental agreements about the good life carried on both among the members of the tradition (those who share in some way the fundamental agreements) and those outside the tradition (those who disagree with the fundamental agreements in some way). These fundamental agreements consist of attitudes, beliefs, and presuppositions. A tradition has, further, a particular purpose that involves pursuing and living out the good life. Finally, a tradition always involves some sort of progress. Given this definition of tradition, what, then, is tradition-constituted reason?

Tradition-Constituted Reason in MacIntyre

Why ought one to believe in a tradition-constituted reason? That is, why should one believe that reason varies with traditions, that it is constituted by traditions, and that the substantive standards of reason vary from one tradition to another? For MacIntyre, one can defend a tradition-constituted reason only by giving examples from history. So his three major works on this issue, *After Virtue, Whose Justice? Which Rationality?*, and *Three Rival Versions of Moral Enquiry*, all provide ample examples from the history of philosophy of what MacIntyre considers to be different rationalities. In *Whose Justice? Which Rationality?*, for example, MacIntyre examines three traditions: one extending from Socrates through Aristotle to Thomas Aquinas, one reaching from Hutchinson through Hume, and one identified as the Liberal tradition.

Rather than repeating MacIntyre's entire work here, I shall defend a tradition-constituted reason along two different lines. First, I will briefly advocate MacIntyre's discussion of the different conceptions of reason found in the moral and political philosophies of Aristotle and Hume, while supplementing that discussion with an analysis of reason in Kant's moral philosophy. Second, drawing from MacIntyre's 1985 presidential address to the American Philosophical Association, I shall garner an argument from language.

The Need for More Than Two Traditions

A brief perusal of the history of moral and political philosophy reveals at least three conceptions of reason. I will focus on the differences in the conceptions of reason in Aristotle and Hume, whom MacIntyre discusses, and Kant, whom he does not. The focus on Kant is necessary to show that there are more than two traditions in moral and political philosophy.

A person could be tempted to argue, given the discussion so far of the Frankfurt School critique of instrumental rationality and the comparison between MacIntyre and Horkheimer, that only two traditions of reason exist in philosophy: a tradition of subjective rationality, or reasons of effectiveness, and a tradition of objective reason, or reasons of excellence. If only these two traditions existed, then the argument would have a different flavor. That different flavor would result from that fact that a motivating concern I share with Horkheimer is the homogenizing or totalizing effect of modernity. Everywhere, modernity reduces freedom for the sake of efficiency. If only two traditions existed, then the battle would simply involve spelling out and defending a reason of excellence. Instead, the battle lies in defending the tradition-constituted nature of reason.

Second, from a practical standpoint, a multiplicity of traditions remains necessary for human life. Traditions can prosper only if they grow through dialogue with other traditions. Such dialogue requires a plurality of traditions, ones that are devoted to goods of excellence. If there were only two, if the sole traditions were those of effectiveness and excellence, not only would a critical theory of society be in jeopardy, but society itself would be in trouble. If traditions can prosper only through exchange and conflict with one another, then the tradition of effectiveness must be supported in order that the tradition of excellence may prosper. Traditions need other traditions in order to grow or else they die. If the tradition of effectiveness were abolished, there would be no tradition with which the tradition of excellence could dialogue. The tradition of excellence must fail, then, because it no longer has another tradition with which to engage in dialogue. Thus, a critical theory of society would be trapped in a catch-22 if there were only two traditions: either destroy the tradition of effectiveness and, in consequence, destroy the tradition of excellence which is the only way to emancipation, or allow the tradition of effectiveness to continue and, in so doing, effectively perpetuate a system of domination.

Of course, a third option presents itself, namely, abandoning reason as a means for liberation. "To put the matter another way: why may one not simply have values—many of which have been acquired in a community experience—and use them without reflection? Does that lack of reflection make the judgments less practical?"[2] Yes, it does. The third option requires abandoning emancipation altogether. One reason why values must be evaluated rests in human action. Human beings act in the name of values upon which they have not reflected, and such action can lead to greater oppression. Those who do not reflect upon their values and actions while also engaging in "emancipatory" practices themselves generally establish new regimes of oppression, as evidenced by the Soviet Union and Cuba. It is true, similarly, that reason has led to systems of oppression. It has done so because of a failure to recognize that reason is fundamentally connected to the good. At this point, I cannot argue for the need for reason in emancipatory practice. It is, as has been said before in unison with Horkheimer and Adorno, the starting point of this work and must be taken as an axiom of praxis.

From the History of Philosophy

MacIntyre's accounts of reason as found in Aristotle and Hume are excellent pieces of exposition. Aristotle, to begin with, held that reason was capable of evaluating ends. For Aristotle, one used dialectic to determine the good and whether one's conception of the good was a worthy one. Book 1 of the *Nicomachean Ethics* proves, in turn, an excellent example of dialectics. Dialectics is the method suited to this subject. Aristotle, thus, begins with commonly accepted conceptions of happiness in his tradition—wealth, health, pleasure, and so on. He then argues against each one of those conceptions by referring to common beliefs about what happiness is and drawing on standards of reason within his society. At the end of book 1, Aristotle synthesizes, finally, a conception of happiness as *eudaimonia*. He then proceeds to describe a doctrine of virtues in which reason can mold and refine the passions. Aristotle emphasizes that one's passions must fit the moment. As is made clear in book 7, the continent person has base desires even if he does not follow those desires, while the temperate person does not have base desires. Aristotle concerns himself not with right action *simpliciter* but with right action that comes from virtue. If the passions are not appropriate, one fails to act virtuously.

Hume, in contrast, holds that reason lacks the capability of evaluating ends. Rationality is, instead, but the slave of the passions. The passions provide the motivations of the agent. Whatever passion is stronger directs the agent to use her rationality to find the most effective means to the goal that person sets. If, consequently, one wants to train the young in proper morals, one does not address the rationality of the young. Rather, one addresses oneself to the education of the passions, bringing to mind different pleasures. For example, one presents awards for bravery when the passions would ordinarily direct a person away from heroic acts.

Kant's conception of reason contrasts with those of Aristotle and Hume. For Kant, rationality neither directs the emotions nor is their slave. The best example of a morally worthy action is one that a person performs in opposition to the emotions. This example shows that passions do not need to be trained in order for an action to have moral worth. In the doctrine of virtue, Kant does hold that training the emotions proves important. Such training is not necessary for moral worth, however, nor is practical rationality centrally concerned with the virtues and emotions. Rather, practical rationality centrally concerns the determination of the will from the rule of law alone.

The three figures provide an informative contrast. First, the relationship between reason and the passions differs for each philosopher. In other words, each conceives of reason differently. Second, dialectics or something like it finds no place in the practical philosophy of Hume and Kant. Kant does use something similar to dialectics when discussing what it is that is good in and of itself (arriving at the good will). He does not, however, give a role to dialectics beyond that. Third, Aristotle, unlike Hume and Kant, thinks that practical philosophy is an inexact science. Moral philosophy cannot be considered a science at all for Hume because he limits science to the exact methods of deductive reasoning. Kant, on the other hand, intends to establish an exact science of morals. When acting morally, a person wills according to universal law, with circumstances and contingencies playing no role in the determination of action. Of final note is how their conceptions of happiness differ. For Aristotle, happiness is fulfillment, whereas for Hume and Kant it is satisfaction of desires. This similarity between Hume and Kant highlights the distinction between their conceptions of reason even more. For Hume, moral education is designed to direct a person's view of happiness by instituting awards and punishments, whereas for Kant, happiness (and such awards and punishments) lead to heteronomous maxims detracting from moral worth. According to Kant,

happiness is the end of human beings, but reason is not directed towards happiness—it is not the slave of the passions.

The three philosophers thus have different conceptions of reason.
They envision reason serving different functions, and the standards of
reason they envision differ between exact and inexact. They promote
different exemplars of reason as well. For Aristotle, an example of reason is using one's reason to seek the good in a particular situation in ac-
cordance with the ultimate good and virtue, whereas for Hume and
Kant an example of reason is, respectively, maximizing one's utility and
using reason to direct one's will in contrast to one's inclinations. The
reasons each philosopher accepts as good reasons are also different.
For Aristotle, a good reason for an action is that it will result in greater
fulfillment, whereas for Hume a good reason for acting is simply some
passion, and for Kant the best reason for performing an action is that
moral duty demands it.

How, then, can these three conceptions be considered conceptions
of the same thing? What is it that the term "reason" identifies in the
three different philosophies? In *Three Rival Versions of Moral Enquiry*,
MacIntyre makes a distinction that can help answer these questions,
namely, the distinction between formal, universal conceptions of rationality and substantive conceptions of rationality.[3] MacIntyre is describing the condition of natural theology during the nineteenth century in
Scotland when Lord Gifford lived. He writes, "And a reading of the
Gifford Lectures of the last hundred years reveals that there has been
among the lecturers no shared standard of value by which such intellectual costs and benefits may be evaluated" (*3RV*, 11). In fact, all of
modern philosophy lacks any shared standards of values, even though
modern philosophers can "elucidate a variety of logical and conceptual
relationships." That is, philosophers in the modern period share a
"minimal conception of rationality," but lack a substantive conception
that they share and agree upon.

Following this line of thinking, one can initially define reason as
those standards of justification and exemplars of reasoning within a
tradition. Modern philosophers and philosophies share a minimal set
of standards of justification (closely identified as logical connections
and conceptual relationships) and some paradigms of reasoning. Yet

they lack a substantive set that allows the justification of differing values and rival first principles and the evaluation of truth of different reasons and conclusions. For example, the categorical imperative is one standard of justification which Aristotle and Hume do not share, and they have no shared set of standards or exemplars by which they can measure the truth of the categorical imperative. Dialectics is an exemplar of reasoning for Aristotle but has no place in the philosophies of Kant or Hume.

Importantly, these three traditions and other traditions of modern philosophy share some minimal standards of justification and reasoning. These are standards borne out by the test of time and which have minimal to no content. Thus, these traditions of Western philosophy prove partially, not completely, different. To some extent, these traditions share a basic understanding of argumentation and of logic which, for instance, Nietzsche rejects and which, some might argue, is not shared by Asian philosophies. Habermas's discussion of reason as the asking for and giving of reasons captures this minimalist notion that MacIntyre points out. It dismisses or excludes what on MacIntyre's and my accounts proves to be the more important and substantial idea of reason as standards of justification and exemplars of reasoning within a tradition. To exclude these is, as I argued in the last chapter, both to deceive oneself about the nature of reason and to undermine the possibility for a critical theory of society.

Taking this position, I reject nominalism. Aristotle, Hume, and Kant do not *name* three different phenomena. Rather, they attempt to name and describe something which proves real and which they share in common to some minimal extent. The task, then, is to lay out more explicitly where they disagree in their description of the singular phenomenon and to evaluate which description bears out the truth. If MacIntyre's diagnosis of modern philosophy proves correct, however, this task remains impossible. Insofar as modern philosophers and philosophies do not recognize that they disagree over substantive reason, irrational debate will remain ineliminable.

The three different conceptions of reason just discussed prove not just different but incommensurable.

For just as some historians and philosophers of science have identified in different periods of the history of physics different and incompatible standards governing rational choice between rival theories and indeed different standards concerning what is to be accounted an intelligible theory, so that between those rival claims there is no way of adjudicating rationally by appeal to some further neutral standard, and just as some social anthropologists have identified rival moral and religious systems as similarly incommensurable, so it appears within modern philosophy there occurs the kind of irreconcilable division and interminable disagreement which is to be explained only by incommensurability. . . . It is not too much to speak of rival conceptions of rationality. (*3RV*, 12–13)

"Incommensurability" names the inability to adjudicate between rival theories because such theories do not share substantive standards of reason and exemplars of reasoning. They may, in fact, differ in their accounts of parts of the world. This incommensurability does not nullify the shared minimal standards of reason that MacIntyre identifies or that we might see in a shared logic. Rather, it points out that this minimal rationality cannot adjudicate between rival moral philosophies or rival philosophies simpliciter.

If any of the three philosophers were to judge the conception of reason held by one of the others (presuming that he could understand it), the verdict would necessarily be "failure." MacIntyre adds that Aristotle would be unable to understand either Hume or Kant because of language. To understand that argument and to determine if incommensurability includes not just an inability to find another's tradition reasonable but in addition an inability to understand it, I must examine MacIntyre's second defense of the claims that reason is tradition constituted.

Language, Reason, and Cultural Variation

In his 1985 American Philosophical Association presidential address, MacIntyre argued that language is an embodiment of standards of reason, particularly in the form of exemplars. MacIntyre's defense rests on three points. First, language may presuppose a cosmology. Second, languages vary across cultures. Third, translations are not always exact.

MacIntyre begins his discussion by holding that "language may be so used . . . that to share in its use is to presuppose one cosmology rather than another, one relationship of local law and custom to cosmic order rather than another, one justification of particular relationships of individual to community and of both to land and landscape rather than another" (RPP 388). Irish of the 1600s and Plato's Greek are examples of such cosmology-laden languages. Using a particular language may not, however, require such commitments to beliefs and ways of life. Twentieth-century "universal" languages like English, French, and German are examples of such cosmology-free languages. Consider this distinction in languages with regard to names and naming.

"If, for example, I speak in Irish . . . of Doire Colmcille—of Doire in modern Irish—the presuppositions and implications of my utterance are quite other than if I speak in English of Londonderry." Doire and Londonderry identify the same particular spot on the Earth. They name it in radically discrepant ways. To begin with, names do not name as such, according to MacIntyre; rather, they name for a particular linguistic or cultural community, "by identifying places and persons in terms of the scheme of identification shared by . . . that community. The relation of a proper name to its bearer cannot be elucidated without reference to such identifying functions." Moreover, the use of these particular names—Doire and Londonderry—"embod[ies] a communal intention of naming"; that is, they presume the legitimacy of a certain political order (RPP 396–97).

It will not do to say that the name "qua name carries with it no presupposition concerning political or social legitimacy" just because strangers (lacking the political presuppositions) might use the name to find directions to the place pointed out on the map (ibid.). The name that the stranger uses is one provided by the community to outsiders and is "parasitic upon its uses by the primary community" (ibid., 390). An Irish Catholic would (presumably) not be angry with a foreigner who asked directions to Londonderry because that person was a foreigner, using a name that did not have the same connotations for the foreigner as it does for the Irish Catholic.

According to MacIntyre, bilingual speakers of cosmology-laden languages must choose between "alternative and incompatible sets of beliefs and ways of life" in choosing to live within one or the other linguistic community. This point explains why the use of Gaelic by Irish political prisoners in the 1970s proved such a powerful unifier for them. In choosing Gaelic over English, the prisoners rejected a certain view of the world and a certain nation's claim to legitimacy. Moreover, MacIntyre continues, the set of beliefs and ways of life tied to a particular language entails particular standards of rational justification and warranters for claims to truth constitutive of that language (ibid.). That is, what is rationally acceptable to one group of language users will differ in key areas from what is rationally acceptable to another group. Not only, then, does the bilingual speaker choose between incompatible sets of beliefs and ways of life; she also "chooses" between incompatible standards of justification. That is, one chooses between different or rival forms of reason.

MacIntyre gives the following sorts of examples to show what he means by cosmology-committed languages: the languages of the Irish of the 1700s, the Zuni Shiwi language, and the Spanish of the *conquistadores*. He continues: "What is from one point of view an original act of acquisition of what had so far belonged to nobody and therefore of what had remained available to become only now someone's private property, will be from the other point of view the illegitimate seizure of what had so far belonged to nobody because it is what *cannot* ever be made into private property" (ibid.).

The Spanish conquistadores brought over ideas of ownership that were alien to Native Americans, and the English brought to Ireland concepts of individual property rights which the Irish could not recognize as reasonable. Consider, continuing with MacIntyre's examples, that some Native American nations thought that one could not own the land. The land belonged to no one and was available for all to use. Such an idea is part and parcel of the belief in the sacredness of Kentucky, which was, to the Native Americans of colonial times, a hunting ground which no one or nation could or should occupy because of its sacredness. Such an understanding of land is foreign to English and Spanish traditions. This misunderstanding is evident in Locke's famous defense of private property.

For Locke, one could, in the state of nature, take for oneself whatever one put to use as long as one left behind enough and as good for others to appropriate or use.[4] Whereas for some Native Americans unoccupied land was able to be used but not owned, for Locke unoccupied land was available to be claimed and worked and thereby owned. Native Americans were committed to a cosmology evident in their language, which held that land belonged to no one. English and Spanish settlers used a language, on the other hand, in which a different cosmology was bound up with the concept "property."

One might ask here, why is it that MacIntyre (and I) can claim that Native Americans were committed to a cosmology as opposed to a morality? Certainly, the Native Americans were committed to a morality that was different from the morality of the European settlers. This morality, however, was based on a certain way of viewing the world. This way of viewing the world was evident in the language that the different nations used, for example, in describing the land. That the land was unownable was not simply a matter of morality but a matter of fact. The European settlers were not simply doing something wrong; they were violating nature.

Another example is the differences between Western European and Native American methods of making agreements. In the West, when agreements are reached a contract is signed. The contract "guarantees" that each partner to the deal will keep her end of the bargain, will honor the contract. Among Native Americans, matters were/are different. Native Americans gave their word and nothing more was needed. In the motion picture *Billy Jack*, the main character gives this distinction punch. He says that to date the American government has made many thousands of agreements with the Indians and has kept none—even though in each case a contract, a treaty, was signed. The point is that Native Americans and "White Men" had different views about what giving someone one's word entailed and required. For White Men, giving one's word had to be followed up with a signed contract that could be broken. For Native Americans, one's given word neither required a contract nor could be broken.

Something similar could be said for the Japanese. When a Japanese individual made an agreement, she did not need to sign a contract in order to "guarantee" that she would uphold her bargain. Honor required that each party to the agreement make good or suffer dishonor. The cosmologies that lie behind the ways these groups reach agreements involve different beliefs and ways of life which, when considered from an alternative cosmology, are unreasonable. For a Japanese, to break one's agreement would go against not only honor but also reason. It would require, moreover, the sacrifice of a body part. To a Westerner, breaking a contract need not dishonor one; and though it might involve sacrifices as they are written into the contract, it would not require the sacrifice of a body part.

Concepts, such as honor, property, keeping one's word, and contract, for instance, are contained in the texts of a tradition. Such texts define the literary and linguistic tradition of that community. Characteristically, according to MacIntyre, poets and saga writers are the creators of such canonical texts, both oral and written. He argues that concepts, as a result, "are first acquired and understood in terms of poetic images" and never leave behind the concreteness first attained in this poetical form (RPP 390). These poems are then supplemented by prose, law books, and so on. This origin means that metaphor can be said to lie at the center of our concepts, ideas, and beliefs.[5]

When two communities meet, communities defined by their canonical texts and metaphors, neither community has linguistic capacity to represent the beliefs of the other tradition because it lacks the appropriate texts and metaphors to do so. Thus, each tradition will abstract the contents of the rival tradition and represent the beliefs of that rival tradition in its own terms. Since these terms and ideas are abstracted from the canonical texts and metaphors of the other tradition, they will necessarily "be lacking in justification" (RPP 392).

A concept like property or contract, on the one hand, or unownable or honor, on the other, can be brought into and used in a language tradition different from its home. When brought into that different language tradition, however, it is separated from the context that originally defined its meaning and made it reasonable. The idea that a contract is something one signs to bind one to an agreement that one has made is intelligible to a person outside of the English tradition. To act on such an idea, however, might appear irrational. For one thing, such an action is wasteful, because contracts are not needed among honorable individuals, and those without honor will not uphold a signed contract regardless. For another, it is an insult, because it suggests that one will not uphold one's honor; the action, that is, implies that one lacks honor.

Consider, as another example, Zande belief in witchcraft. E. E. Evans-Pritchard's extensive study of Zande beliefs about witchcraft has been the focus of much debate concerning the possibility of divergent forms of reason across cultures.[6] The Zande believe, among other things, that some people are witches; that these witches can cause pain, hurt, and even death through mystical forces; that one can tell if someone is a witch by performing an autopsy on the person and discovering witchcraft substance (an elusive substance to describe, according to Evans-Pritchard); and that witchcraft substance is passed on through kinship ties.

Beliefs in witchcraft are intelligible to contemporary Americans and to nineteenth- and twentieth-century anthropologists. When one reads Evans-Pritchard, however, one gets the sense that he does not think the Azande are acting reasonably. Why might that be?

Although English speakers have the concept of witchcraft in their language, and can represent witches in their cosmology, this concept differs from the Zande concept of witchcraft. Further, Westerners and Azande treat their concepts of witchcraft differently. The texts of Evans-Pritchard's era and our own present time depict belief in witchcraft as irrational. Witchcraft can be seen as a reprehensible practice of which one may accuse outcasts or other innocent people in order to condemn them, or can be seen as the beliefs of an illiterate and uncultured people, for example, people of the Middle Ages. That is, Westerners see beliefs in witchcraft as beliefs akin to those held by earlier English speakers who are considered to be superstitious and irrational. Past beliefs in witchcraft are paradigmatic of superstitious beliefs. Belief in witchcraft, although intelligible to us, is unreasonable to us.

Just as the differences between Aristotle, Hume, and Kant are in-commensurable, so too are the differences among cosmology-laden language users incommensurable. Aristotelian, Humean, and Kantian rationalities are incommensurable insofar as, when one philosophy's standards of justification are translated into the forms of alternative philosophies, those standards appear unreasonable. The concepts and cosmologies that are tied to particular languages-in-use are incom-mensurable in a similar fashion. Although the ideas of honor and of witchcraft can be translated into the English language and be intelli-gible, those concepts do not appear reasonable to English speakers, who are committed by their language to a cosmology different from the ones embedded in the Japanese and Zande languages. Similarly, a Na-tive American during the colonial period could understand the English idea of property, but the idea and the actions which follow from it would appear unreasonable—just as Native American uproar at the ap-propriation of land by English settlers would be unreasonable to those same settlers.

I began this discussion with the claim that only some languages are cosmology laden, while others are universal languages; yet I have ig-nored the issue of universal languages throughout. Someone might argue that if a universal language or languages existed, surely they could provide a way out of the seeming relativism of cosmology-laden languages. This argument is different from what Habermas argues. He argues that languages have universal features (like truth, justice, and rationality) that provide a point upon which a rational and universal ethics can be built. MacIntyre's discussion of modern languages, like English, can accept Habermas's claims about universal features of lan-guage and still contend that we live in incommensurable languages.

First, even if we can translate many ideas and images from other languages into English, many expressions exist which cannot be trans-lated. In *Dependent Rational Animals*, MacIntyre avails himself of the terms "wancantognaka" and "misericordia" to capture ideas that are not quite translatable in English. Yes, MacIntyre can explain those ideas in English, but their untranslatability extends beyond providing some sense of their meanings. It further entails capturing a sense of the world of the cosmology-laden language. I can talk about Doire Comcille or Londonderry, but my use of either name in English does not commit, as it would in Gaelic, to a certain conception of the world. What modern languages like English lack is reference to some cosmology of values and meanings.

Moreover, modern languages like English developed by ridding themselves of commitments to standards of rational justification which one would find in traditional languages, like Gaelic or Lakota. "For the relevant kinds of controversial subject-matter, all too many heterogeneous and incompatible schemes of rational justification" are offered by a culture of a modern language (RPP 405). The existence of modern languages, then, does not constitute a way out of the tradition-constituted nature of reason. Rather, it proves the extent to which reason both is constituted by and constitutes tradition. It is constituted by tradition because it relies, at least in part, on those idioms and metaphors that arise from living in the world. It constitutes the tradition by developing those idioms and metaphors and by instantiating some uses of reason as standards and exemplars as part of the language.

On the one hand, when a language becomes universal it abandons any commitments to a cosmology, and, in so doing, it loses the ability to allow its users to appeal to standards of reason. Those standards no longer inhere within the language; language users, then, have nothing to appeal to when they reason. On the other hand, a universal language, as universal, allows the incorporation of all standards of reason into its system. This incorporation is evident in the very ability of a universal language like English to translate the very documents of diverse traditions into one language—documents which appeal to and embody incommensurable standards of reason. Thus, at one and the same time, users of universal languages have a dearth and a plethora of standards of reason to which to appeal. This situation becomes all the worse because, having a plethora of standards of reason but lacking a commitment to any, users of universal languages cannot choose reasonably between the different standards available to them. They must have already accepted some standards of reason in order to reasonably choose between the different standards presented to them. *Ipso facto*, they have not accepted any standards because their language abandoned appeal to standards when it became universal. Thus, within this wealth, language users starve; they cannot reason because they have been deprived of the very commitments that make rationality possible.

The preceding discussion shows not only that conceptions of reason differ but also that they differ because the standards of reason within a tradition differ. Aristotle, Hume, and Kant differ about the standards of reason, not simply reason per se. Similarly, Native Americans and European settlers differed over the standards of reason. Such differences prove incommensurable because they spring from disparate conceptions of reason that are part and parcel of a tradition. Thus, all language users are de facto committed to some standards of reason or other, whether they acquire those standards from a cosmology-laden language or from somewhere else. The following section will consider in more detail what exactly reason is—that is, what the standards of reason are.

Standards of Reason: Supplementing MacIntyre with Kuhn

In the previous section, I defended MacIntyre's claim that some languages are committed to cosmologies and that those which are embody their own standards of reason. On MacIntyre's account, cosmology-laden languages commit their users to (1) sets of beliefs, (2) ways of life, (3) a cosmology, and (4) specific modes of rational justification and specific warranters for claims of truths (RPP 390). For the Native Americans, for example, the relevant beliefs include ones about the purpose of land, ownership, and sacredness. Their approved ways of life include ways of life that are largely nomadic and which refuse to lay claim to any land, and the cosmology is one which includes theories about the origins of the universe, the role of human beings, and the sacredness of land. The relevant Zande beliefs, meanwhile, include ones about witchcraft, kinsmanship, and death. Approved ways of life involve the use and abuse of witchcraft, the entirely separate use of magic or sorcery, performing autopsies to discover witchcraft substance, and the role of vengeance. Their cosmology includes witches, sorcerers, witchcraft substance, poison, and so on. What, however, are specific modes of reasonable justification and specific warranters for claims of truth?

This question seems to have no answer in MacIntyre's discussion, particularly his discussion in the presidential address to the APA. He suggests simply that such standards are to be found in the canonical texts of a tradition, and that what is found in such texts is justificatory arguments. What are some examples of such justificatory arguments?

Setting the reader up for his arguments about different traditions of reason in philosophy, MacIntyre claims that "to be practically rational, so one contending party holds, is to act on the basis of calculations of the costs and benefits to oneself of each possible alternative course of action and its consequences. To be practically rational, affirms a rival party, is to act under those constraints which any rational person, capable of an impartiality which accords no particular privileges to one's own interests, would agree should be imposed. To be practically rational, so a third party contends, is to act in such a way as to achieve the ultimate and true good of human beings" (*WJWR* 2). These arguments can certainly be found in the canonical texts of the philosophical traditions of utilitarianism, Kantianism, and Aristotelianism. Do they, however, constitute modes of reasonable justification? If these count as examples of modes of reasonable justification, then what should we be looking for in the traditions of the Native Americans and the Azande? Native Americans, for example, might hold that to be practically reasonable one should act in such a way as to honor mother earth. Azande might, on the other hand, hold that to be practically reasonable one should act in such a way as to guard against and take revenge upon witchcraft.

In order to clarify the answer to this question, that is, what are specific modes of reasonable justification, I turn to Thomas Kuhn's notion of disciplinary matrix. Kuhn's notion draws out exactly what reason is in a tradition and helps point to phenomena one should look for within a tradition in order to grasp descriptively its reason.

In *The Structure of Scientific Revolutions*[7] the expression "disciplinary matrix" embraces symbolic generalizations (both universal laws and definitions), shared commitments to beliefs and models (such as "heat is the kinetic energy of the constituent parts of bodies"), values (e.g., accuracy and simplicity), and paradigms (exemplars). Several points about such matrices should be noted. First, paradigms are what MacIntyre describes when he refers to exemplars of language use in a community. They provide a basis from which to extrapolate and create new uses. According to Kuhn, for example, a paradigm provides a standard way of viewing a problem: examining how one would solve a certain problem leads one to apply the method for solving that problem to another problem. Second, since symbolic generalizations refer to definitions as well as laws, definitions will differ among competing disciplinary matrices. Third, although values might be shared among competing disciplinary matrices (just as they are shared amongst different cultures), how those values are used, interpreted, and related to each other will vary across matrices. Finally, shared commitments to beliefs and models undergird grand differences between disciplinary matrices, differences which can and do result in different worldviews, different pictures of the world—in some sense, they result in different worlds.

Consider the concept of disciplinary matrix as applied to the Zande belief in witchcraft. Zande values include truth and vengeance. The Zande concern for truth is found in their use of the poison oracle to verify a previous oracle. When someone is hurt or killed among the Azande, the family of that person might visit a priest to discover who used magic to hurt or kill the family member. The priest poisons a chicken to determine assignation of guilt. If a poison oracle pronounces that Beta is responsible for Alpha's death, a second oracle is consulted to see if the first oracle pronounced accurately. A priest poisons a hen and says, "Die if Beta killed Alpha with witchcraft." Regardless of what happens, the priest then poisons another hen and says, "Live if the first oracle was right." The poison oracle is consulted for numerous questions. One of these questions, however, as just noted, is the question of whether someone used witchcraft to kill another. The value of vengeance is evident in that sort of questioning, because the oracle is being consulted in order to determine who is responsible for another's death so that that person can be killed himself or, at least, pay retribution to the deceased's family.

What, then, counts as a paradigm in the case of the Azande? A paradigm is an exemplary way of solving a problem that might apply to further uses. One takes the method for solving one problem and applies it to another. The use of the poison oracle, then, counts as a paradigm. It is used to determine the person responsible for someone's death or for particularly bad misfortune and for other questions which arise during the life of the Azande. In this case, the poisoning of the chicken constitutes a practice among the Azande.

Another example of a paradigm in the case of the Azande is the operation to find the witchcraft substance. If someone is accused of being a witch and dies, that person's corpse is examined for witchcraft substance. If witchcraft substance is found, that person is known to be a witch, and his (immediate) family members are also known to be witches. This method for investigating one question has been used to investigate a similar, but slightly different question. If a live father, for instance, is accused of witchcraft and he has a son die, he may have the son examined for witchcraft substance in order to clear his name. If witchcraft substance is found in the deceased son, the father is humiliated and everyone knows he has witchcraft substance because of how witchcraft substance is passed on. The questions are different, but the methods for answering the questions are the same.

So far the discussion has looked at the Zande belief in witchcraft in terms of its cosmology, values, and paradigms. What of the symbolic generalizations that Kuhn claims are part of a disciplinary matrix? Such generalizations are said to be universal laws and definitions. No problem occurs in looking for definitions in traditions. Here, of course, symbolic generalizations must not be understood only as written. They can also be carried in the spoken language of a particular tradition and incorporated into its oral storytelling. Among the Azande, for example, one finds oral definitions of witchcraft substance, of witches, of sorcerers, of kinship, and so on.

The notion of universal law, by contrast, brings in different issues. Insofar as Kuhn is specifically addressing scientific traditions and my argument addresses cultural traditions, locating universal laws within the latter traditions becomes unnecessary. Obviously, scientific traditions should contain universal laws; science is, after all, a search for such laws. Cultural traditions, on the other hand, do not seek universal laws necessarily. Perhaps some nonscientific traditions do invoke universal laws while others do not. Kantianism, for instance, does appeal to a universal law—the categorical imperative; the Aristotelian tradition, however, holds that such universal laws do not exist outside of science.

This discussion has focused on standards of reasons. Such standards include "warranters for claims to truth." Such warranters will differ from tradition to tradition. These warranters are the practices that are seen as leading conclusively to the truth in the different traditions. Among the Azande, for instance, the second poison oracle qualifies as a warranter of truth. What the notion of warranter to truth points out as opposed to standards of reason is the role of the notion of truth in MacIntyre. The search for truth proves fundamental to MacIntyre's conception of a well-functioning tradition. The importance of truth will serve as a hedge against claims about relativism in chapter 5.

Thus Thomas Kuhn's notion of disciplinary matrix, with its concomitant notions of paradigm, symbolic generalizations, and values, elucidates MacIntyre's discussion of tradition-constituted reason by giving specific content to MacIntyre's notion of standards of reason. MacIntyre's notion of tradition and his understanding of standards of reason parallel and can be captured by Kuhn's discussion of a disciplinary matrix, exemplars, and paradigms. The four aspects of MacIntyre's cosmology-laden languages can be mapped onto disciplinary matrices as exhibited in Table 3.1. Table 3.2 shows the different sorts of things included within a sufficiently broad conception of rationality and how those are spelled out with respect to the Zande belief in witchcraft.

Table 3.1. Disciplinary Matrices and Cosmology-Laden Languages

Disciplinary Matrix	Cosmology-Laden Languages
Cosmologies	Cosmology
Exemplars and Paradigms	Modes of Reasonable Justification
	Warranters of Truth
Symbolic Generalizations	Concepts, Beliefs
Values	Values
Practices	Ways of Life

Table 3.2. Zande Witchcraft as a Disciplinary Matrix

Disciplinary Matrix	Cosmology-Laden Languages
Cosmologies	Naturalistic, Mystical
Exemplars and Paradigms	Poison Oracle, Autopsy
Symbolic Generalizations	Witchcraft, Witchcraft Substance, Magic
Values	Truth, Vengeance, Merit
Practices	Good Magic, Vengeance

Tradition-Constituted Reason and Critical Theory

Substantive reason, on MacIntyre's account, consists in standards and exemplars of reasoning used in the giving of and asking for reasons. Does this account of reason provide resources for a person concerned with emancipation? Given the argument that a critical theory of society aimed at emancipation requires a substantive reason, one can ask, does MacIntyre's account of reason allow one to judge ends as well as means? An appropriate route to answering these questions would be to look at what resources MacIntyre's tradition itself has. MacIntyre places himself within a Thomistic-Aristotelian tradition. At first glance, this tradition seems to pose problems for someone who is interested in a reason capable of judging ends as well as means.

In book 3 of the *Nicomachean Ethics*, examining what is involved in making a decision—in deliberating—Aristotle is quite clear: deliberation is about things we can do (1112a31). Further, human beings "first lay down the end, and then examine the ways and means to achieve it" (1112b16). Again, "deliberation is about the actions a [person] can do, and actions are for the sake of other things; hence we deliberate about what promotes an end, not about the end" (1112b11–12). Yet I have argued throughout that reason must be capable of evaluating ends.

About this passage, MacIntyre holds that even if Aristotle denies we deliberate about ends, he affirms that "we reason non-deliberatively about ends and about that first end which is the *arche*" (*WJWR* 132).

Deliberation is a construction of an argument which begins with an *arche* and ends with a product Aristotle calls *prohairesis*. *Prohairesis* is a desiring thought or desire informed by thought (*WJWR* 136). Further, Aristotle holds that one can deliberate about proximate ends as means toward the ultimate end. About the ultimate end, happiness, one cannot deliberate.

Although it might seem, based on the above passages, that Aristotle agrees with what McIntyre terms the modern understanding of reason, according to which goods cannot be ordered reasonably, he in fact does not agree. On the modern account, "the individual human being confronts an alternative set of ways of life from a standpoint external to them all. Such an individual has as yet *ex hypothesi* no commitments, and the multifarious and conflicting desires which individuals develop provide in themselves no grounds for choosing which of such desires to develop and be guided by and which to inhibit and frustrate" (*WJWR* 133). Such an individual would have various desires—for money, for fewer work hours, for favor with her church. How does the individual choose between these desires? Each desire appears to the modern individual equally worthy of pursuit because no rationale presents itself for choosing between the different desires. The pursuit of one over another is left up to individual tastes. Aristotle would consider this modern individual to be deprived of the ability or power to make rational evaluations and choices. "Because it is the *ergon*, the peculiar task of human beings to evaluate, to choose, and to act *qua* rational beings . . . human beings cannot be understood in detachment from their necessary social context, that setting within which alone rationality can be exercised" (*WJWR* 133).

MacIntyre holds that the modern individual does not have the ability to be reasonable in the Aristotelian sense. The modern individual can certainly determine which means best satisfy a particular desire or end. So she is rational in one sense. Yet the modern individual cannot reasonably arbitrate among different ends. This, of course, is precisely the problem with modernity and the enlightenment as discussed earlier. Subjective rationality, the dominant form of reason in modernity, does not allow the individual or society to judge ends.

It is clear, however, that Aristotle thinks that human beings can reason about ends. Human beings can use their reason "in forming [their] desires and in acting" (1095a10–11). Further, almost all of book 1 of the *Nicomachean Ethics* is an attempt to arrive at a definition of the good using reason. Aristotle does not use emotion or desire to decide what the good is. He instead provides the student with reasons for considering *eudaimonia* to be the end of human beings.

What are the resources for judging ends on Aristotle's account? The major resource is a social context. This social context must be understood as a "form of social order whose shared mode of life already" orders the "goods to be achieved by excellence within specific and systematic forms of activity, integrated into an overall rank-order by the political activity" of the citizens (*WJWR* 133). Within this social order and its ordering of goods, one can ask what the good to be pursued is, both in particular situations and over one's entire life. The means of reasonable evaluation is dialectic. Dialectic, in turn, is part of *phronēsis*. *Phronēsis*, or practical rationality, is the "exercise of a capacity to apply truths about what it is good for such and such a type of person or for persons as such to do generally and in certain types of situation to oneself in particular situations" (*WJWR* 115–16). In other words, *phronēsis* consists in applying to one's specific situation a general rule for types of persons or persons in general. *Phronēsis*, it should be noted, is not reducible to rule following, though it "involves . . . the application and extension of rules" (*WJWR* 116).

Dialectic is a necessary part of the relationship between the ordered goods in a tradition and phronetic activity. The social order or tradition already orders goods. These goods provide the basis for *phronēsis* insofar as *phronēsis* involves applying the truths about these goods to actions for certain types of people (artists, journalists) or in certain situations (finding a drowning victim). Dialectic, on the other hand, allows individuals and society itself to question the ordering of those goods. Dialectic empowers the individual to investigate that ordered set of goods and determine for herself the right ordered set of goods, both in general and for specific situations and specific types of persons. Dialectic involves "the confronting of alternative and rival opinions . . . by each other" in order to determine which opinion "best survives the strongest objections which can be advanced on the basis of others" (*WJWR* 118).

Consider Francis. He is the son of a merchant; he likes to party with his friends, spend money, and enjoy the good things in life. He is aware of the poor and knows his church demands that the rich feed and clothe the poor. He confronts two sets of ordered goods. One set prioritizes wealth, pleasure, honor, and glory (for Francis dreams of being a great soldier) above that of caring for the poor. The other set prioritizes love of neighbor and God above wealth, pleasure, and glory. The two sets of ordered goods are tied to different beliefs and different ideas about what counts as the good life. The first set, characteristic of the merchant life, holds the following beliefs: money is the highest good because it allows one to live a life of pleasure, one should seek glory both through the accumulation of money and through soldiering, and life should be spent in pleasure as much as possible. The second set includes the beliefs that one should love others as Jesus modeled, that money distracts one from the important things in life, and that love and charity are the highest goods. The two sets of ordered goods entail rival conceptions of the good life: the merchant sees the good life consisting in the pursuit and acquisition of as much capital as possible; the friar sees the good life consisting in living modestly and focusing on the realization of world justice. They also present different role models: the rich Italian merchant and the poor Jesus.

Francis must choose between these two sets of ordered goods and ways of life. To make a decision, he garners arguments for and against each ordered set of goods. These arguments might include, on the one hand, Epicurean arguments about pleasure or the arguments of poets and minstrels of the high medieval period who travel from town to town singing about pleasure. Or they might include arguments from the Bible, arguments from doctors of the church. Today, they could include arguments from social Darwinists, from Smithians, or an argument from Marxism. He will also garner arguments for and against different goods within the individual sets. These might include arguments for the value and power of money to achieve other ends, such as influence, health, and women, or arguments about the power of love and simplicity. On the basis of these arguments, he might do a number of things. He might decide that the life of the merchant is right and that he should live as an Italian merchant; he might decide to join a monastery or become a priest; or he may create a lifestyle never seen before.

He will also have to affirm or reorder a set of goods. He might affirm the set of goods given to him by one of the dominant modes of life in society, or he might decide that, although that overall position is right, its ordering of goods needs to be modified. Or he may develop a different set of ordered goods from the two lists and other experiences he has enjoyed. Throughout this elaborate process, however, he will constantly draw on the arguments and beliefs available in his society and the sorts of heroes that are honored there. Such drawing-on constitutes using reason in the form of dialectics.

Francis can do these things only if he is reasonable, that is, if he has access to a set of standards and exemplars of reason. Such standards and exemplars, as I have argued throughout this chapter, come from the society. Thus, Aristotle, and with him MacIntyre, are right to hold that any society that expects its members to choose a standpoint independently of its ways of life fails to be reasonable. That is, such a society denies to its members any standards or paradigms of reason. A liberal society presents its members with multiple sets of goods but fails to provide them with the ability—reason—to choose between those sets or judge them in any way. A liberal society, because it maintains neutrality concerning conceptions of the good and particular goods, does not provide its citizens with the context to reason. Such a liberal society does not make any commitments.

Now, as mentioned above, whether MacIntyre actually believes such a modern individual exists is questionable. Most likely, he thinks such an individual is a fiction of contemporary liberal society. The whole point of *After Virtue* is that even in American liberal society there are commitments to certain beliefs. These beliefs include the belief that redistribution of resources through taxation is unfair to those who "earn" the resources and the belief that the rich should be taxed to help those in poverty. Other beliefs include the belief that schools should teach morals to children or the belief that moral education is something not only best, but only rightly, left to parents. Such beliefs are conflicting. Moreover, and more importantly, these beliefs go undefended and are left unchallengeable except on a purely ideological level. I am not saying that no debate about these beliefs occurs. A modicum of debate does exist, but the debate generally begins and ends with the mere assertion of the basic beliefs without any real examination of such beliefs. Argument proves impossible in American society because the conflicting positions remain incommensurable as defined above. The rival parties do not share standards or exemplars of reasoning or evaluation of truth claims by which they can evaluate arguments from a shared standpoint.

This lack of a shared set of standards and exemplars entails certain realities for our "democracy." The dynamics of political advertising reduce any serious debate to a mere assertion of views without serious and respectful consideration of those views or the opposing views. As avowedly neutral concerning conceptions of the good, the liberal society cannot provide reasons or arguments for its commitments, not because it denies that it has such commitments (although it does deny this) nor because it lacks arguments for its commitments (although, as generations proceed, such arguments disappear). Rather, the liberal society fails to provide its members with standards and exemplars of reason because it denies that such standards and exemplars hold for all people at all times. The real problem with a pseudo-neutral-liberal society is that it denies that universal standards and exemplars of reason exist which its members should accept, but incorporates some nonetheless.

Substantive reason, then, on MacIntyre's account, is thinking and acting on the set of standards and beliefs of a particular social order. This substantive reason includes reason's self-evaluation. Reasoning about ends is investigating the goods of a society for their adequacies and improving on them where possible. Such reason involves the use of standards and beliefs. Thus, I define substantive reason as a set of social practices that involve the asking for and giving of reasons, the evaluation of those reasons and the asking for and giving of such evaluation, and, importantly, the evaluation of the good. However, the use of such reasoning raises an immediate problem both for MacIntyre and for the critical theorist.

Problems with MacIntyre's Account

Two problems arise in view of the discussion so far and the aim of this book. The aim of this book is to set out a theory of reason that can ground a critical theory of society. That conception of reason must be not simply formal or instrumental but substantive. The consideration of MacIntyre's account of tradition-constituted reason as a basis for this theory opens up two lacunae that need to be filled in to make MacIntyre's account useful for critical theory, if it can be made useful. First, although MacIntyre explains what it means for an individual to engage in reasoning and dialectic, he fails to ask and answer the following question: is such reasoning necessary for emancipation and available in all societies or traditions? Second, although MacIntyre argues that conceptions of justice and reason depend on each other for justification within a tradition, he neglects to spell out in detail what the relationship is between reason and justice, or the good more broadly, within traditions.

Traditions of Enquiry and Cultural Traditions

MacIntyre claims that only appeal to reason and reasonable justification provide the possibility of "unmasking and dethroning arbitrary exercises of power, tyrannical power within communities, and imperialist power between communities" (RPP 397).[8] Such appeal to reason, moreover, occurs when a tradition provides the resources to examine several conceptions of the good from various traditions.

A question arises in light of this claim: to what extent do individuals actually engage in such reasoning practices? To what extent is self-reflection, leading the examined life, an activity which occurs in everyday life? Although one might want to agree with MacIntyre, St. Thomas, and Aristotle that the unexamined life is not worth living, such a life seems to be par for the course for the vast majority of society.

Indeed, a critical theory of society must be interested in addressing this issue. Consider, for example, the life of the average person in the United States. Consider that the average person in the United States does not vote. Why? Because the average person is not interested. In fact, many of our comedies poke fun at those who "think too much." On the popular television show *Friends*, Ross was a paleontologist who could never find happiness because he overthought every decision. In the 2000 presidential election, many people said they would not vote for Al Gore because he was too stiff. We know that individuals are reluctant, at best, to engage in any sort of critical thought.

Another question arises at this juncture: how should a critical theory of society respond to the fact that a majority of people either do not have the opportunity to lead an examined life or are not inclined to do so? MacIntyre suggests that arbitrary exercises of power should be exposed and either removed or corrected. Yet he himself does not address the issue of the prevalence of leading an examined life in contemporary society or the value or need to do so. His arguments deal with what constitutes reason and how to defend a tradition-constituted reason and not with the role or value of such a reason. This issue needs to be addressed, however, if one is to engage in critical theory.

Moreover, the examined life is not an unquestioned value in philosophy. Some philosophers either neglect to mention its role in their theories or have no place for it. These philosophers include liberals, Humeans, and Kantians. Liberals must remain neutral concerning the good life. This neutrality means, however, that liberalism cannot promote the examination of life because such examination constitutes a conception of the good and of the good life. Committed to neutrality concerning the good, liberalism cannot commit to a particular version of the good—the examined life. I do not think that the liberal could consistently promote the examined life as an instrumental good which allows one to determine which set of goods to choose. Such a promotion entails the value of examining goods in opposition to living unreflectively with those goods inculcated in one by family, church, or society. Whether a Humean can ask about or be concerned with the examined life, and if so, to what extent, remains unclear. Morality is a matter of presenting rewards and punishments so that some passions appear stronger in an individual than do other ones. Little place is left for the value (for noneducators) of an examined life, because such a life necessarily means using reason to choose one's way of life, and precisely this use of reason is absent from Hume's philosophy. Kant, finally, concerns himself more with considerations about what is right than about what is good. Although Kant requires the individual to examine whether her choices are morally worthy, he leaves unasked the question of whether that life is good, and if so, to what degree it is good, or whether it is one good among many. Indeed, whether such a question can be raised in Kantian moral philosophy is unclear. The only absolute good, according to Kant, is the good will. How is that will, however, to be judged good?

Voltaire questioned the value of leading an examined life during the Enlightenment period. As we saw earlier, in the "Story of a Good Brahmin," Voltaire pictures a Brahmin who supposes that part of the contentedness he observes in a poor woman doing her laundry arises out of the very fact that she leads an unexamined life. Voltaire, one of the representatives of the Enlightenment, used this story to question the value of an examined life.

The concerned critical theorist who wants to appropriate MacIntyre's tradition-constituted reason to ground critical work aimed at emancipation is left with questions: To what extent are traditions of enquiry and their associated reasons outside the needs of a critical theory of society that is aimed at the concrete lived experiences of people who do not engage in enquiry and self-examination? Is an examined life necessary for emancipation? If so, how does one bring to individual people the resources for examination despite their thoroughly oppressed society? In short, does one, in embracing a tradition-constituted reason as propounded by MacIntyre and explained in this chapter, distance oneself from the very population one aims to engage for the purposes of emancipation?

We should keep in mind two things when answering these questions. First, Horkheimer and Adorno discuss the issue of culture and pop culture in relation to human emancipation in the *DOE*. They carefully note the dialectic of culture, showing, for instance, that modern individuals recognize a sales pitch when they see one, even as disguised as movies or songs, but still they purchase the product anyway. Much more has to be done to consider how culture and pop culture realize and hide the desire for emancipation in modern individuals who consume it. (My essay "Eucharist and Dragon Fighting as Resistance" attempts this from a MacIntyrean point of view.) Second, we have to keep in mind the tremendous workload that modern Americans maintain. In a world wherein it takes two incomes plus to support a family and work hours increase (while productivity increases and salaries stagnate), people simply lack the time and energy to exercise their *phronēsis* in a political community. This lack of time is a major impediment to human emancipation in a consumerist society. Both of these points must be kept in mind in any further work that addresses how tradition-constituted reason grounds critical political activity and engagement.

The Relationship between Reason and the Good in MacIntyre

The second issue which arises for a critical theorist is the relationship between reason and the good in MacIntyre's theory. It arises because a critical theory of society needs a well-formed substantive conception of reason. Substantive reason is needed insofar as a critical theory of society seeks a reason which will allow individuals to examine their ends and which will allow society to examine its ends. Such examination necessarily involves questions about the good. As discussed, a tradition-constituted reason does empower the individual to evaluate ends by enabling him to investigate an ordered set of goods.

The exact relationship between reason and the good, however, must be spelled out at the level of tradition. As we saw in the discussion of Aristotle, Kant, and Hume, each one's conception of reason and the good and the relationship between the two differed from the others'. In the next chapter, I will discuss cultural traditions, which will highlight this fact even more. MacIntyre's theory on which I am building does not embrace a universal conception of the good or a universal conception of substantive reason. MacIntyre explicitly states that to each determinate form of reason there corresponds a determinate form of justice (*WJWR* 321). Reason and justice are linked. Given that they are, what allows a critical theory of society to hope in any particular substantive reason for emancipatory purposes?

A critical theory of society is concerned with a link between reason and emancipation. Horkheimer's own discussion does not bring this point out clearly. Horkheimer holds, as does MacIntyre, that what is lacking in modernity is a substantive reason, a reason by which individuals might judge conceptions of the good. In making this claim, however, Horkheimer is presuming that the good is universal and, moreover, that the good involves emancipation. In rejecting a universal conception of the good, are we committed to rejecting a conception of the universal good?

The answer will turn out to be no. Each tradition identifies its conception of the good as good for everyone. It is universally good. In denying a universal conception of the good, the danger lies in reducing the good to a relative concept. The next chapter will examine how each tradition makes claims about a universal good, and chapter 5 will explain how this argument does not reduce to a relativism about the good. We shall see how reason connects to a conception of good that does not reduce the good to a relative concept and how that conception provides for the emancipatory function of reason. This argument depends on the argument that reason has substance.

MacIntyre has shown that reason has substance. His discussion of different philosophical traditions in the three works *After Virtue*, *Whose Justice? Which Rationality?*, and *Three Rival Versions of Moral Enquiry* shows that the substantive reason of each tradition has particular commitments. MacIntyre's discussion points to the necessary historical character of the good, but not to the interdependency of reason and the good. If reason is truly useful for liberatory purposes, however, it must be connected to the good, which is emancipatory at core. A connection to the good allows reason to point the way not only to pursuing the good life but also to distinguishing emancipatory ways of life from oppressive ones.

| The best place for a critical theorist to look for a conception of reason once Habermas's communicative rationality is rejected is to a tradition-constituted and tradition-constitutive reason such as is proposed by MacIntyre. Such a conception of reason can be defended through examples from the history of philosophy which represent different and competing conceptions of reason (as evidenced in the comparison of Aristotle, Hume, and Kant) and through examples of cosmology-laden languages such as were used by Native Americans, Irish, and Azande in previous centuries. This defense becomes even more convincing when supplemented with Kuhn's notion of disciplinary matrix. The next chapter addresses one of the two issues raised from the perspective of a critical theory of society about a tradition-constituted reason, namely, does a substantive reason, as conceived by MacIntyre, provide the needed material for a critical theory of society that unites reason and the interest of freedom?

4 | A Substantive Reason

I have argued that reason is substantive because it is an aspect of a socially and historically embodied tradition. Given this, the relation between substantive reason (the standards of reason) and the good must be spelled out by delving into particular traditions, which is the task of this chapter. This task has as its telos forging a path out of the modern impasse to a genuinely emancipatory substantive reason. Failure to explain clearly the connection between reason and the good will jeopardize this telos and the possibility of a critical theory of society. After first reviewing the distinctions between rationality, substantive reason, and reasons, I will discuss in turn tradition, the good, reason, and the mutually constitutive nature of reason and the good.

Formal Rationality, Substantive Reason, and Reasons

I have maintained a clear distinction between reason and rationality. "Rationality" names the kind of reason that focuses on means and ends, that categorizes, or that lays out the relations between concepts. That is, "rationality" refers generally to those processes of the individual mind through which an individual classifies objects and events and thinks in an instrumental fashion. This type of reasoning includes traditional logical principles, such as the principle of noncontradiction and *modus ponens.*

Substantive reason, in contrast, names the whole toolbox of reasoning within a tradition. As stated in the previous chapter, substantive reason comprises thinking about and acting on the set of standards and beliefs of a particular social order. As discussed, the social practices of reason involve standards and exemplars of reasoning. These standards and exemplars constitute an element of the tradition or disciplinary matrix. As such, they are informed by the other aspects of the tradition, including the values and symbolic generalizations, the general social practices and ways of life, and the larger cosmology—in short, everything included in Table 3.1 in the previous chapter. In turn, they provide reasons for those same aspects and allow members of the tradition to evaluate those aspects. This chapter will examine these relationships in detail for several traditions.

Exemplars of reason—of giving and asking for reasons—might include a scientific method or the Zande poison oracle, or the method a judge uses in deciding a case. Contemplating these exemplars reveals essential features of all exemplars. First, all exemplars of reason are socially established procedures. Second, they comprise procedures that model a kind of thinking for specific situations. Thus, whereas a scientific method is used for specific scientific or experimental situations, the Zande poison oracle is appropriate for situations in which mystical forces are expected or thought to be at work. Third, exemplars have different social functions: whereas, for instance, the scientific method has the function of producing a verifiable empirical result, and the Zande poison oracle functions to determine the presence of magic in a situation, the legal method functions to determine guilt or justice. Fourth, these procedures justify their own results. Because exemplars are socially established, they have been tested by society and/or at least accepted by society as how one should reason. If one uses one of these methods to provide reasons for one's actions or beliefs in their contexts, then the results of those methods in those contexts are accepted as legitimate. To question those results would be to question the exemplar itself and, thus, to question their social legitimacy and use.

Unlike substantive reason, reasons are not practices. They are neither methods nor procedures, are not limited to specific situations, have more than one function, and do not by their nature and function automatically justify the results of the activity. A reason is simply a statement that is meant to justify a specific action, belief, or the like. A reason is anything which one thinks will justify one's actions or beliefs to others.

Some reasons are socially established—that is, one can feel certain that one's use of them in particular situations is right and will be accepted by others. In deciding a case, for example, a judge refers to other cases—other socially sanctioned reasons for a decision. A judge might find a reason in a prior court case, for example, that evidence obtained from a forced plea is tainted. The judge then inserts that reason into her procedure for determining what the law calls for in the particular case. Similarly, a Catholic theologian such as St. Thomas Aquinas will refer to biblical statements, statements from other religious figures, and statements from "the philosopher" in his arguments. In these two cases, reasons have social standing. That is, members of the tradition recognize these reasons as worthy reasons in the given situation. Members of a tradition accept them prima facie.

Other reasons do not have such social standing. For example, I might give as a reason for buying a particular album that it is relaxing, while my wife might offer as a reason not to purchase the album the fact that our bank account is low on funds. These types of reasons, unlike court decisions and biblical statements, do not have social standing—that is, they do not have the same prima facie acceptance that the first type of reasons have. Similarly, the social establishment of a reason depends on the circumstance. A court case will not have the same standing within a church setting as it does in the courtroom, nor likewise will the biblical statement have the same standing in the courtroom as it does in theology.

Reasons can be used in multiple situations. The fact that our bank account is low on funds can be used as a reason to decide not just whether I should purchase an album but also whether I should pay to have the bushes trimmed, or, alternatively, give to a charity. A directive from the *Bible*, for example "Give alms," might be used both to justify giving alms and to argue against buying a new album.

Traditions

Traditions, Cosmologies, and Ways of Life

As stated in the previous chapter, standards and exemplars of reason, both formal and substantive, are found in the canonical texts of a tradition. These "texts" appear in the social embodiments of the fundamental agreements, that is, in the utterances (oral, written, and pictorial) and actions of a tradition. These fundamental agreements unify the tradition. The pertinent arguments with insiders and outsiders are arguments about the fundamental agreements. History, then, constitutes a history of those arguments and social embodiments.

Fundamental agreements include agreements about cosmologies, laws, customs, and relationships of both individuals and communities to each other and to the environment. Thus, the Lakota of the colonial period had commitments to a different relationship between human beings and the land than did the English settlers,[1] and the Azande had different commitments concerning cosmic order than did Evans-Pritchard. Beliefs and ways of life flow from such cosmologies. These cosmologies, then, prove basic to the other aspects of the tradition in that cosmologies lay the framework in which all of the other aspects fit.

Traditions certainly involve a view of the cosmos. Having a view of the cosmos entails having a view of humanity's relationship to and position in that cosmos. A view of the cosmos, if it is to be of the cosmos, involves a view of the whole including the relationships of the parts, or at least the major ones, to the whole. To qualify that claim by adding "or at least the major parts" does not detract from my point. Humanity either is or is not a major part of the cosmos. In either case, the view of the cosmos has within it a view of humanity, insofar as it views humanity as a part of the cosmos.

It follows, then, that a view of the cosmos also necessarily involves a view of humanity's relationship not only to itself—of one people to another—but also to the environment and nature. The beliefs about the relationship between humanity and the environment and nature may be unconscious, but they are there nonetheless to inform the other beliefs and ways of life which constitute the general cosmology of the tradition. Such views inform the practices which compose a tradition's ways of life. Ways of life comprise practices that are justified because of the view people have of their particular place and role in the cosmos when the cosmos is considered to encompass relationships not just of parts to whole but also of parts to one another (of groups of human beings and communities to other groups and communities).

Consider some examples. The nomadic way of life of the Lakota rested on their beliefs about their relationship to the whole; how they saw the land rested on how they viewed Mother Earth. Mother Earth existed as something not to be owned but to be cared for.[2] In contrast, European, especially English Protestant, settlers believed that unoccupied land was wasted land; such beliefs figured greatly in, for example, Locke's arguments for private property. It is better to own and cultivate land to increase its productivity than to let it sit fallow or grow wild.

Zande witchcraft vengeance, meanwhile, was a way of life for the Azande, a way that depended on their beliefs about both the nature of the cosmos, in particular, the existence of magic in that cosmos, and the nature of unfortunate accidents. Consider the following analysis offered by Evans-Pritchard about Zande belief in witchcraft.

> In speaking to Azande about witchcraft and in observing their reactions to situations of misfortune it was obvious that they did not attempt to account for the existence of the phenomena, or even the action of phenomena, by mystical causation alone. What they explained by witchcraft were the particular conditions in a chain of causation which related an individual to natural happenings in such a way that he sustained injury. The boy who knocked his foot against a stump of wood did not account for the stump by reference to witchcraft, nor yet again did he account for the cut by saying that it was caused by witchcraft, for he knew quite well that it was caused by the stump of wood. What he attributed to witchcraft was that on this particular occasion, when exercising his usual care, he struck his foot against a stump of wood, whereas on a hundred other occasions he did not do so, and that on this particular occasion the cut, which he expected to result from the knock, festered whereas he had dozens of cuts which had not festered. Surely these peculiar conditions demand an explanation.[3]

The boy understood that knocks against wood and bumps happen. He also knew, however, that such cuts did not usually fester. Festering on this occasion, consequently, had to have a cause. A conception of what is natural lies dormant within this demand that the festering must have a cause that is unnatural. An understanding about how things work in the universe further underlies the need for an explanation. The use of witchcraft as an explanation, moreover, depended on a view of the world that recognized that some people chose witchcraft as a way of acting.

When, furthermore, someone dies among the Azande, they want an explanation. Someone, let's call her Alpha, dies. Alpha's family wants to know why this happened. They go to a priest. They ask the priest, "Was witchcraft the cause of Alpha's death?" The priest then consults an oracle. He poisons a hen. He asks the hen a name. If the hen dies, then the priest knows that the person attached to the name given to the hen used witchcraft on Alpha. Suppose the priest tells Alpha's family, "Yes, Beta used witchcraft on Alpha." The family then seeks out a different witch. They seek authorization from the priest and the prince to have vengeance witchcraft. They then have the witch perform vengeance witchcraft on Beta. Vengeance as a way of life among the Azande depends on the shape of their fundamental agreements about witchcraft.

These three different practices show how practices, or ways of life, relate to traditions: they are parts of traditions. The cosmologies of those traditions provide the necessary background to give definition and meaning to those ways of acting. That is, the ways of acting rest on a certain cosmology and the beliefs that constitute part of that cosmology.

Interrelationships between Cosmologies, Beliefs, Ways of Life, and the Good

The beliefs and ways of life of a tradition, then, constitute some of the fundamental agreements of a tradition. The chart that compares MacIntyre's cosmology-laden languages with Kuhn's disciplinary matrices captures those fundamental agreements. That is, then, the fundamental agreements of a tradition are simply the elements of a disciplinary matrix mentioned above and in the previous chapter. Those elements, however, included standards and exemplars. Nothing as yet has been said to suggest that the fundamental agreements include those standards and exemplars.

If it is true that traditions involve commitments to cosmologies that undergird ways of life, it is also, and maybe even more, true that cosmologies necessarily entail conceptions of the good, or the choice-worthy. What members of a tradition see as choice-worthy determines their ways of life. The nomadic life depends[4] on viewing the uncultivated earth, as uncultivated, as good. The appropriative life depends on viewing the earth as good only when cultivated.

A tradition's fundamental agreements, then, involve cosmologies, beliefs, and ways of life. All of these facets interrelate within a tradition. For example, the realm of possible beliefs a person might have is defined by the cosmology of that person's tradition. The history of philosophy easily demonstrates this fact. Take, for example, the work of Étienne Gilson on the concept of god in philosophy. Plato, Aristotle, and other ancient Greeks, for instance, could not conceive of the Judeo-Christian God, because the Greek cosmology, even as understood and developed divergently by different Greek philosophers, had no place for the concept of *being* apart from individual beings (i.e., apart from particular substances).[5]

Conversely, beliefs can help determine a cosmology. Many beliefs are formed from experiences—experiences interpreted, of course, by a particular cosmology. Yet one can deny some interpretations of experience only for so long. One example of the limits of a cosmology's influence on belief involves early Christian beliefs about the second coming of Jesus. Early believers expected Jesus to return almost immediately, and in any case before the "present" generation had passed away. As time went by, this belief proved wrong, which meant that the cosmology had to change. Rather than believing in the immediate apocalypse, the Christian tradition had to explain why the second coming had not occurred. This explaining involved developing a new conception of the cosmos and its eventual demise. It entailed the tradition becoming more adequate to human experience, such adequacy being the core of truth (discussed in the next chapter).

Examples of beliefs changing cosmologies are easier to find on the individual level (e.g., religious conversions and changing views of race relations). Moreover, beliefs are more easily determined by cosmologies than vice versa, partly because beliefs derive from experiences interpreted through cosmologies and partly because changing a cosmology involves changing a large set of interconnected beliefs. Such large change is psychologically daunting and, therefore, seldom occurs.

A cosmology includes a view of what is good and evil. Some leeway is open here, though, for an intuitive sense of the good to effect those more deeply held beliefs. By intuitive, I mean people intuitively associate good with pleasure and evil with pain. These associations affect the general view of the cosmos, including the more sophisticated— that is, noninstinctual—conception of good and evil. On the one hand, these intuitive beliefs about what is good and evil help determine and inform conceptions of the good. Here the physical environment comes into play. Of course, the interpretations human beings offer in this regard can vary greatly. Some traditions could view a volcanic eruption as a message from good gods, and others as a portent of evil from evil gods. The general view of the cosmos both is shaped by and shapes the interpretation of such natural events. Cosmologies evolve. Such evolution will be shaped in turn by the beliefs about good and evil already available to the members of the tradition from their basic cosmology. Perhaps it is the belief in a good god that allows a tradition to interpret a volcanic eruption as a message from such a god. Or it might be a belief in evil gods that allows a tradition to interpret a volcanic eruption as a message that the gods want virgin sacrifices. Alternatively, it could be past experiences with volcanic eruptions kept alive in the tradition which have led them to believe that all higher powers are evil or, alternatively, stern yet good.

On the other hand, beliefs about the good encourage some interpretations of natural events over others. Beliefs about the sacredness of all things can lead a tradition to interpret life-threatening natural phenomena as good. For example, some people might interpret the occurrence of forest fires due to lightening strikes as means nature employs to regulate its own growth. They might then, on this interpretation, attempt to help nature control her growth by starting their own forest fires under controlled conditions. Such an interpretation and practice is not available to members of a tradition who see natural powers, like lightening, as belonging to evil beings. Thus, a tradition's conception of the good and its conception of the cosmos are mutually determinative and, through a process of historical reflection and experience, coexist in a sort of equilibrium.

A community's conception of the good, then, establishes ways of life as appropriate in a tradition. The relationship between ways of life, on the one hand, and beliefs and cosmologies, on the other, is more complicated. Ways of life are not determined solely by a tradition's cosmologies and beliefs. What ways of life are established in the tradition as appropriate—as opposed to ways of life simpliciter—depends on the cosmologies and beliefs of that tradition. These beliefs and cosmologies determine *appropriate* ways of life. They do not necessarily determine all possible ways of life that are found in a particular tradition. Having a homosexual lover was a possible way of life for the twentieth century even though the cosmologies of Americans did not deem it appropriate (and, for the most part, still do not). Certainly, someone could imagine that in a Puritan tradition, for example—which is so close-knit and in which everyone knows both everyone else and what everyone does—cosmologies and beliefs define the possible ways of life found in that tradition. Once a community becomes large enough that not everyone can keep track of what everyone else is doing, the ways of life found in a tradition will partially deviate from those deemed appropriate. If Plato's reports on Socrates are accurate, Socrates did not engage in sexual activities with other Greek men and, so, stands as just one example of a deviant way of life in a particular tradition.

Just as cosmologies and beliefs inform appropriate ways of life, appropriate ways of life can come to inform particular cosmologies and beliefs. A prime example of this reverse influence is the Roman Catholic practice of Communion, adopted, according to the Christian gospels and the Acts of the Apostles, as a way of forming the early Christian community. It arose out of a religious observance of Passover that Jesus celebrated with the apostles the night before he was crucified. Later, the practice became a way of identifying the risen Jesus (for example, on the road to Emmaus) and identifying with other Christians. Because of this identifying function, the practice of Communion became a ritual for building community: Jesus said to repeat the act in remembrance of him.

During the Middle Ages, the practice helped define Roman Catholic belief and cosmology. Catholics disputed what happened during the practice: did the bread and wine really become the body and blood of Jesus? The belief in the gospel testimony was central, of course, but without the practice there would be no need to change the cosmology to include the notion of transubstantiation. Here, rather than the cosmology determining the act, the act determined the cosmology, encouraging the adoption of an Aristotelian metaphysics. A theory was needed to explain how bread and wine continued to appear (for the most part, miracles aside) as bread and wine when it was really human flesh and blood. Aristotelian notions of substance and form provided some answer. Importantly, the cosmology also influenced other aspects of the practice, including the turn in which the church declared that only priests could perform the sacrament. This change in practice at another level led to the elevation of the ordained priest over lay members of the church in a new way.

Thus, one can see that the relationship between a tradition's cosmologies and beliefs and its ways of life is complex. One could imagine a way of life that was judged neither good nor bad (perhaps smoking in the eighteenth century). The cosmologies and beliefs can determine appropriate ways of life. In most traditions, appropriate ways of life are only a subset of actual and all possible ways of life in the tradition. Ways of life can, in turn, determine particular beliefs and cosmologies. The example of the history of the Roman Catholic practice and theology of Communion demonstrates this point. Beliefs and cosmologies are more closely connected to each other than they are to ways of life. Of course, if ways of life can transform cosmologies, they necessarily can change beliefs. Indeed, it is perhaps through changing individual beliefs that ways of life can change whole cosmologies. Working with African Americans changed the beliefs of individual white Americans in the 1960s and 1970s, which led to a change in cosmology.

In the relationships between cosmologies, beliefs, and ways of life, conceptions of the good can and do play central, formative roles. Not only does the conception of the good help determine cosmologies and appropriate ways of life, but it informs the ways members of a tradition will interpret and judge the cosmologies, beliefs, and, even more, ways of life of other and competing traditions. Yet although the conception of the good determines the evolution of cosmologies, beliefs, and ways of life within a tradition, the traditions that result are not monoliths.

Diversity within Traditions: Against a Monolithic View

When speaking about a tradition, one always characterizes it according to certain predominant features: in the Zande tradition, belief in magic and witchcraft; in the Lakota tradition, a belief in the sacredness of land and a commitment to a nomadic lifestyle;[6] in the English settler tradition, a certain appropriative relationship to nature; in the Roman Catholic, a belief in transubstantiation. Such characterizations, however, are always oversimplifications.

To even talk or write about traditions clearly and concisely, one must make them appear monolithic. Though one generally speaks of traditions as homogeneous in beliefs, variations of beliefs will occur among the members of any given tradition. A tradition is defined in terms of its fundamental agreements. Those fundamental agreements, however, are always contested. A tradition is an ongoing argument among insiders, as well as with outsiders, about those agreements. So people within a tradition will always be questioning whether its particular view of the cosmos is the right view, or whether that conception of the good really captures the good, or whether a standard of reason really counts as a standard of reason.

How, then, one might ask, does one characterize a tradition? That is, how does one determine the borders of different traditions? Kuhn holds that a "paradigm is what members of a scientific community share, *and,* conversely, a scientific community consists of men who share a paradigm."[7] Paradigms, again, are "shared examples" which guide the practitioners in their scientific work. In other words, paradigms are just those standards of reason that members of a tradition share. Such a view of the defining characteristic of a tradition coheres with MacIntyre's view. For example, MacIntyre characterizes moral traditions according to their standards of reason. Utilitarianism, Kantianism, and Aristotelianism are each characterized by particular paradigmatic examples of reasoning.

If the argument of this chapter is correct, however, such a view does not tell the whole story, for standards of reason are determined in part by a tradition's conception of the good. If standards of reason are a defining feature of a tradition, then the conception of the good must likewise be a defining feature. That conception of the good determines what the particular standards of reason are within that tradition. The conception of the good, that is, determines the defining characteristic of a tradition. Traditions that share standards of reason must also share conceptions of the good—of what is choice-worthy or objectively valuable.

Till now I have left out an aspect of traditions that makes determining borders even more complicated: the fact that if a tradition is a historically and socially embodied argument, that argument will be, in part, about the very identity of the tradition. The boundaries of a tradition are determined in a dialectical encounter both among the members of the tradition and with those who live outside it. A priori and analytic arguments will not suffice to determine the identities and boundaries of traditions. Such identities and boundaries must be hammered out, as it were, only in the development and process of concrete, historical argumentation.

Rather than thinking about what feature is universally shared within a tradition, it is better to think of a tradition as setting certain constraints on the historically and socially embodied arguments over its fundamental agreements. These constraints are found in how the components of the tradition—the view of the cosmos, the ways of life, the conception of the good, and the standards of reason—interact with one another to set limits to how the debate can proceed.

Consider two examples.

First, consider the work of Étienne Gilson.[8] While I understand some controversy exists over Gilson's thesis, I take his argument as definitive of the issue. Gilson argues, for instance, that the ancient Greek cosmology had no room for a conception of the Hebrew God. The Greek understanding of the world could and did conceptualize being only in terms of substance. That is, the Greeks could not conceive of being apart from concrete instances; they could not conceive of being as something apart from existents. The Hebrew definition of God, however, relies on such a separation. When Moses asks the burning bush, "Who should I say sent me," God answers, "I am Who am." According to Gilson, this pronouncement is the first and unique understanding of God as something apart from and not dependent on the universe. Whereas the Greeks could conceive of God only as something within the universe of contingent things, the Hebrews conceived of God as outside and independent of the universe. Hence, Greek arguments about the gods were constrained by their cosmology, a cosmology that did not admit of being apart from substance.

Second, a discussion of whether Aristotle's political philosophy included a notion of rights provides another example of how cosmologies and conceptions of the good can constrain debates. Several scholars have recently argued that Aristotle had a notion of rights that prefigured the notion of natural rights in Hobbes, Locke, Rousseau, and other social contract theorists.[9] These arguments ignore the fact that Aristotle lacked a concept that would be necessary for rights talk. Modern political philosophers conceive of human beings as atoms in a void, but Aristotle could not so conceive them. Although Aristotle did have access to the notion of atoms, such a notion was so alien to his conception of the good that he could not conceive of human beings as atoms. Human beings were defined as human only within a community. Existing outside of a community, they could not be considered human beings, but only beasts or gods. Hence, whereas Aristotelian arguments about justice were constrained by a cosmology that saw human beings as essentially social animals, many modern philosophical arguments are constrained by a cosmology that views them as solitary individuals. The preconceptions of those who advance such arguments even constrain their reading of Aristotle (just, of course, as my conceptions might constrain my reading of Aristotle).

These two examples show that traditions provide parameters for debate. They can set limits to what can be conceived. These limits can be set by the general picture of the cosmos or by a conception of the good, or even by the standards of reason within the tradition. Rather than hampering debate, these limits provide the very conditions for reasonable debate. Reasonable argumentation must presume some fundamental agreements. When people cannot identify any fundamental agreements, they cannot debate but must fight or go their individual ways. Such a claim should not be novel or surprising.

Traditions, then, are historically and socially embodied arguments about fundamental agreements among insiders and between insiders and outsiders. The borderlines of a tradition are not protected from such debates. The fundamental agreements include notions of the cosmos, conceptions of the good, ways of life, and standards of reason.

The Good

Philosophical Good: Aristotle, St. Thomas, Kant, Hume, Bentham, and Mill

If the borderlines of a tradition defy determination, the concept of the good also proves difficult to capture. A priori and analytic arguments do not work here. The conception of the good differs among traditions, just as the standards and exemplars of reason differ between traditions. All share some formal element—that the good is choiceworthy. Just as formal elements of reason cannot capture what is really meant by reason or give direction with respect to actions, a formal definition of "the good" cannot capture what the good is, capture how it relates to and determines the standards and exemplars of reason, or, finally, provide direction in action. To develop a more substantive conception of the good, then, I must examine the conceptions of the good found in various philosophical and cultural traditions. This analysis reveals that a conception of the good in a tradition is defined in terms of a conception of human nature. Generally, we see the good as the best that is achievable for human beings conceived as such and such creatures within a tradition.

Philosophers on the Good

The Aristotelian tradition provides a paradigmatic example of how the concept of the substantive good is defined in relation to a conception of human nature.[10] Aristotle holds that the good is the proper functioning of a thing. The proper function of human beings is reason. Thus, the good for human beings is excellent reasoning. Excellent reasoning provides the foundation for *eudaimonia. Eudaimonia*, or happiness, names that condition of self-fulfillment or self-realization that comes from the excellent functioning.

Scholars debate the exact activities of the excellently functioning human being. Some hold that Aristotle thought that contemplation of the divine was the highest good; others hold that he thought that political activity was the highest good; and still others hold that he thought that a combination of contemplation and political activity was the highest good. However these debates are decided does not matter. What matters is that these conceptions of the highest good depend on a particular conception of the human being. The human being is both a political animal and an animal capable of reason, or of contemplating the divine. Human beings also have functions that correspond to their being political and contemplating the divine. All answers about what the good is for Aristotle must take into consideration his conception of the human being.

As it is with Aristotle, so it is with St. Thomas Aquinas. For St. Thomas, the *summum bonum* is contemplation of the divine, which is *beatitudo* or happiness. Such contemplation, on the Thomistic account, takes the form of unity with God. Such unity proves impossible on the Aristotelian account because Aristotle did not conceive of the human being as something able to unite with the divine. On the Thomistic account, however, the human being was created for the purpose of living in union with God. Happiness is the ultimate good of human beings, and it consists in the fulfillment of all desires. Human beings, moreover, have a desire to know God. Thus, happiness consists, in part at least, in knowing God.[11] The conception of the human being as a creature with a particular desire determines what the good is for human beings.

The notion of desire brings out how different are the various moral and political traditions of the great philosophers. Moreover, it highlights how different conceptions of desires and of the human being determine the conception of the good for these various philosophers.

Kant, for example, has a unique conception of desire, rationality, and the good for human beings. The human being, on Kant's account, is an entity which occupies a position in two different worlds—the phenomenal and the noumenal. In the phenomenal world, the human being is determined in his actions by his desires. In the noumenal world, the human being is determined by his rationality. The will must be made consistent with the noumenal world. What the person wills, if it is to be morally right willing, must be determined by rationality. (I leave aside here the discussion of whether rationality alone, or rationality plus desires, determines the will.)

The highest good is "that whole which is no part of a yet larger whole of the same kind."[12] That perfect good, for human beings, is happiness in proportion to virtue. On Kant's account happiness is the fulfillment of desires, but "that complete well-being and contentment with one's condition which is called happiness make[s] for pride and often thereby even arrogance."[13] Such fulfillment does not constitute the highest good. Human rationality was not designed for such an end, but for determining the will according to the moral law alone.[14] What is good in and of itself, then, is the good will—the will that is determined by rationality. Virtue is the determination of the will according to moral law.

The perfect good, however, cannot be achieved in the present life, according to Kant. Thus, human beings must, according to practical rationality, presume an afterlife in which happiness is accorded to individuals in proportion to their virtue. Virtue itself is the supreme good, that is, the "supreme condition of whatever appears to be desirable and thus of all our pursuit of happiness."[15]

Contrasting Kant to Hume makes this role of the conception of human nature in determining the conception of the substantive good even more obvious. For Hume, passions are the controlling or determining elements of decisions. The good, on the Humean account, is simply pleasure, which he defines as the satisfaction of desire. Evil, conversely, is pain. Thus, for Hume, one knows the morally right thing to do not from some law of rationality but from a faculty of moral sentiment: "Since morals have an influence on the actions and affections it follows they cannot be derived from rationality." Morals cannot follow from rationality because "rationality is wholly inactive."[16] Indeed, according to Hume, "no action can be virtuous, or morally good, unless there be in human nature some motive to produce it, distinct from the sense of its morality."[17] Yet the only motives Hume admits in human nature are desires and passions. Thus, virtuous action is possible, for Hume, only on the condition that some prior desire acts as motive for that action. The moral good, then, rests on or arises from simple human desires; it is defined in terms of what is possible for human beings in light of human nature. That good is the satisfaction of desires. The role of education is to train the human being to value some desires over others by, for example, praising various acts to encourage them and condemning other acts to discourage them. Approbation brings pleasure; condemnation brings pain.

Consider as a final contrast on the philosophical level the difference in opinion between Jeremy Bentham and J. S. Mill on the nature of the good. Bentham is similar to Hume, defining good and evil in terms of pleasure and pain; pleasure is the condition of happiness, and pain of unhappiness. The good is synonymous with happiness;[18] so the good is pleasure. Pleasure and pain are the sole motivating factors of the human being. Indeed, the principle of utility directs one to choose that action which produces the greatest overall happiness, that is, the greatest pleasure and the least pain. The good, happiness, for human beings is pleasure on Bentham's account. For Mill, in contrast, it is better to be Socrates dissatisfied than a pig satisfied. Though Mill claims that he agrees with Bentham, the difference is obvious. Mill argues that happiness is pleasure and absence of pain, but he develops, in addition, a hierarchy of pleasures. Bentham never acknowledges any such hierarchy. Each has a different conception of what is possible for human beings, a different conception of human nature, that in turn defines what the good is for human beings. For both Bentham and Mill the conception includes the notions of pleasure and pain and, moreover, what causes pleasure and pain. Further, one understanding of the human being allows Bentham to hold that all pleasures are equal, while a different understanding allows Mill to conclude that some pleasures are worthier than others—those pleasures which are particularly human (such as the use of reason). That is, if one's conception of human nature includes a notion of pleasure and pain, then how one defines pleasure and pain becomes simply a more refined aspect of the conception of human nature.

A Formal Conception of the Good

From this analysis of various philosophers' conceptions of the substantive good arises an element of a formal conception of the good: all substantive conceptions of the good are defined in relation to substantive conceptions of what the best possible achievement is for the human being. Formally, conceptions of the good arise from a conception of human nature. These conceptions differ substantively and prove incommensurable because of the rival conceptions of human nature on which they are based. Incommensurability does not mean that such conceptions have nothing in common, but rather that despite such commonalities, individual philosophers cannot reach agreements over ranking of the goods or over how the highest good can be defined. Formally, these philosophers name the same thing, while substantively they name different things.

The greatest distinction between Kant, Hume, Bentham, and Mill, on the one hand, and Aristotle and St. Thomas, on the other, concerns autonomy. For Kant, Hume, Bentham, and Mill, one of the greatest goods, if not the greatest good, is autonomy. Autonomy is not, however, significant for Aristotle or St. Thomas. Autonomy requires a notion of will that Aristotle lacks. St. Thomas does have the notion of will, a notion introduced by St. Augustine; yet freedom of the will is subordinate to the need to control the fallen nature of humanity. On the Thomistic account, the fallen nature of human beings means that they must be trained in the virtues. On the more modern account, by contrast, if the fallen nature of humanity is recognized, it is recognized as a reason for autonomy because the ultimate nature of the good cannot be known for certain by human beings. A conception of the powers of human knowledge, then, plays a role in how each of these philosophers specifies the good.

In sum, these discussions highlight that the substantive conception of the good within any particular tradition is determined as the best that human beings can achieve, as this is conceived on the basis of the particular conception of human nature held by each philosopher. Human nature, in turn, is a part of the conception of the cosmos, as argued above. The beliefs about human nature form some of the fundamental agreements held by the members of a tradition. Further examination of the Roman Catholic, Zande, and Lakota traditions will support this understanding of the relation between a tradition's conception of human nature and its conception of the good.

The Good for Roman Catholics, Azande, and Lakota

One will notice immediately a difficulty in discussing the good for these various cultural traditions. My analysis of these cultural traditions proves necessarily piecemeal. I have not captured, and could not within a reasonably sized book, even one of these traditions in all of its aspects, much less all three of them. Still, connecting what has been discussed about them might suffice to confirm, or at least to avoid contradicting, the finding in the last subsection, namely, that the conception of the good is always the conception of the best that a human being can achieve given a particular understanding of human nature.

The substantive human good for the Roman Catholic is union with God. Such union is achieved through leading a virtuous life, following the Golden Rule and the Ten Commandments more generally, and participating in and being a part of a religious community. The act of Communion is an integral part of participating in the community and of being with God. Through the ingestion of bread and wine, the body and blood of Jesus Christ, God becomes part of one's own body. Excommunication is ostracism, a separation not just from the church, God's community, but also from the various sacraments, including Communion, and from God himself. It occurs only in response to the greatest evils. Excommunication is an extreme measure, however. A more common measure, and one that is self-imposed, is abstinence from Communion. Catholics who have sinned mortally are forbidden to receive Communion. Having deliberately separated themselves from God and his people by their mortal sin—for example, refusing to pay a just wage—they are not suited for Communion until they have been reconciled to God and his people through the Sacrament of Reconciliation (confession). Such sin is then, in essence, the separation of a person from God. Evil is that separation. Good is union with God.

This union with God is the best state for human beings, according to Roman Catholic doctrine. The divine vision is the *summum bonum*. This *summum bonum* is the most complete or best state for human existence—union with "that than which nothing greater can be thought," something greater than human beings—God himself. Nor does the union of God with human beings add anything to God's essence, to his perfection. Such union does, however, mark the zenith of human accomplishment. The conception of human nature within the Roman Catholic tradition, then, is of a being capable of union with God. The human being is fallen, in that humanity once, in Eden, shared the vision of God, but no longer shares it; humanity, or at least individual human beings, can receive grace which allows them to experience the vision of God once more.

The Azande and their tradition contrast informatively with Roman Catholics and theirs, since the Azande represent a (non-European) African people. Of the three traditional conceptions of the good that we are considering, the Zande is the most difficult to understand. The tradition of magic and witchcraft among the Azande is a small part of their total tradition. While witchcraft and magic are ubiquitous in Zande lives, discussing the tradition of the Azande in terms of witchcraft and magic severely limits what can be said about their way of life as a whole and about their general conception of the good. Still, some research has focused on the relationship between witchcraft and morality among the Azande.[19] A. B. Saran, for instance, holds that the whole practice of witchcraft influences all of Zande life, including notions of good and evil. "The Azande morality, i.e. 'good' or 'bad', 'right' or 'wrong', is so closely related to their notions of witchcraft that it may be said to embrace them."[20] Evans-Pritchard, furthermore, gives some clue about the idea of the good life for the Azande. He notes that for them the good life consists in raising good crops, having good neighbors and faithful wives, and living peaceably.[21] Notions of evil are tied to their understanding of misfortune. For the Azande, misfortune has to be explained.[22]

Witchcraft and sorcery can disrupt or destroy a good life. According to Evans-Pritchard, "witchcraft, oracles, and magic are like three sides to a triangle. Oracles and magic are two different ways of combating witchcraft." Magic, however, comes in two forms: good and bad. "Witchcraft and sorcery [bad magic] are opposed to, and opposed by, good magic."[23]

The difference between bad magic—witchcraft and sorcery—and good magic does not derive from the effects. Witchcraft and sorcery are not bad because they harm others. Rather, the difference is that good magic "settles cases as judiciously as princes" and bad magic does not judge equally.[24] The question that determines whether the magic is bad or good is whether the magic affects an innocent or guilty person. Magic is good—"receives the moral and legal sanction of the community"—only if it "acts regularly and impartially." Magic is bad, and stupid, when it slays or harms others "without regard to the merits of the case."[25]

Magic, when good, is used only when the injured does not know who injured him. If the injured knows who injured him (either from an eyewitness or from some oracle, such as the poison oracle), then the injured takes the matter before the prince (or judge). If he does not know who injured him, then he uses good magic to exact retribution, for magic searches out who is guilty and punishes him. Bad magic (sorcery and witchcraft), in contrast, is aimed at specific known people. This aim shows that magic is bad, for if there were a legal case against the person at whom the bad magic is aimed, then the sorcerer would be morally bound to refer the matter to the courts.

Although this distinction between good and bad magic provides some insight into the mind of the Azande, the distinction has not yet been related to a conception of the good itself. Evans-Pritchard interprets the distinction as one between a situation in which the injury is deserved and one in which it is not. While insightful, this interpretation does not provide much in the way of a conception of the good. It does suggest, though, that the good for the Azande at least includes a sense of justice, or fairness.

A more telling aspect of magic practices lies in another way good magic is used. Good magic can be used to protect the work in which an Azande is engaged. Thus, an Azande may hang particular good magic over his hut door, or perform certain magic rituals before undertaking a journey, or place good magic over his crop. These uses of good magic aim to prevent or block the use of witchcraft and sorcery. The idea is that if someone is out to get me and to cause me harm or injury through witchcraft or sorcery, such harm can be blocked by the use of good magic, which can both block the harm and wreak vengeance on the person intending harm. Again, the idea behind Zande beliefs in witchcraft and sorcery is that these explain why things go wrong or why harm befalls someone. The boy who stubbed his toe (from the example earlier in this chapter) blamed it on bad magic because he took normal precautions and still something bad happened to him. Witchcraft and sorcery are seen as explanations for why bad things happen.

This understanding of bad and good magic suggests that the use of good magic helps the Azande achieve the best that they can achieve under normal conditions by blocking interference from those who harm. People who wish others harm are bad on the Zande view. Individual Azande can plant a good crop or maintain a good home as long as others do not harm them. Good magic protects the work of the Azande so that it can be the best possible. Bad magic explains the presence of misfortune, that is, the inability to achieve the best. The best that the Azande can hope for is living a good life, that is, having good spouses and good crops and living peaceably with others. A good life is one without misfortune.

Among the Lakota the role of the conception of human nature in defining the conception of the good in a tradition is clearer, because the Lakota are always discussed in light of or against the background of Anglo-Europeans. This background highlights the distinct characteristics of the Lakota tradition.

As discussed, the Lakota saw all things as sacred. The good life was one in which the Lakota lived in harmony with Mother Earth and all her creatures. The Lakota believed that if they took proper care of the earth and its creatures—which meant not overhunting, overgathering, or destroying in any way—then Mother Earth would take care of them in return. The nomadic way of life was essential to this vision. Mother Earth provided the buffalo in ample number for the sustenance of the Lakota. Reliance on the buffalo meant, however, that the Lakota needed to follow the buffalo where it could graze. A certain harmony was maintained in the relationship.

The good for the Lakota, then, relied on their conception of themselves and the world. Human beings were just one other aspect of the world, of the earth, among others. Mother Earth, in turn, cared for all of her parts. The best that the Lakota could achieve was to maintain harmony with the land. If they broke that harmony, they would suffer; for instance, Mother Earth would send them harsh weather and little food. So the Lakota could not hope for something better than being the children of the earth and living in harmony with all of its creatures. The Lakota conception of human nature is that human beings are children of the earth who can either live in harmony with or in discord with the earth. Their conception of the good follows from this view of human nature, for the good is living in harmony with the earth—that is the best they can achieve.

The typical English Protestant settler, in contrast, saw the world differently. The world was there to be conquered and dominated by (white) human beings. After the fall of Adam and Eve, a contest ensued between nature and humanity. Human beings had always to strive to get what they needed from the earth through hard toil. The earth did not care for them, but rather contested them at every step. European and English Protestant settlers also saw themselves as not equal to but superior to nature and its creatures. Human beings were given the power—rationality—to conquer and control nature so as to make it serve their needs. This modern mind-set embraced the notion that because of their ingenuity human beings would no longer need to fear the uncontrollable powers of the earth. Rather, they would discover the secrets of the earth and control it.

The good for the English Protestant settlers, then, relied on their notions of themselves and of the universe. Human beings could extract more from the earth by using their brains and their toil to maximize what the earth was capable of producing when properly cared for. Such proper care meant controlling it (generally, white males controlling it, since they were the superior race—another aspect of their view of human nature). The best that the settler could hope for, then, was what he could extract from the earth given his own individual sweat. He must contend with a planet that no longer served his needs, but which he could tame to serve his needs. Such taming meant that the English Protestant settler had to own his particular property. Success with his property meant that he was good; failure meant that he was lazy and of no account. Success also was a sign of favor with God, or election to the saved.

These cultural traditions—of the Roman Catholic, the Azande, and the Lakota in contrast to the English settler—exhibit a common, or formal, feature of conceptions of the good. Formally, the conceptions capture the idea of the best that a human being can hope for given her tradition's particular view of the nature of the human being. Substantively, these conceptions prove to be rival and generally incommensurable. All conceptions of the good are conceptions of what is best; but this best is spelled out within the tradition. One cannot really say anything specific about the good without saying so from within a particular tradition; no one can step outside of a tradition and say anything meaningful, and yet more detailed, about those traditions than what has been said here. Since, moreover, conceptions of what is best rest on a particular conception of the human being, as the conception of the human being changes, so does the conception of the good. The examination of the various moral traditions in philosophy led to the same conclusion.

Reason

The central question is whether reason is genuinely suitable for the pursuit of enlightenment and emancipation or whether those who seek emancipation must accept the pessimism about reason so powerfully expressed in Horkheimer and Adorno's *Dialectic of Enlightenment.* This question, so I argued along with Horkheimer, must be understood as asking what the connection is between reason and the good. Accordingly, I now address the question by investigating particular standards and exemplars of reason within the traditions discussed.

Reason in Relation to Tradition

Commitments to cosmologies and the good provide the substantive elements of reason. They fill out, as it were, the standards of reason within the tradition. Exemplars are more than the exemplary ways of life that one might find in a tradition. Such exemplary ways of life are ones lived by those considered heroes, saints, and everyday leaders. The exemplars of reason, on the other hand, are the ways people think about or through a situation. For example, the mother-child relationship is an exemplar for the Lakota, the law of property and contract for the Anglo-European, consulting the poison oracle for the Azande, and the citing of sacred Scriptures and church fathers for the Roman Catholics because they are models by which people in those traditions reason, judge, or think in diverse situations. The Lakota use the mother-child relationship as a model in judging how to use the land. The contract is a model used by Anglo-Europeans for thinking about general human relationships. Consulting the poison oracle is a model for the Azande for finding out about mystical forces at work in their lives. Again, referencing the sacred Scriptures and the church fathers is a model used by Roman Catholics for contemplating all decisions. These exemplars are not reducible to exemplary lives, though exemplary lives include plenty of such standards and exemplars of reason. Just as the good Lakota always thinks of the Earth as her mother and proper Protestant Anglo-Europeans think of relationships in terms of property laws, so careful Azande always consult the poison oracles, and saints always reference the Scriptures and fathers.

The above ways of life—seeking vengeance, nomadism, appropriating land, and partaking of Communion—prove reasonable within their tradition because they meet the standards of reason in those traditions: the traditions' exemplars and paradigms. The nomadic way of life appears reasonable given the exemplary ways of living in the Lakota tradition, just as the appropriation and cultivation of unowned land appears reasonable according to ideas, exemplars, and values in the tradition of English Protestant property laws. Again, seeking vengeance is reasonable according to the exemplars and values available to the Azande in their tradition.

The exemplars and paradigms of a tradition, then, are its very standards of reason. They are in effect the gold bar which all reasoning aims to meet. They are that by which a member of a tradition judges whether she or another member of the tradition is reasonable, and, importantly, they are the standards by which a member of a tradition first inquires into the reasonableness of her own tradition and of the standards of reason themselves. She refers to these standards as standards of reasonable activity when she herself attempts to reason through some situation or when she is trying to decide if someone else is being reasonable. Exemplars, in the form of ways of life, are a basic mode of action for members of society so that they do not have to stop and think about what they are doing; they provide shortcuts for approaching life when a member of a tradition no longer has time to deliberate about them.

The exemplars of the mother-child relationship, property contract, consulting a poison oracle, and referencing sacred Scripture and the church fathers are examples of how the standards of reason have content. To focus on the standards of reason exclusively would be a distortion, however, for they do not show how one can evaluate ends. Reason includes asking for and giving reasons for actions and beliefs, but it also, and most importantly for my argument, involves evaluating those beliefs, those conceptions of the good, and the very standards of reason themselves. To say that reason has substance means that reason allows the individual and the society to judge ends as good or bad, right or wrong. Reason that is instrumental or devoid of content—that is, rationality—cannot judge ends as good or bad because it has no conception of the good by which to judge.

That reason needs some conception of the good in order to judge ends as good or bad may seem circular. Yet one cannot judge the activity of some being (human, plant, animal, or planet) as healthy or unhealthy unless one has some conception of what health is for that particular being. Similarly, one cannot judge whether some action or belief is good or bad unless one has some prior conception of what the good is for the particular being who acts or believes. Reason is the means by which human beings make such judgments. Reason, then, must have some content from which to make these judgments of good and evil. Evaluation involves weighing these things against each other— weighing beliefs against beliefs, conceptions of the good against conceptions of the good, and standards against standards, but also beliefs against conceptions of the good, and conceptions of the good against standards of reason, and vice versa. All of these weighings, further, involve reflection on one's own experiences and the experiences of the tradition. Such evaluation is not possible, however, with subjective rationality, for neither instrumental nor formal rationality can compare or judge qualitative aspects but only quantitative aspects.

That content is found in the various aspects of the fundamental agreements in any given tradition, particularly in the conception of the good. These aspects include exemplars, symbolic generalizations, cosmologies, values, and ways of life. Exemplars and paradigms are the very standards of reason within a tradition. Exemplars and paradigms are the ways members of the tradition have reasoned before that consistently (though not always) had good results. Symbolic generalizations are laws or, more generally, principles and definitions that have emerged from those exemplars or from the overall experiences of the members of the tradition. Cosmologies provide the framework within which and through which traditions develop and their members act on their exemplars, symbolic generalizations, values, and ways of life. The conception of the good is articulated in terms of the values of the tradition. Those values help determine what become exemplars of reasoning because they establish the baseline of what counts as a good or bad result. Ways of life, finally, are modes of living that have historically expressed some of those values and resulted in achieving the good.

Commitments to these various standards of reason—exemplars and paradigms—and to the other fundamental agreements of a tradition—values, cosmologies, and ways of life—are what allow human beings to qualify or not qualify as reasonable actors. The best defense of this position lies in exposing the substantive reason of those bound by subjective rationality. Subjective rationality makes commitments to exemplars ("objective" instrumental reasoning), symbolic generalizations (law of supply and demand), cosmologies (atomism), values (self-preservation), and ways of life (consumerism/consumption). The exemplars of subjective rationality include such formal, logical procedures as *modus ponens*, *modus tollens*, and so on. They might also include, depending on various factors, the categorical imperative (if one trusts the Hegelian critique of Kant) or the principle of utility. Finally, general scientific exemplars of reasoning might be included under the exemplars of subjective rationality.

This last claim proves most controversial, incidentally, for it relates to Kuhn's observations about scientific revolutions. To explain these scientific revolutions, Kuhn devised the notion of a disciplinary matrix, which embraces values and cosmologies. Given the definition of disciplinary matrix found in Kuhn and expounded here and the account of reason offered here, it follows that a disciplinary matrix yields a sub-stantive conception of reason. The arguments I laid out against subjective rationality have held that subjective rationality opposes such a substantive conception of reason. How, then, can the exemplars of science be included within the exemplars of subjective rationality? They cannot unless subjective rationality is itself a form of substantive reason. The point that should be emphasized is that the exemplars of scientific reasoning are supposed to be formal and instrumental.

The tradition bearing subjective rationality involves more than just exemplars of reasoning; it also involves symbolic generalizations, values, and ways of life. The symbolic generalizations of subjective rationality, *qua* substantive reason, might include definitions of utility, of the good will, of the good, of reason, and of passion or emotions. The values of subjective rationality include, first and foremost, self-preservation. Horkheimer hints at this throughout his discussion of subjective rationality, particularly in *The Eclipse of Reason*. He also, however, hedges between claiming that subjective rationality is strictly without content and claiming that it judges ends according to the mode of self-preservation.

Finally, the tradition that carries subjective rationality also includes ways of life. Foremost among them is pursuing ends without questioning their ultimate worth. This way of life involves following passions and attempting to satisfy desires. It is reinforced by and itself reinforces the value of self-preservation—whether self-preservation is understood in terms of this world or another. Again, Horkheimer and MacIntyre implicitly describe the pursuit of self-preservation and desire as how people in modernity conduct themselves (or how certain people in ancient Greece did). Horkheimer fails, whereas MacIntyre succeeds, however, in making the leap to seeing the pursuit of self-preservation and the satisfaction of desires as a way of life.

The failure to see the value of self-preservation and the pursuit of the satisfaction of desires as values that inform the standards of reason within subjective rationality prevents Horkheimer from viewing subjective rationality as a particular kind of reason with content. Or perhaps his focus on the inability to judge ends in modernity blinds him to the possibility that not judging ends constitutes a particular way of life in modernity supported by a conception of reason which judges that way of life to be the most reasonable. In either case, a revision of Horkheimer's critique of modernity via MacIntyre is in order.

In *Whose Justice? Which Rationality?* MacIntyre identifies liberalism as a tradition. It is characterized by interminable debate concerning alleged principles of shared universal rationality. It includes a self that "moves from sphere to sphere compartmentalizing its attitudes" (*WJWR* 337). Most significantly, it assigns the public arena for the expression of individual or group preferences. This view of the public sphere entails that the market is the "dominant institution in a liberal economy" (336). Significantly, "in the practical reasoning of liberal modernity it is the individual qua individual who reasons" (339).

In other words, the modern liberal tradition of rationality—subjective rationality—constitutes a tradition with the features I have outlined in previous chapters. MacIntyre's analysis sublates Horkheimer's analysis into an internal critique of subjective rationality. It overcomes while preserving the previous analysis of subjective rationality. This sublation entails further demonstration that all reason is substantive, even that of subjective rationality. What distinguishes subjective rationality, as previously stated, is two things: first, that it preferences the pursuit of self-preservation over all other ends, and, second, that it denies its substantive character. Thus, I still argue that the failure of modernity to bring about emancipation is due to subjective rationality. Subjective rationality must be understood, however, as another form of substantive reason.

Reason and Judgments of Worth

I argued above that the standards of reason are the exemplars and paradigms found within a tradition. Such exemplars and paradigms have relationships to the other fundamental agreements. If my argument is right, then this account of the standards of reason has ramifications for how reason itself should be understood. In particular, much can be said about the relationship between judgments of worth and judgments of reason.

Preliminarily, I have been using the term "reason" to name a set of social practices that involve the evaluation both of reasons and of the good. Reason must also involve the ability to evaluate the reasonableness of actions and beliefs. One is reasonable, on this thick understanding, when one can, not only give reasons for one's actions, but also understand those reasons as good and understand one's processes of arriving at one's beliefs, actions and reasons as the sort of processes one ought to use if one wants to be reasonable. Further, one is reasonable on this thicker understanding when one can evaluate the ends being pursued as either the right or wrong sort of ends, that is, when one can evaluate whether such ends are worthy of pursuit. Reasoning is, in short, a normative activity. That is, in giving and asking for reasons, one is asking why something should be the case—not simply why it is the case, but also why one should have this belief, why one should act in such and such a way, why one should see X as a reason for the belief or act Y, why such and such is the right way of determining the proper way of acting or believing, but also why one should pursue this R rather than this S.

A child, for instance, can give a causal explanation for some event, say, for why she hit her sister. Generally, such causal explanations do not make the act reasonable. The parent attempts to help the child reason through the situation by explaining why she should have not hit her sister and under what conditions one is permitted to hit another. Again, one can give a causal explanation for why there is thunder, for example, God is bowling in heaven. Such a causal explanation is not seen to be reasonable, however, but rather as a means for calming a child.

Part of teaching a child to reason, then, involves teaching that child the standards of reason within one's tradition. These standards are highly normative—they serve to make it the case that something should be believed or done. They are able to serve this normative purpose because they are the exemplars embedded in the parent's tradition. The conception of the good plays an important role in showing the child how to reason as well. Parents teach their children that people/children who think in the wrong ways are not good people or, at least, that such thoughts are bad or mean. Those who share the cosmology of the tradition believe these standards help one lead a happy or fulfilling life.

As discussed, the good determines specific standards, which is not, incidentally, to claim that it determines all standards. Reason, in other words, is determined in part by the good. The Lakota provide an easy and obvious example from which to draw out how the good determines the specific exemplars and paradigms of reason within a tradition.

When a Lakota attempts to decide what is reasonable vis-à-vis treating the land, he thinks, for instance, of how one would treat a relative or a mother. One would not sell one's mother. Neither would one sell land. Indeed, to think of land as something to sell can make no sense on this account of land. The land is not something to be owned, just as one's mother is not something to be owned.

For English Protestant settlers, the matter is different. A settler approaches land in the following way. He finds land that is left fallow; it has not been plowed or cared for. No signs mark it as owned—there is no fence, no post with a name or sign marked on it, nothing that can be interpreted by the Englishman as a mark of ownership. So the settler thinks something such as the following: "Here is land that is unowned. God put us here to till the Earth, to be fruitful and multiply. In order to be fruitful and multiply, one must work land, grow crops, and raise livestock. I have no land at present to work. Therefore, I will take this land and toil upon it, making it mine as I serve God." The train of thought is reasonable given the disciplinary matrix within which the English Protestant settler operates. The conclusion, furthermore, is reasonable given the settler's understanding of what makes something reasonable, namely, that it instrumentally serves some preestablished good. As with most ways of life, it may be that no one has spelled out or thought about the acquisition of property in quite this way, except perhaps if she has been challenged (by outsiders or in extreme circumstances, for instance). Rather, the settlers saw this acquisitive way of life as reasonable; it was how a good Englishman acted.

What is the good for the English settler? Again, goods are most often articulated as values. The good for the settler can be articulated, in part, in terms of the values of hard work, ownership, service to God, being fruitful and multiplying. These values constitute the good of dominating the earth, though such an overarching good includes more than what I have listed here. The point, however, is that the elements that, in part, constitute the good for the settler determine what is reasonable as well.

To be clear, I should emphasize that my claim is not simply that what counts as a good reason is determined by the conception of the good within a tradition, but rather that the good determines not just what counts as a good reason for some belief or action but what standards count as exemplars or paradigms of reason. The various goods within the English Protestant settler tradition determine that appropriating land is reasonable; they thereby also establish such appropriation as the paradigmatic approach to land and land-ownership.

The Lakota could not recognize such a paradigm as reasonable, let alone as an exemplar of reason. In the Lakota tradition, the paradigmatic approach to land is based on the relationship to one's mother. A mother is not something that can be owned, but someone who cares for one and for whom one cares in return. Various duties and virtues attend to the mother-child relationship and also apply to one's relationship to the land. So the very act, for instance, of looking for signs of ownership does not even occur to a Lakota. The fact that land is unowned does not become a premise for any syllogism or argumentation in the Lakota tradition.

This tradition-embedded nature of the standards of reason, then, entails that judgments of reason are tied up with judgments of goodness. One cannot separate one's evaluations of the reasonableness of an action from one's evaluations of its goodness. The standards of reason that an individual uses in his tradition incorporate the good, articulated as values, held within that tradition. When judging whether an action is reasonable, one in effect delivers an evaluative judgment of that action. Reason is essentially normative. To separate the evaluative aspect from the reasoning aspect of judgment is to undermine the whole enterprise of reason, because reason is partly constituted by the values held sacred within one's tradition.

The failure of modernity, then, lies in its narrowing of what judgments are permissible in this arena by virtually separating the evaluative aspect from the reasoning aspect. Subjective rationality denies that it can evaluate the goodness of ends; it separates that evaluative ability from reason itself. Such a separation is a mask, however, for in reality subjective rationality claims that the good is effectiveness. Thus, judgments of reasonableness are reduced to judgments of the effectiveness of beliefs and actions. The reduction of reasonableness to effectiveness, has, in the process, led to greater and greater subjugation and suffering in modernity, the total abandonment of freedom, because people are unable to reason—to evaluate the goodness of the goals set in society by various institutions—most importantly, government and economy. The questions of reason in modernity are limited to "how can we effectively reach this or that goal?" not "is this goal worth pursuing?"

If the standards of reason entail standards of goodness, that is, if judgments of reason depend on conceptions of the good, how does one make judgments of goodness? Are these simply nonreasonable (i.e., unjustified) feelings or tastes? If they were, then reason itself would be based on simple tastes and, thus, would be unreasonable. Tastes cannot be evaluated. This concern lies behind much of the criticism aimed at Kuhn's history of scientific revolutions.[26] In defending his theory, Kuhn holds that even though value judgments lie behind much of the incommensurability between the worldviews of different disciplinary matrices, they do not undermine the possibility of reasonable judgment among different (scientific) traditions. As I will show in the next chapter, Richard Bernstein defends this position. According to Bernstein, accepting Kuhn's account of science requires not an abandonment of the reasonableness of science but a change in the accepted understanding of reason.[27] This book provides such a different conception of reason.

I want to be quite clear here. In asking why one goal should be sought rather than another, it is not enough to say that it will satisfy further goals, for that answer remains at the level of rationality rather than reason. Rather, one must show that the goal is the right goal to pursue; that is, one must show that the proposed goal is worthy of pursuit. To be reasonable, then, is to pursue worthy goals.

In essence, then, substantive reason is a process of evaluation. It is a process of evaluating reasons for actions, beliefs, and ways of life according to the standards embodied in a tradition, standards which are themselves dependent on the conception of the good in the tradition.

We evaluate goals (being a millionaire), beliefs (transubstantiation) and ways of life (witchcraft practices), and do so using the standards of reason and belief found already in tradition. We cannot judge whether a person is reasonable or not without looking at the actions and beliefs of that person in light of the standards, cosmologies, values, ways of life, and conception of the good in that person's tradition.

Two questions arise at this point. First, how does such evaluation work when a tradition includes more than one conception of the good? Or how do multiple conceptions of the good affect reason? Second, what happens when someone belongs to multiple traditions?

When multiple conceptions of the good are found in a tradition, the agent must determine which conception of the good she is most attuned to; she might choose one of the available conceptions of the good in her tradition, or she might take from them to develop her own conception of the good. Of course, such evaluation occurs only when the good becomes a question for the agent, which is rarely. Usually, the good is articulated in terms of values which the agent upholds or which are expressed in various ways of life that the agent can choose to live or in which she can engage. The value of courage, for example, is a value embodied in, among other things, the soldiering way of life. Multiple conceptions of the good, then, multiply the ways of life available to members of a tradition. Disputes about the good in a tradition can then be disputes about what way of life is best. Thus, an Aristotelian might debate about whether it is better to be a politician or a philosopher. Such debate might occur without reference to the ultimate good, however.

Disputes about the best way of life are played out in cultural traditions as well. Such ways of life might be ranked as good or better. For example, before the 1960s, in the Roman Catholic Church the priestly way of life was ranked as a far better way of life than those available to lay people, or nonpriests. The same is not true today (or, at least, not as true). This change in perception about what is a better way of life depends partly upon a renewed emphasis on the value of laity (nonpriests) and the role of the priest in the church as a whole. Vatican II, for example, involved a change in the conception of the good life that required more participation of the laity in prayer life, Eucharistic celebration, and parish management. This change in how the priestly life was viewed is an example of a dispute within a tradition about the best way of life.

Conversely, debates about the best way of life are liable to raise issues about the conception of the good in a tradition. Such debates about the best way to live might cause an agent to proceed to a higher stage of reflection in which she questions not simply the best way of life but the values which lie behind the various ways of life available to her. This reflection on values might reveal the underlying multiplicity of conceptions of the good in her tradition. At this point, the agent might decide that such debates are beyond her understanding and concern, and she might simply choose to follow in her father's footsteps or in a way of life that she is already pursuing. Or the agent might engage in deliberation about the best conception of the good. She might do this by comparing the various models who have lived different ways of life, or the results of leading certain lives, or the various values as they are realized in her tradition. Such comparisons are comparisons that center on the different conceptions of the good as they might be articulated in the tradition. She might, on the other hand, reflect on the different conceptions of the good and of goodness within her tradition. She could then decide on a conception of the good to pursue and coordinate values to uphold without necessarily choosing a way of life. In either case, although the agent must eventually decide how to live if she wishes to live at all, these questions might, and indeed probably will, remain with her for her entire life.

Once an agent has settled for herself the debate about conceptions of the good, she will generally utilize those standards of reason which are most aligned with her conception of the good and good way of life. Living a particular life means thinking as a person living such a life thinks. Of course, some people will choose to redefine how to live a particular way of life so as to honor values at odds with those realized in how that way of life is normally lived. Some laity within the Roman Catholic Church, for instance, might decide to live a celibate life even though they are not priests. Alternatively, some priests might choose to live a noncelibate life (for as long as they can get away with it). Such choices can impose considerable strain on the mental powers of the agents.

Traditions with multiple conceptions of the good, then, embody standards of reason that may fluctuate with those particular conceptions. Agents choose to utilize certain standards when they choose which conception of the good is theirs. Of course, agents usually do not choose a conception of the good but rather take one over or inherit one from others (relatives, friends, heroes, cultural stories, etc.). Such choice involves evaluating the conceptions of the good available in the tradition. Substantive reason as I have defined it, however, is suited for such evaluation, unlike the subjective rationality that is dominant in modernity.

The second question, regarding the issue of a person who belongs to multiple traditions, is a slightly different matter. MacIntyre holds that such a person must at some point make a choice between the traditions. MacIntyre must be right about this, particularly if the traditions that an agent carries on are significantly different from each other. Such significant differences will create conflicts regarding conceptions of the good, the values that articulate those conceptions, and the standards of reason that are informed by those conceptions of the good. At such moments of conflict a person must choose among traditions.

Finding agents who occupy more than one tradition is not difficult in modern times. One need only think about the situation of Native Americans, for instance. Many Native Americans still live on reservations and attempt to continue their native traditions. Of course, such traditions are different from what they were in the past. It might be, as I will discuss in the next chapter, that such change is a natural part of the growth of traditions. In any event, many Native Americans are attempting to reclaim their past by remaining on a reservation rather than assimilating to the general American culture. During the early twentieth century, things were not as easy for Native Americans. At that time, the United States government used various means to force their assimilation. Such means included mandatory public schools for them where they were taught the English language, American manners, and American ways of life. People who were raised in such circumstances were caught between two different cultures: the culture of their Native American tribe and that of the general U.S. population. The novel *When the Legends Die* by Hal Borland (1982) depicts this situation nicely.

One need not look at indigenous cultures to find people who occupy multiple traditions. Roman Catholics who are sent to public schools occupy two traditions: the Roman Catholic tradition of their parents and the consumerist tradition of capitalist America. Here, again, a strong rivalry exists between the two traditions. The agent is presented with heroes and ways of life that value humility, solidarity, simplicity, and so on, while also being confronted with heroes and ways of life that value pride, individualism, and acquisitiveness. To put the contrast starkly, whereas in the one tradition a person is encouraged to adopt a simpler, less lavish lifestyle in order to live in solidarity with the poor throughout the world, in the other one is encouraged to express one's individuality through the acquisition of a variety of commodities.

A person who occupies positions in both of these traditions, just as a person who carries on both a Native American and the "American" tradition, will eventually have to choose between the two traditions or live a schizophrenic life. To choose not to choose between the two traditions condemns one to acting from the perspective of both traditions chaotically. While some decisions and reasoning will follow the exemplars of one tradition, others will not, and vice versa. One might also attempt to bring insights from one tradition to another so as to incorporate them there and redefine a preexisting way of life for one of the traditions. Such "learning from" is an essential part of traditions.

Whenever an agent carries on in more than one tradition, he must reasonably evaluate those traditions' conceptions of the good if he is to lead a reasonable life. A person who lives in a multivalent tradition—one with multiple conceptions of the good—may but need not so evaluate conceptions of the good, but only the ways of life and values attending those conceptions. One who inhabits multiple traditions is more likely to evaluate the conceptions of the good directly because that is where one attains greatest clarity in debates between the traditions. The debate is a matter not of which value gets a higher ranking but of choosing one set of values over another, an articulation of one conception of the good over an articulation of a quite different one. Of course, one can evaluate these conceptions only by using particular standards of reason, which are themselves embedded in a tradition.

Thus, these two situations—the case of the multivalent tradition and the case of the person who occupies multiple traditions—raise issues about how reasonable decisions are made concerning questions of the good. In each case, one might possess multiple and competing standards of reason to use in adjudicating conceptions of the good. Within a multivalent tradition, the standards used will have to be weighed as well as the conception of the good. These standards should be able to effectively judge each other as long as the tradition is not in crisis, with its very standards of reason in question. If choosing between different traditions, the agent must either see how each fares on its own standards or find some common standards between the two which will allow for adjudication. The issue of evaluating standards of reason will become clearer in the next chapter.

Reason and the Good

Table 4.1 compares some of the standards of reason found in three traditions discussed in this chapter: the Zande tradition of witchcraft, the Lakota tradition of unowned land, and the Roman Catholic tradition of transubstantiation.

Constructing such a chart highlights the extent to which traditions possess standards of reason and in what those standards consist. Just as the Scriptures provide a reason for acting and believing in Roman Catholicism, so too do poison oracles and the mother-child relationship provide good reasons for acting among the Azande and Lakota, respectively.

The conception of the good is captured in the various values mentioned under each tradition. These values and conceptions of the good give content to the paradigms and exemplars found in each tradition. Again, they define what is best given each tradition's understanding of human nature. This chapter has investigated very specific ways of life within each of these traditions: transubstantiation and Eucharistic communion for Roman Catholicism, witchcraft for the Azande, and landownership for the Lakota. These are only aspects of much richer traditions full of many different ways of life, values, and standards of reason. Thus, the chart should be thought to capture not a whole tradition but only a slice of a tradition.

Table 4.1. Comparative Chart of Fundamental Agreements of the Azande,
the Lakota, and Roman Catholics

Disciplinary Matrix	Azande	Lakota	Roman Catholic
	Witchcraft	Relationship to Land	Religion
Cosmologies	Natural and Mystical	Natural Wholism	Monotheistic, Creation, Providence
Exemplars and Paradigms	Autopsy, Poison Oracle	Respect Mother Earth, Mother-Child Relationship	Dialectic, Scriptures, Tradition
Symbolic Generalizations	Witchcraft, Witchcraft Substance	Mother Earth, *Wakan*	God, Substance, Real Presence as Transubstantiation
Values	Truth, Vengeance, Merit	Truth, Nature, Freedom, Harmony with Nature	Truth, Knowledge of God, Union with God
Practices	Good Magic, Vengeance	Nomadism, Hunting/Gathering	Eucharistic Communion, Eucharistic Adoration

The chart, then, shows what I have been arguing for the last few
sections. Traditions give content to reason by grounding the standards
of reason in a conception of the cosmos and a conception of the good.
The good thereby provides substance to reason, which a critical theory
of society has searched for all along.

Because reason is connected to the good in this way, it can be used
to evaluate not only individual goals but societal ones. Reason is filled
with the content of a way of life. It pronounces judgments about ends
because it can draw on the order of the good and judge those ends in

light of that order. When Aristotle, for instance, judges contemplation to be good and reasonable, he is making that judgment in light of his conception of the universe. This conception also contains a conception of the nature of human beings, according to which the use of reasonable faculties is the highest human good and contemplation is the best use of those reasonable faculties.

Reason's Influence on the Good

Just as the conception of the good can determine the standards of reason, so too can the standards of reason determine the content of the conception of the good. In other words, substantive reason and the substantive good are mutually constitutive, just as reason and tradition are mutually constitutive. This mutually constitutive relationship proves not vicious but virtuous, since it is only through that relationship that reason can be critical. On the one hand, the conception of reason within the tradition may help fill out what the good is for the tradition. On the other hand, the activity of reasoning is used to evaluate the good and, as so used, can determine the content of the good along either pragmatic or moral lines.

Reason and the Conception of Human Nature

Every tradition includes a view of the cosmos, which includes a view of humanity. Every tradition must also include a view of reason. What is the function of reason in the tradition? What does reason allow one to do? Where does reason fit into the life of humanity? The tradition must address these questions, because reason is an essential feature of humanity. In addressing them, the tradition fills out one aspect of its view of human nature. The tradition must decide, for instance, whether reason belongs only to humanity or whether it also belongs to other creatures or to God or the gods.

Answering these questions can significantly influence the content of the good. A brief look at the history of moral philosophy easily highlights this. How particular philosophers viewed reason determined what the good was for human beings. For example, the good on either an Aristotelian or a Thomistic account included living a life of reason. These accounts viewed reason as the essence of humanity, and such an essence brought with it its own virtues that were peculiar to human beings. Reason for both of these traditions involved more than rationality; each included a more substantive account of reason that spelled out how people were to live reasonable lives. Thomas Hobbes and David Hume contrast nicely here. For both thinkers, reason was simply subjective rationality, "reckoning" in Hobbes's words. For both, the good did not involve any sort of theoretical contemplation or any life of reason. The good was the satisfaction of desires. J. S. Mill, like Aristotle, finds reason to be a higher good: for Mill, as we saw earlier, it is "better to be Socrates dissatisfied than a pig satisfied," because reason was important to human beings and must therefore be included in a conception of the good. Kant, finally, provides the most obvious example here. For Kant, because human beings have reason, the good could not be happiness. Nature would have implanted in human beings instinct alone if the ultimate goal had been to get human beings to satisfy their desires.

In a certain sense, a chicken and egg question arises in this context. What came first: the importance of reason or the conception of the good? Such a question cannot and need not be answered. Conceptions of the human being and of the good are developed simultaneously and in tandem. Philosophers do not, any more than nonphilosophers, sit down and compose these conceptions linearly. Rather, these conceptions develop simultaneously, mutually influencing each other. On this point, Kant was exactly right: all the questions of philosophy reduce to the question "What is the human being?"

Reason and the Evaluation of the Good

I have argued in this chapter that judgments of reason are tied up with judgments of worth. I have also held that such a claim means that the conception of the good in a tradition helps define the standards of reason in a tradition. One should not conclude from this claim that reason is simply a rubber stamp on conceptions of the good: the account of reason I defend shows that reason evaluates conceptions of the good. Therefore, it can change the conceptions of the good in a tradition. It is this evaluative aspect that proves essential for a critical theory of society.

In the first place, standards of reason are not simply determined by the conception of the good in a tradition. Many other factors influence those standards, including all the elements of the tradition—the view of the cosmos, the view of humanity, and ways of life.

Second, the relationship between reason and the good must be understood with regard to where that relationship occurs—in a tradition. A tradition is an argument about the good, an argument with insiders and outsiders. Arguments about the good proceed along reasonable grounds. Members of the tradition are bound to argue about what the good is and what it requires. Such arguments will undoubtedly lead to changes in the conception of the good itself.

The Roman Catholic tradition provides an example. The focus of the Catholic Church has always been otherworldly. Certainly there was a concern for the needy in this world. The approach of the church had been one of offering up one's worldly sufferings for glory in heaven. The introduction in the Middle Ages of the notion of human rights was a step away from such a total focus on the hereafter. Rights were introduced as a means to defend the needy in this world. The people of this world have a right to a decent standard of living, including some minimal property. More recently, the Second Vatican Council, as mentioned above, invited the laity to be involved more in the prayers and activities of the church. In particular instances that invitation has meant urging people to get more involved in the affairs of this world. The church sees part of the good life as consisting in addressing injustices in this world to make it a better place. The liberation theology movement has a significant role in turning the attention of the church to this-worldly concerns. Liberation theology, however, is a fringe movement, and the mainstream approach of the church has been that work done in this world should always be carried out in a manner that reflects a belief that the next life is its ultimate goal. In this example, the change in the conception of the good is very subtle. The good always has been and always will be about achieving the vision of God. That good defines the ultimate end of human life; however, to attain it we must help the poor and needy in this world. The church has increasingly emphasized the second part of this good in recent centuries, while the good itself is one unified idea.

The arguments within the Roman Catholic tradition about the good, moreover, utilized the very standards of reason available in that tradition. The invention of the notion of rights appealed to Scriptures and tradition. The liberation theology movement defends itself by utilizing the very same standards of reason utilized by more conservative influences of the church—including Scripture and tradition, as well as dialectical reasoning available from its more philosophical influences. Without those standards of reason, the debate over the conception of the good would have been less fruitful and persuasive.

Of course, evaluations of the good might result in abandoning some values and adopting others (since the good is articulated in terms of values). If one considers the contemporary Western medical profession a tradition, one can see debates about euthanasia to be tied essentially to debates about the good. The issue is one of the values of self-preservation and life versus the values of living a self-determined life free of intolerable pain. The history of medicine is a history of people attempting, among other things, to save lives. Saving life always means extending life. Modern times have taken this power in unforeseen directions—extending life even in the face of severe chronic pain. Doctors and moral philosophers debate the good: is the good simply living, or is it living well, and what constitutes living well? These debates involve the use of reason in sorting through myriad facts, situations, and values. Reason, informed by a conception of the good, cannot simply rubber-stamp a value, but must evaluate it in light of other values. Further, if the tradition contains multiple conceptions of the good, then at moments of conflict reason must adjudicate between those conceptions. Changes in understandings of the good might result from the process in which reason evaluates the good. Such evaluation, incidentally, also relies on other elements of the tradition, including its history, that is, its experience, which is when truth enters. In certain cases, what now appears good and reasonable will sometimes not have appeared reasonable in earlier times because those times lack the historical consciousness that the present possesses.

Reason might also bring about a change in a tradition's conception of the good through interaction with another tradition. The Roman Catholic Church, for instance, gives more value now to self-determination than it did in earlier times. This change in values is a result of its historical encounter with liberalism. Similarly, engagements with the feminist tradition have caused various moral and political traditions to rethink their conceptions of the good. Marxism, for instance, today must address issues of sexism and racism. A tradition must change and grow through interaction with others if it is to remain viable. Such change will inevitably involve reasonable alterations in the tradition's conception of the good.

The standards of reason, then, involve more than the conception of the good and the values held sacred in a particular society; they also include exemplars of reason, definitions, and other symbolic generalizations, and a view of the cosmos. Reason evaluates conceptions of the good in terms of their whole fit, as it were, into the particular tradition. Reason gains content from the conception of the good in so doing, but this conception can in turn change through reasonable deliberation. One reasons to clarify positions and ideas, to critique and defend. One uses conceptions of the good in that critique to evaluate aspects of the good. So, for example, someone living in a tradition that values both equality and freedom can use reason to arbitrate between those two values. Reason is not simply a rubber stamp on conceptions of the good.

Being reasonable, then, is more than asking for and giving reasons. One can give reasons, and even ask for reasons, without being reasonable. One might give as a reason for scratching one's finger the fact that it itches. Being able to provide that as a reason does not make one reasonable, however, if in scratching one's finger one destroys the whole world.

Anyone writing in the United States about "cultural" traditions and reason today must consider the attacks of 9/11. If the terrorists or their organizers could speak to us, they would undoubtedly be able to give reasons for their actions. Still, one would want to know whether these persons reflected on and evaluated those reasons and their goals with the resources made available within their tradition. We might also look into the revolutions that swept across North Africa and the Middle

East during the first part of 2011. Did the leaders of the Egyptian army, for instance, reflect on their reasons for supporting the people? Did the United States, NATO, and the United Nations reflect on the reasons for supporting the rebels in Libya as well as the reasons for not supporting the rebels in Bahrain or Yemen?

The "War on Terror" must be considered in answering these questions. Yet the "War on Terror" cannot be considered apart from the culture of death that seems dominant in American life. Until one examines the war on terror and the culture of death—the cultural beliefs that lie behind them—the actions taken in response to terrorists attacks or to rebel uprisings (including the war on terrorism, its expansion, the incarceration of thousands of Arab Americans and immigrants, and the bombing of Libyan forces) will be unreasonable. Reason requires that the reasoner evaluate her own goals and reasons for acting as she does. The military-industrial complex supporting and supported by the dominance of subjective rationality prevents any such evaluation.

| As a set of social practices that involves evaluating both reasons and the good itself, reason has a forensic aspect: refining, criticizing, and developing the conception of the good, the view of the cosmos, and the conception of reason itself, among other things. This forensic aspect involves the tradition in reflecting back on itself and its own set of arguments as well as looking at the arguments presented by other traditions to clarify its own conceptions. Reason is a recurring, self-referential activity.

Most importantly for the purposes of a critical theory aimed at emancipation, substantive reason on this account is capable of judging ends, because of the content it gains from a tradition's conception(s) of the good. It judges ends in light of that conception or those conceptions. Reason, consequently, is not limited simply to serving the passions. It is capable of determining whether one has good reasons for believing, acting, and so on, as one does. It can thus judge the ends one pursues on the basis of whether there are good reasons for pursuing those ends. This conception of reason allows one to evaluate and criticize the ends of individuals, of their own society, and of other societies. A critical theory of society cannot escape from this or that society, this or that conception of the good, this or that set of standards and exemplars of reason. Rather, critical theory is necessarily embedded in this society, this conception of the good, and these standards and exemplars of reason.

One serious challenge immediately arises for a conception of tradition-constituted reason, that of relativism. I will argue in the next chapter that a tradition-constituted, substantive reason, by pointing to truth—or adequacy to experience—provides for reasonable debates within and between traditions and for "learning from" other traditions, and thereby escapes the false dichotomy of relativism/objectivism.

5 | Beyond Relativism

Reasonable Progress and Learning From

But where then does this leave us when it comes to the matter
of judging our rationality, our form of life, our culture in rela-
tion to those of others? . . . [H]ow are we to condemn Nazis, or
Serbs, or the present government of China, or the sentiments
and actions of . . . terrorists? . . . [H]ow are we to call into
question and reject our friend's decisions and actions when
we discover that she has embezzled money from her doubtless
oppressive and exploitative employer in order to pay off the
$10,000.00 balance on her credit cards which had been run
up by a man who claimed to be a friend, but who has now ab-
sconded?

—Araminta Stone Johnston, "Theory, Rationality,
and Relativism"

Whether we talk about the military-industrial complex that hides the loss of hundreds and thousands of innocent lives in the language of "collateral damage,"[1] or we discuss deals made between the U.S. Immigration and Customs Enforcement and agribusinesses that limit the number of "illegal" immigrants the agency can pick up from their businesses each night,[2] or we look at the thousands of female human beings, mostly children, sold each year in the sex-trafficking business, or the laws which give corporations rights to free speech but deny that corporations can be punished for the illegal practices of their chief officers—in each case we are discussing activities that harm indi-vidual human beings. *Any philosophy that justifies or supports such de-structive practices, policies, beliefs, and ways of life is immoral and wrong.*

This statement clearly challenges my argument that reason and morality go hand in hand and, moreover, that reason is relative to tra-ditions in the sense that no objective standards of substantive reason exist that apply across traditions or that allow one to judge traditions other than the one of which one is a member. Substantive standards of reason and principles of morality and political theory, I have asserted, are justified or not within their home traditions. My thesis and theory of substantive reason do not abet destructive practices, policies, beliefs, and ways of life.

I will show this, first, in a simple defense of the theory against the charge of incoherence, leveled by Donald Davidson and like-minded theorists against any theory that presumes there are incommensu-rable anythings, particularly languages. Davidson's argument misses the point. Translating languages uncovers the underlying rival substan-tive reasons working in rival traditions.

Second, I will examine the role of truth in the philosophy of Mac-Intyre, who argues that each tradition seeks truth and that truth is an essential element of any tradition-constituted reason. MacIntyre rejects as false the objectivism/relativism disjunction that Richard Bernstein pointed out as underlying many contemporary discussions of relativ-ism. MacIntyre escapes the objectivism/relativism dichotomy by focus-ing on epistemological crises.

Finally, through an examination of Charles Taylor's Gadamerian fusion of horizons, which he sees as a continuation of MacIntyre's ar-guments, I show how traditions can learn from one another. The the-ory of substantive reason defends itself as a theory by which evalua-tions of reason and the good occur not only within but between traditions. It obviates the objectivism/relativism dichotomy by accept-ing the tradition-constitutive nature of reason—that is, recognizing both reason's foundation in tradition and its capacity for evaluating the good and the standards of reason in a tradition.

The discussion of truth and learning from proves essential for a critical theory of society, since such a theory must be able to make truth claims about unjust, inhumane practices. That these claims are made from within a particular tradition should not undermine the critical potential of a theory of substantive reason. Further, that traditions can learn from one another through dialogue and thus morally advance makes such dialogue a useful tool for critical theorists, who can utilize it in progressive politics and ethics to advance human welfare in different concrete traditions. A theory of substantive reason, then, enables a critical theory of society to criticize existing forms of domination and power.

The development of a tradition-constituted reason adds a greater urgency and thoroughness to an account of substantive reason: urgency because the theory shows how reason works at the everyday level—the level of the plain person, in MacIntyre's words; thoroughness because one can apply the notion of tradition as an argument about fundamental agreements to cultural traditions, like that of the Lakota.

This distinction, further, entails that I have a slightly different understanding from MacIntyre's, which should be clear from the last chapter. I hold that all traditions reflect in some way a cosmology, even if in brief form. My use of the term "tradition," then, may be more specialized than MacIntyre's use when he refers to fly-fishing as a tradition without a cosmology.[3] This terminological distinction should not detract from our basic agreement about the tradition-constituted and tradition-constitutive nature of substantive reason.

The Very Idea of a Conceptual Scheme

A conceptual relativism such as I have advanced presumes that there are different conceptual schemes. The idea of a conceptual scheme is that each individual has a blueprint by which she takes given data and organizes it. Different blueprints will result in different layouts of the data. A blueprint is the set of concepts an individual has. Thus, an affirmation of conceptual schemes means that "different people can use different sets of concepts to organize the given."[4] Donald Davidson attacks the very idea of such a scheme on the ground that it is incoherent. Having examined both Davidson's argument and a more general formulation of it made against the theory of tradition-constituted reason, however, I will show that Davidson's argument is incoherent itself, because it reduces understanding to a matter of translation and because the issue is not simply a matter of understanding but of recognizing the reasonableness of a claim.

Davidson's Argument

In arguing against conceptual schemes, Davidson rejects what he calls the third dogma of empiricism, a dogma that identifies a "dualism of scheme and content, or organizing system and something waiting to be organized."[5] Bernstein reformulates Davidson's concern: "The very idea that there is something that is known (uncontaminated by different conceptual schemes) and the various schemes for conceiving or knowing it is suspect."[6] It is not the case, on Davidson's account, that there is something out there which is then interpreted by different conceptual schemes.

Davidson's method of attack is to define what a conceptual scheme is in order to show that the concept has no content. That is, he claims that the term "conceptual scheme" is a meaningless term that injects confusion into debates about intercultural understanding. His argument takes the following form. Suppose a person cannot tell whether she sees one or two chairs before her. In such a case, she has no criteria for individuation of chairs. Lacking such criteria for individuation, she really does not have a concept of chair at all.[7] Likewise, because there is no principle for individuating conceptual schemes, there is no concept of a conceptual scheme. The concept of conceptual scheme is, for all intents and purposes, empty and should not be used in philosophical analysis.

How can I tell the difference between two radically distinct conceptual schemes? According to Davidson, the belief in conceptual schemes rests on a paradox: "Different points of view make sense, but only if there is a common coordinate system on which to plot them; yet the existence of a common system belies the claim of dramatic incomparability."[8] In other words, I can only know that there are different conceptual schemes if I can, in some way, compare them so as to mark them as different. If I have some way to compare them, however, they cannot really be incomparable. If I cannot make the comparison, then how could I possibly know that I am comparing two of the same thing— whether it be conceptual schemes or whatever? A more familiar way of making this argument is to point out that one could not recognize another conceptual scheme as such unless it shared some essential features with the conceptual scheme one already has. In fact, Davidson continues, Whorf, Kuhn, and Quine all make their comparisons using one such coordinate system.

The question then becomes, for Davidson, how does one determine the limits for conceptual contrasts? Again, the problem is that belief in conceptual schemes implies that at some point, one cannot compare two different conceptual schemes. So the natural question to ask is, at what point is that limit reached? To answer this question, Davidson turns to the issue of translation. He holds that "we may accept the doctrine that associates having a language with having a conceptual scheme. . . . If conceptual schemes differ, so do languages."[9] Thus, to study the limits of conceptual contrast, one must discern the limits of translation. One must find, then, the criteria for translating from one language to another.

Davidson continues his argument by targeting possible criteria of translation. He divides his argument into two parts. First, he considers the possibility of complete failure of translation between languages. Neither MacIntyre nor I have claimed that any languages are completely untranslatable. Further, at issue for a tradition-constituted reason is not so much language but tradition, which includes cosmologies, values, ways of life, and standards of reason. This point will prove pivotal later in the discussion. For now, I shall ignore this first part of Davidson's attack on the idea of conceptual schemes.

Davidson also attacks the very idea of a conceptual scheme given partial untranslatability. In this case, one needs to examine criteria for translating and understanding other peoples. Davidson holds that when interpreting the speech of others both alien and kin, interpreters must be guided in their translation by the principle of charity, which states that when interpreting others, an interpreter presumes that the others' beliefs, on the whole, make sense or are rational.

Consider Davidson's example: "If you see a ketch sailing by and your companion says, 'Look at the handsome yawl,' you may be faced with the problem of interpretation." The difference between a yawl and a ketch is subtle: on the yawl, the second mast is aft the rudder, while on the ketch, the second mast is forward the rudder. "One natural possibility is that your friend has mistaken a ketch for a yawl, and has formed a false belief. But if his vision is good and his line of sight favorable it is even more plausible that he does not use the word 'yawl' quite as you do. . . . We do this sort of off the cuff interpretation all the time . . . to preserve a reasonable theory of belief."[10]

How is one to understand the friend's use of the word "yawl"? Your friend's use of the term suggests that he thinks the jigger is in a different place than you think it is. You can interpret your friend to have a false belief, to use the term which points out where the jigger is differently than you, or to be ignorant about what a jigger is (or the distinction between a ketch and a yawl). The principle of charity says that you interpret your friend in such a way that he does not have an unreasonable belief.

Although this example is rather trivial, Davidson's point—that one must assume some sort of agreement between one's beliefs and those of another whose language one is interpreting—applies to less trivial examples. We must assume agreements on beliefs if we are to have any knowledge of beliefs of others at all.[11] From a practical standpoint, charity of interpretation is forced on the interpreter because one must begin from somewhere when trying to understand a foreign language.

Davidson's take on charitability in translation leads him to write, "If we choose to translate some alien sentence rejected by its speakers by a sentence to which we are strongly attached on a community basis, we may be tempted to call this a difference in schemes; if we decide to accommodate the evidence in other ways, it may be more natural to speak of a difference of opinion. But when others think differently from us, no general principle, or appeal to evidence, can force us to decide that the difference lies in our beliefs rather than in our concepts."[12] For Davidson, in such a situation of disagreement one could not determine whether it was the beliefs or the concepts that differed. Since one cannot pick out definitively that it is the concepts that differ, one cannot give any content to the notion of a conceptual scheme. For Davidson, there simply is no matter of fact that is true. The term "conceptual scheme" cannot be demarcated. Davidson concludes that "in giving up the dualism of scheme and content, we do not give up the world, but reestablish unmediated touch with the familiar objects whose antics make our sentences and opinions true or false."[13]

Davidson's discussion hinges on an ability to distinguish between beliefs and concepts. I will return to this issue in the discussion of MacIntyre's response. First, however, I will examine how John Haldane and Paul Kelly have reformulated Davidson's argument to specifically address MacIntyre's tradition-constituted reason.

Haldane and Kelly each reformulate Davidson's argument in order to apply it to MacIntyre's defense of a tradition-constituted reason. Both ask how MacIntyre can tell the difference between two radically disparate traditions, or more generally, between traditions at all. Haldane argues that MacIntyre must show that there "are points of separation beyond these spatio-temporal ones which constitute incommensurable differences." He also notes that MacIntyre uses linguistic difference to mark the incommensurability of traditions. MacIntyre holds that understanding a second culture may involve learning a second first-language. Learning a second first-language involves coming to grips with what can be said in one language but not in another. Haldane then rephrases Davidson's point to address MacIntyre's notion of learning a second first-language. "Either such learning involves translation of terms from one language into those of another or it does not. If it does, then in what sense did the foreign language represent an incommensurable cultural difference, as opposed to an interesting variant of a common human culture? If it does not, then how does one know what one is saying, or indeed that one is saying anything coherent at all?"[14] As stated, the dispute boils down to whether one can make sense out of the idea of understanding a language that is incommensurable, here equated with untranslatable.

Kelly takes a similar tack. "If we can do this [learn a second first-language] then in what way is the language of one community radically incommensurable with another? Surely if the concepts of one community were genuinely incommensurable with those of another then we would be at a loss to understand them at all, and past tradition would remain completely mysterious to us."[15] Note Kelly's language here: he takes aim at a defense of "radically incommensurable" languages. Yet, again, neither MacIntyre nor I have defended radically incommensurable languages or traditions. We hold, instead, that rival traditions prove partially incommensurable because some standards and exemplars of reason, among other things, prove incommensurable. Haldane and Kelly, in fact, recognize this point without understanding quite what it means. Both point out that in his analysis of other traditions and cultures MacIntyre is able to say much about those other traditions and cultures.[16]

Haldane's and Kelly's arguments mirror Davidson's criticism. Davidson holds that because one has no criteria by which to distinguish conceptual schemes, the very idea of a conceptual scheme is questionable. He makes this argument with reference to the procedures of translation. Haldane, also referring to the procedures of translation, argues that MacIntyre provides no criteria for identifying incommensurable languages. Lacking such criteria, the very idea of incommensurable languages is jeopardized. Kelly, on the other hand, argues that only the inability to learn another language would prove incommensurability. In fact, however, MacIntyre is able to discuss these other traditions, so he must be able either to translate those traditions himself or rely on someone who does. In either case, the languages of the tradition are translatable, showing that traditions are not incommensurable.

These Davidsonian arguments put the following questions to the theory of substantive reason for which I have argued: Is it possible to distinguish incommensurable traditions without relying on a scheme/content dualism? Is it possible to make sense of the idea of incommensurable languages that one can understand or translate into each other? Is it possible to hold that traditions are incommensurable while discussing them within one particular tradition? How is it possible to recognize or provide criteria for determining incommensurable traditions or incommensurable concepts? The answers to these questions depend, first, on whether one means radically or partially incommensurable. They depend also on the fact that language translation does not capture the issue at hand.

MacIntyre's Reply to Davidson

MacIntyre's reply to Davidson shows that what's at stake is not language translation but the partial incommensurability of standards and exemplars of reason. Although language is a key element in reason and reasoning activities, traditions are not reducible to languages, and the most important aspects of traditions are not parts of languages.

MacIntyre makes four replies to Davidson, but I will consider only two, which he provides in his 1985 APA presidential address.[17] First, he likens Davidson's rejection of the scheme-content dualism to Hegel's rejection of the same, stating that Davidson repeats the substance of Hegel's rejection. MacIntyre finds it surprising, however, that Davidson rejects the very idea of a conceptual scheme. MacIntyre claims that to accord any truth to relativism (and he thinks it must have some truth because it is such a perennial challenge to reason and philosophy), one must formulate relativism in such a way as to leave "no opening for any scheme/content or scheme/world distinction" (RPP 385).

MacIntyre then lays out his argument for the cosmology-ladenness of languages, recounted in chapter 3 above. Some languages commit their users to certain beliefs, values, and standards of reason. For example, "Doire Colmcille" and "Londonderry" do not name the same thing. There is no same thing for them to name. To posit such a sameness would be to posit some neutral thing out there which is then organized or synthesized by different conceptual schemes. It would be to contravene the Hegelian and Davidsonian rejection of scheme/content dualisms.

MacIntyre holds that his view does not rest on such a dualism. No one has access to some subject or thing sans conceptions. That is, our access to the world is already through concepts that "presuppose the truth of one set of claims rather than the other" (RPP 394). Communities have criteria of sameness and difference by which they recognize they are making claims about the same thing. According to MacIntyre, two different traditions can realize that they are discussing one and the same subject matter over which they advance different claims.

The Lakota and the U.S. government recognize that they have a dispute over the Black Hills in North Dakota. For the Lakota, this land is sacred, the center of the world; but the U.S. government does not see the land the same way. This disagreement cannot be phrased as a difference of beliefs, because part of what makes up the differing beliefs is differing concepts. This difference in concepts means that the Lakota could never take monetary reparations for the loss of the sacred land. It would be demeaning.

Similarly, Jews, Christians, and Muslims—the people of the book—disagree over the nature of Jesus. In discussing whether Jesus Christ is the Son of God or not, all three recognize that they are discussing the same thing: the status of the individual Jesus Christ in relation to another individual, God (the God of Abraham and Isaac, the God of the Hebrew Scriptures). The three religions are not referring to something that exists apart from their interpretations. Rather, they are arguing about what actually exists, but they do so within the confines of their traditions, which have already conceptualized the terms of the debate in such a way that their conceptualization presupposes the truth of one set of claims about what exists over another. The Christian understands Jesus only in terms that already determine the answer as to whether Jesus is the Son of God. MacIntyre's first response to Davidson, then, relates Davidson to Hegel and holds that he (MacIntyre) does not violate Hegel's proscription against scheme/content dualisms.

In *Whose Justice? Which Rationality?* MacIntyre notes that Davidson holds that a tradition with beliefs radically different from our own is not something that can be recognized as a tradition. MacIntyre also, however, finds little in Davidson that contradicts his own theory. Indeed, he thinks that what Davidson's argument shows is that some shared meanings, ideas, concepts, and so on must exist in order for the process of translation to begin. MacIntyre concedes that any two languages or two sets of thoughts have something in common (*WJWR* 371). He rejects, as I have discussed earlier, any notion of radical incommensurability, though Davidson, Haldane, and Kelly all seem to imply MacIntyre accepts such a notion. If anything, MacIntyre has been overly charitable in his discussion of these issues by not simply denouncing the idea of radical incommensurability as one he does not accept.

Instead, in the face of these claims about the incoherence of his view, MacIntyre elucidates his account. In particular, he spells out the features of a language that make it translatable and untranslatable, which he discussed in his 1985 APA presidential address. Such features, as noted in chapter 3, include naming and extrapolation from poetic images. Naming and poetry cannot be translated, for both are heavily dependent on the background beliefs, cosmologies, and standards of reason that are present in a given cosmology-laden language or tradition. Reading a translation of a poem from a different language highlights this partial incommensurability: we can grasp most of the meaning of the poem without really capturing the heart of the poem.

MacIntyre reaffirms this point in addressing Haldane's and Kelly's objections to his theory of a tradition-constituted reason. He repeats Haldane's question: how is it possible, when facing incommensurable sentences in (partially) incommensurable languages, that one either knows what one is saying or that one says anything coherent at all? "[V]ery easily." Each natural language includes standards that determine what is coherent and what is meaningful in that language, and these standards prove internal to that language. According to MacIntyre, a person capable of speaking two incommensurable languages recognizes when those languages are incommensurable because he recognizes when something said in one language cannot be said in the other language. Similarly, when attempting to articulate something from one tradition in the terms of a rival tradition, a person recognizes that the second tradition lacks the very "concepts, idioms, or modes of argument necessary for the statement of those claims."[18] Indeed, it might transpire that one recognizes, because one is at home in two different traditions, that the traditions are too much at odds to make some statements of one tradition plausible in the rival one. As an example, MacIntyre holds that Latin had to be enriched by Cicero so that certain things sayable in Greek—things that challenged traditional Roman beliefs—could then be said in Latin.

A summary by Michael Krausz gets at the essence of MacIntyre's reply to Davidson. According to Krausz, MacIntyre, unlike Davidson, distinguishes between translatability and understanding. On MacIntyre's account, "one can understand two cultures or appropriate 'portions' thereof while not being able to translate between them. . . . [T]he bilingual needs to be able to do this in order to determine as he does what is not translatable from one culture to another. Just as untranslatability does not entail a limit on understanding, understanding does not entail translatability."[19] Krausz here highlights one of MacIntyre's central claims that his critics seem to miss: the person fluent in two languages may not be able to translate every sentence, word, or concept of one language into the other language. Indeed, one's skill in and knowledge of another language is shown precisely in being able to point out what words and phrases are not translatable.

Critique of the Debate

Krausz's discussion raises the central question of translatability. MacIntyre responds to his critics by engaging them in discussions of translation. MacIntyre has some important insights about translation in these responses, for example that untranslatability does not necessitate scheme/content dualism and that one can understand an alien language without being able to translate it wholly into one's native tongue. The discussion of translation, however, occurs within a larger discussion about understanding and substantive reasons.

Haldane and Kelly are responding in particular to MacIntyre's notion of a reason of traditions. They target this issue in terms of translation. In other words, they suggest that what mark rival traditions are languages. While MacIntyre's discussion includes a discussion of language translation, however, his arguments concern not language translation but rival, incommensurable tradition-constituted reasons. For instance, MacIntyre argues that one finds proof of tradition-constituted reason because some languages are cosmology-laden. Thus Haldane argues that "MacIntyre is dismissive of Davidson's interpretative argument but yet invokes a linguistic criterion of cultural difference: roughly, a culture is distinct from one's own to the extent that understanding what speakers belonging to it are saying involves learning the meaning of their words as terms in a second language. But this suggestion invites a reapplication of the Davidsonian argument."[20] This reading of MacIntyre proves inadequate given all that MacIntyre has written on the tradition-constituted and tradition-constitutive nature of reason.

Although Haldane holds that MacIntyre is dismissive of Davidson's argument, he gives no evidence of such dismissiveness. Indeed,
MacIntyre's replies to Davidson discussed in this section seem to take
him seriously. Second, being able to say something in another language
and knowing that it is coherent does not necessitate being able to translate it into one's native language. Many people find Hegel's *Phänome-
nologie des Geistes* coherent without being able to adequately translate
the title, particularly the term "Geist." In conjunction with this point,
MacIntyre notes that one masters another language just when one real-
izes what can be said in one language but not in another. Even if the
question was one of translation, then, Haldane's argument seems
to falter.

Kelly and Haldane think that traditions are demarcated by languages. MacIntyre's reply to Davidson might encourage this approach
if that is the only thing one focuses on. The issue is not one of language,
however. Indeed, Davidson's argument fails to apply because he as-
sumes that "having a language" means "having a conceptual scheme.
The relation may be supposed to be this: if conceptual schemes differ,
so do languages."[21] What could such a supposition mean, however?

It could mean that for every conceptual scheme there corresponds
a distinct natural language with its own syntax and words. Thus,
conceptual schemes would be associated with natural languages like
English, German, French, and so on. Such a supposition implies that
all English speakers throughout time have had the same conceptual
scheme. If this were the case, however, then Davidson would be in
error to seek criteria of translation as evidence for conceptual schemes.
The lack of such criteria of translation would not be sufficient to show
that there are no conceptual schemes because it would be possible that
the same language has multiple conceptual schemes. If such schemes
are possible, then the issue is not one of translation, because the rival
conceptual schemes already share the same language.

On the other hand, Davidson's supposition could mean that different conceptual schemes mean different languages where any change
of the meaning of a word or the syntax of the language marks a change
in language. Here, the idea would be that those who spoke English
before the discovery of the Heisenberg principle spoke English$_{bh}$ and

those who spoke English after the discovery of the Heisenberg principle spoke a totally different language, English$_{ah}$. Thus, we could not speak of German being a different language from English, but of German$_x$ being a different language from English$_x$. If Davidson wanted to understand languages on this level, then he would have to answer the following question: is it beliefs or concepts that change the language? Either answer to this question will raise problems, however. If Davidson were to argue that a change in language is brought about by a change in beliefs, then he would be left with the absurd situation that people who think they speak the same language but have different beliefs would speak two different languages. The idea here is that anytime people's beliefs were different, they would be said to speak different languages. So the number of languages would soon proliferate beyond counting.

Michael Lynch makes a similar point. He argues that if languages were conceptual schemes, as Davidson thinks, then that "would imply that people who spoke the same 'extensional' language would automatically share the same scheme. Yet, this strikes me as quite implausible. A Hinduist and myself may 'assign the same extension' to the term 'cow' and yet have radically different *concepts* of a cow" (emphasis original).[22] The conclusion that one reaches, then, when one believes that languages are demarcated by beliefs is implausible or absurd.

If, however, Davidson wants to hold that it is conceptual innovation that marks a change in language, then he has ceded the victory to those who believe in conceptual schemes. To assert that concepts mark changes in languages would be to assert what Davidson wants to deny, namely, that there are conceptual schemes. Davidson might simply decide to hold that different beliefs mark different languages. If he were to do so, while I could not argue against him, I would feel justified in dismissing such an absurd conclusion.

To argue as Davidson does, then, leads to various difficulties. On the one hand, he could argue that languages coordinate with conceptual schemes in such a way that conceptual schemes imply different natural languages. I believe this is the line that Davidson actually does take. However, such a tack denies the very real possibility that one language might have several conceptual schemes. Traditions are not limited or coextensive with languages, however. One could speak about a liberal and a conservative tradition, both of which are traditions in the English language. Or, one could speak about an Appalachian and Western tradition, both of which share the English language. On the other hand, Davidson could assert that conceptual schemes do not coordinate with natural languages but with languages as they are spoken. To take this tack leads him into an absurdity (that people who think they use the same language actually speak different languages because they have different beliefs) or to cede the debate to those who believe in conceptual schemes. Davidson, then, is wrong to associate conceptual schemes with languages in the way he does. The demarcation of conceptual schemes or of tradition is not language.

Davidson anticipates this objection. "If conceptual schemes aren't associated with languages in this way, the original problem seems needlessly doubled, for then we would have to imagine the mind, with its ordinary categories, operating with a language with *its* organizing structure. Under the circumstance we would certainly want to ask who is to be the master."[23] This argument suggests that languages have an organizing structure apart from the mind.

If I agreed with Davidson that the mind has one organizing structure and language a different one, then I could see the problem to which this argument points. However, I cannot make any sense out of the idea that language has an organizing structure apart from the mind. Indeed, what would the structure be organizing? Surely, language does not organize reality on this view, for that immediately violates the scheme/content dualism. Maybe he means that it organizes the mind, which would lead to the problem of determining who the master is (the mind or the language). Why must one believe that language organizes anything, however? This assumption is an unnecessary one that leads the idea of conceptual schemes to difficulty; one need not maintain this assumption, however. Thus, there is no difficulty with denying what Quinean relativism asserts and Davidson accepts, namely, that conceptual schemes are to be associated with languages.

Where does the debate stand at present, then? Davidson has attacked the very coherence of the idea of conceptual schemes by associating language with such schemes and then looking for criteria of translation in order to demarcate the schemes. He fails to find a fact of the matter, declaring that since there is no fact of the matter, no one can have a clear concept of conceptual schemes, and thus, it is an empty concept. Kelly and Haldane have applied Davidson's argument to MacIntyre's notion of a tradition-constituted reason. In similar fashion to Davidson, they associate traditions with languages and focus on issues of translatability. MacIntyre could be less charitable in his reading of these critics by forcefully denying that he is writing specifically about language. Regardless, the preceding argument has shown both that MacIntyre's and my argument for a tradition-constituted reason cannot be reduced to that of language translation and, further, that conceptual schemes cannot be associated with languages in the fashion needed by Davidson without leading to irresolvable problems. Davidson's argument fails in its purpose of showing that the concept of a conceptual scheme is incoherent. What does this conclusion mean for Kelly's and Haldane's (and like-minded) attacks on the notion of a tradition-constituted reason?

Neither MacIntyre nor I have formulated our defenses of tradition-constituted reason simply with reference to language traditions. We have referred to cosmology-laden languages; but we have also referred to universal languages, which have no commitments to cosmologies. These universal languages can express different conceptual schemes and different traditions. Just as, then, a language might embody several different conceptual schemes, a language might embody several different traditions. Latin, for example, embodied both an Augustinian and a Thomistic tradition during the Middle Ages. To challenge the coherence of conceptual schemes or traditions in terms of issues of translatability, then, is to misconstrue the very nature of traditions.

Davidson-minded thinkers might retort, however, that I have still not shown whether differences pointed to between traditions are differences of belief or differences of conceptual schemes. More appropriate for the purposes of my argument, they might argue that I have not shown there is a fact of the matter as to whether the differences I have pointed to are differences of belief rather than differences of standards of reason. One could argue, perhaps, that I argue that a difference in standards of reason is really a difference in belief supported by the same standards of reason.

On the one hand, Zande witchcraft and the Lakota notion of *wakan* seem obvious examples of differences in concepts.[24] Neither of these concepts/categories seems to have an equivalent in English. I do not deny that one could explain, in a roundabout way, what each term means. Rather, the claim is that English does not have terms that function in the same way. The witchcraft of the Middle Ages and of Salem is not the witchcraft of the Azande. Zande witchcraft, while evil, has nothing to do with worshiping an evil being or generally bringing about the destruction of society. Lakota *wakan* is not to be confused with the soul. The Lakota do not believe that individual human beings have individual *wakan*.

On the other hand, I have discussed several examples of different standards of reason. The most obvious are the differences between the Lakota and the English Protestant settler. They do not simply have different beliefs; they think and act on rival sets of standards and beliefs of a particular social order. Different concepts of land and property entail different standards of reason by which the individuals of the rival traditions act and judge their actions as reasonable or not. Thus, if it is examples of different conceptual schemes and different standards of reason that one requires, they have been provided.

One might retort, however, that it is not examples of such conceptual schemes or standards of reason that the critics want. Rather, they want some universal criteria of demarcation. Someone might argue that the "use of the concept of a tradition and of that history of development recounted within each tradition as a constitutive element of it requires an independent philosophical grasp of that concept and of the criteria for its use and application." To require such criteria is to require not only what my argument cannot supply but what no philosophy can supply, namely, a priori, universal criteria. All debates occur within a tradition. The very concept of a tradition is one that proves tradition-constituted.[25]

A priori criteria of demarcation for conceptual schemes and for traditions cannot be supplied because of the very nature of the argument. Davidson's argument is essentially a search for such criteria. It must, then, fail, as I have shown it does. If one wants to demarcate conceptual schemes or traditions, one must do so from within a particular tradition. A rival conceptual scheme is just one that I note is different from mine. A rival tradition is just one that I recognize as such.

Finally, one might question my continual use of the notion of a conceptual scheme. I have already denied the scheme/content dualism. Yet that dualism is essential to how this section has defined "conceptual scheme." This section needs not to define the notion of a conceptual scheme but only to defend the coherence of that notion. Such a notion must avoid the two pitfalls of accepting the scheme/content dualism and reducing conceptual schemes to languages. Whereas Kant's model violates the first requirement, Quine's violates the second.[26] Theirs are not the only games in town. Michael Lynch, for example, develops a neo-Kantian notion of conceptual scheme in light of Wittgenstein's work. Whether such a neo-Kantian notion will eventually suffice is a question for a different work.

Beyond Relativism: Evaluation, Epistemological Crises, and Truth

Beyond Relativism

In developing a conception of substantive reason, I have shown that such reason involves much more than means-end or formal rationalities, and my argument has proven that claim throughout. I have not only given reasons for my conclusion but also evaluated those reasons and the conceptions of reason proffered by different philosophers, such as conceptions of subjective rationality, communicative rationality, and a reason of traditions. My argument gives reasons for its conclusions, for example, by holding that different theories have different conceptions of reason and the good and by analyzing different philosophical and cultural traditions.

If everything in the last paragraph is true, then I still must show that a substantive reason can be marshaled as a tool for a critical theory of society. The reader may object at this point, however, that before I discuss this issue, I must first decisively remove the specter of relativism. Do not the conclusions of my argument lead to relativism concerning reason and morality? As one sympathetic critic notes, since the publication of *After Virtue,* MacIntyre has repeatedly defended himself against the charge of relativism.[27] I will use his defense to support the claim that my own version of tradition-constituted reason does not lead to relativism.

Richard Bernstein relates the issue of relativism to what he calls Cartesian anxiety, the fear that if we human beings, as fallible creatures, are bereft of universal grounds for our beliefs—our knowledge and morals—we will be left in darkness. Bernstein describes a specter that lurks in the background of Descartes's *Meditations,* which is an account of a journey of the soul. That specter "is not just radical epistemological skepticism but the dread of madness and chaos where nothing is fixed, where we can never touch bottom nor support ourselves on the surface. *Either* there is some support for our being, a fixed foundation for our knowledge, *or* we cannot escape the forces of darkness that envelop us with madness, with intellectual and moral chaos."[28] Either we have grounds for our beliefs or we face madness.

Bernstein claims this anxiety lies behind the dichotomy of relativism and objectivism. Objectivism is the belief that "some permanent, a-historical matrix" exists "to which we can ultimately appeal in determining the nature of" reason. Relativism, on the other hand, is the belief that all such fundamental concepts as reason or truth can be understood only "relative to a specific conceptual scheme, theoretical framework, paradigm, form of life, society, culture," or, one can add, tradition.[29] From the perspective of Cartesian anxiety, if we find the permanent, ahistorical matrix that grounds our beliefs, we escape madness; if, on the contrary, we abandon the search for such grounds, we have chaos.

This anxiety has been with philosophers throughout time (it was named for Descartes not because it was new with him but because his philosophy exemplified it so well), and it remains with us today, says Bernstein. At the same time, Bernstein wants to paint a way out of the either/or of objectivism versus relativism. To escape this either/or, we must exorcise the Cartesian anxiety. The either/or of objectivism and relativism misleads and distorts, by forcing our conceptions of truth and reason into molds that do not quite suit them. To demonstrate this,

Bernstein examines movements in postempiricist philosophy of science (including, Kuhn, Popper, and Lakatos), the philosophy of the social sciences (particularly Winch), and the hermeneutic tradition (as reconceived by Gadamer). He concludes that some philosophers in all three fields are moving away from the search for a solid ground for truth and reason. These philosophers recognize the historical embeddedness of reason and truth. In showing that chaos and disorder do not result, they thereby exorcise the Cartesian anxiety.

These theories break away from the either/or of objectivism versus relativism because they do not accept the Cartesian project. According to Bernstein, the exclusive disjunction of objectivism and relativism makes sense only on a Cartesian or like-minded framework. That is, once philosophers abandon the search for an Archimedean point, they no longer need to concern themselves with the issue of objectivism versus relativism. The dichotomy of objectivism and relativism makes sense only when one denies that comparison and difference are mutually compatible. That is, when one holds that things can be (partially) incommensurable (that is, that they have rival and competing standards of reason) and yet compared and evaluated, one no longer need fear falling into chaos because one's judgments lack ultimate ground. Evaluation can proceed only from the grounds available to the agent. This last claim should be evident from the course of the argument that substantive reason resides only within a tradition. Therefore, the very possibility of evaluation relies not on the actual possession of some ultimate, ahistorical and permanent matrix, but on the best efforts of agents who begin within the historical and finite nature of human beings. These very methods of evaluation, moreover, point to possibilities for "learning from" others.

The very idea of evaluation entails a rejection of relativism while accepting the truth of relativism. In his 1985 presidential address, MacIntyre insists that relativism remains a recurrent problem for philosophy because it relies on a partial truth. That partial truth rests, as I showed in chapter 3, on the reality that substantive reason is both tradition-constituted and tradition-constitutive. Just as Popper, Kuhn, and Lakatos reject an "objective" Archimedean ground of evaluation, so too MacIntyre sees the notion of rational principles that provide certainty as "mythical beasts."[30] Yet he insists that the rejection of such mythical beasts does not entail that we must accept relativism. Rather, he provides an analysis of substantive reason that shows how substantive reason includes a power to evaluate and how agents within traditions can recognize the inadequacy of their own standards of reason and their tradition.

The concept of truth proves pivotal here. Even though reason is constituted by tradition, MacIntyre holds that the agents of each tradition make claims to truth.[31] Truth is "the perfected understanding in which enquiry terminates."[32] That is, truth implies some ability to say how things really are in the world. Truth entails that what an agent claims proves true regardless of the particular standpoint from which she makes that claim. When an adherent to a tradition—Roman Catholic, Azande, Lakota—makes a claim to truth, that adherent means to make a claim about how the world is regardless of what her particular perspective might be. When the Lakota claim that the Black Hills are sacred, they do not mean sacred for them; they mean that the Black Hills are, in fact, for everyone *Paha Sapa*—the center of the universe.

On this point, MacIntyre agrees with Habermas. Every tradition, for MacIntyre, and every language, for Habermas, includes an ability to distinguish between how things seem and how things really are.[33] Because each tradition makes this distinction, when an agent in a particular tradition makes a claim to truth, she is necessarily committed to making a claim as to how things really are, not simply how they seem to be. If she were only making a claim as to how things seem to be, then she would make a claim about seeming rather than about truth. MacIntyre takes this fact further than Habermas does, however.

Habermas uses the congruence of languages on the role "truth" plays in each language to defend a universal-pragmatics of language. This analysis leads him to defend a formal rationality that, as I showed, lacks awareness of its own value commitments. MacIntyre, however, takes the idea of truth to argue that agents of traditions are committed to making truth claims. This means traditions prove their validity or their truth based on how things really are. This claim to truth places a particular burden on members of traditions when they make truth claims. "It is the onus upon the adherents of each particular rival tradition of showing, so far as they can, that, if and only if the truth is indeed what they assert that it is, and if and only if it is appropriated rationally in the way they say it must be appropriated, can we adequately understand how, in the case of each rival moral standpoint, given the historical, social, psychological, and intellectual circumstances in which that standpoint has been theoretically elaborated and embodied in practice, it is intelligible that this is how things should seem to be to the adherents of those other standpoints."[34] They must be able to explain why those other traditions see things the way they do, when in fact things are not the way they see them.

In short, truth does not bear out as relative to each tradition. Rather, substantive reason proves relative to tradition. Yet agents retain a power to evaluate their own tradition-constituted explanation of reality, in part, through engagement with the world. Experience amounts to a check on the claims to truth. We see this fact in the development of scientific traditions that tests their claims to truth against experience. To see how MacIntyre appropriates this understanding of science, we must turn to his discussion of epistemological crises.

MacIntyre's Account of Epistemological Crises

Stages of Traditions

To defeat the challenges of relativism, in *Whose Justice? Which Rationality?* MacIntyre outlines a series of stages that a tradition must undergo to remain viable. In the first, stasis, members of the tradition give unquestioning deference to the canonical texts and authority figures of the tradition. A possible second stage, disruption, can occur if the tenets of the tradition are called into question. Stage two can be precipitated by several kinds of events, including (1) the canonical texts being interpreted in incompatible ways; (2) the tradition becoming obviously incoherent; (3) new experiences showing that the tradition lacks means for formulating or justifying new answers to new or perennial questions and ways of life; or (4) two traditions meeting or merging, giving rise to new problems and incompatible concepts (*WJWR* 355). In this second stage, then, inadequacies are discovered in the tradition without any correlative rectifications of those inadequacies.

In stage three, then, members of the tradition try to reformulate it, reevaluating it to answer the inadequacies discovered in stage two. Members who accept the reformulation can make judgments of truth and falsity about the tradition and its cosmology by comparing their old view about the world and about the concepts that were central to that view with their new understanding of it and of the concepts central to that new understanding. In making this comparison, they can understand how their previous understanding of the world was inadequate. It was inadequate in that it did not allow action in the world to fulfill the expectations of actors. The previous understanding of the world can be and is judged false because it does not correspond to present understanding. Present understanding, meanwhile, is judged true insofar as the tradition does not so change that retrospective inadequacy appears once again. Truth, then, attaches to those beliefs that to date have withstood historical questioning and change in the tradition, that is, have been judged by experience to be adequate to the world. Judgments of what counts as surviving that historical questioning will themselves be subjected to further rational debate and evaluation. Claims about how the world is and what the standards of truth are must withstand dialectical questioning. Here, "dialectical" refers to those processes by which a tradition evaluates and compares its beliefs about its central claims.

At this point of development, having undergone the initial three stages of evolution and having evaluated its own ideas of truth and evaluation, a tradition is, MacIntyre declares, a form of enquiry. It will, at this point, "have recognized intellectual virtues" (*WJWR* 358). Questions about these virtues and about their relationship to virtues of character will generate conflicting answers within the tradition. At this point, as well, a tradition may conclude that another tradition has or is undergoing similar sorts of conflicts. The judgment that these conflicts are similar is made from within, according to the standards of the tradition making the judgment. Traditions may, moreover, define areas of overlap and disagreement between themselves and other traditions based, again, on their own understanding of issues, arguments, and so on.

It might come to pass, consequently, that a tradition begins to question and investigate its own methods of enquiry. It will want, for example, to develop a theory of truth or of reason, which it did not have explicitly before. The answers and theories arrived at will differ for various traditions. The divergent conclusions those traditions come to on substantive matters such as justice and practical rationality will underlie those variances. Still, MacIntyre claims that, at least to some extent, if a tradition is one of rational inquiry, it will generally recognize what it has in common with other such traditions. As these traditions develop, "common characteristic, if not universal, patterns will appear" (*WJWR* 359). Traditions of enquiry *qua* traditions of enquiry will recognize what they share with other such traditions. Further, *qua* traditions of enquiry, they will find common, even universal, patterns. One example of a common pattern that MacIntyre finds in the traditions that he discusses in *Whose Justice? Which Rationality?* (Aristotelianism, Augustinianism, Thomism, Scottish Enlightenment philosophy, and liberalism) is giving authority to logic in practice and belief. Other common patterns include reference to established authority, adherence to coherence, reference to previous beliefs in the tradition, and the presence of dialectics. Significant for MacIntyre's further argument is the claim that the beliefs of a tradition will be presently less vulnerable to attack and rejection than are their predecessors.

So far, I have discussed only how a tradition changes within itself. This discussion contravenes relativist claims that rational progress is impossible and the perspectivist claim that the concept of truth should be abandoned, while denying the objectivist position of relying on some fixed, ahistorical, permanent ground of reason. Each tradition must prove adequate in accounting for its members' experience of the world, and this adequacy is the criterion for reason and for (apparent) truth.

Still, one can ask, What resources does MacIntyre provide for understanding intercultural comparisons?

According to MacIntyre, every tradition has certain unresolved problems and issues that it strives to resolve, and the degree to which it resolves them constitutes the reasonable progress of the tradition. As mentioned above, these problems and issues involve interpreting canonical texts, dealing with incoherences that develop in the tradition, encountering and merging with rival traditions, and failing to resolve problems in the face of new experiences. It is possible for a tradition, according to its own standards, to fail.

A tradition of enquiry might come to recognize that according to its own standards it no longer makes progress. Or it might come to a view that its methods of enquiry are barren or that competing answers to central questions in the tradition resolve those questions rationally (*WJWR* 361–62). Moreover, its current methodology and exemplars may uncover new, heretofore unseen, inadequacies, incoherences, and problems that agents judge they lack resources to explain or resolve. Recognizing that these problems arise on the basis of the standards of reason in the tradition remains salient. The tradition fails not on the standards of other traditions but on its own standards. MacIntyre's argument all along has been that traditions may always fail on the standards of reason of rival traditions. A tradition experiences an epistemological crisis just when it fails to make progress according to its *own* standards of reason and progress.

Communication between and action by members of a tradition occur because they have an understanding of the world by which they interpret and act within it. We can refer to this basic understanding as a *schema*. It consists in the tradition's beliefs and cosmology. This schema says what is in the world and defines possible actions within the world.

Not only does a schema enable human beings to communicate and act; it can also lead to error. Just as a tradition in science may, through the various assumptions and research methodologies underlying it, lead the scientist astray in her search for an understanding of the world, so too can the schema of tradition lead the individual actor astray both in acting and in understanding the world and the actions of others. An actor is led astray when her assumptions or schema call for particular actions while her social context calls for quite different ones. Almost everyone can probably recall some time when they acted on the basis of assumptions which proved wrong and which, thus, led them to get "egg on the face."

Schemata can confuse action and interpretation in another way, moreover. A person might encounter a situation in which a plurality of schemata is available by which to interpret the actions of others and the situation in which one finds oneself. These different schemata might yield "mutually incompatible accounts" of the situation (EC 454).

The following simple example might make these claims clearer. Albert has certain relatives and friends who are always making derogatory comments about him, always with a smile and a laugh. They insist that such comments are really signs of affection; they mean nothing by them. Albert might, then, operate according to a schema in which these comments are seen as signs of affection. He acts appropriately, then. Since he is not as witty as his relatives and friends, he simply laughs at the jokes himself. Of course, one day Albert might come to think of matters differently. He might seek psychological counseling. This counseling might suggest to him that this "joshing" is really hurting him and not in fact friendly kidding around at all. Albert is simply hanging out with the wrong people (even if they are relatives). He might then come to see the comments as insults and attacks on his person. He will react appropriately then. He will either ignore such attacks and find new friends (and only see relatives at Fourth of July picnics), or he might develop a skill of giving witty retorts. Regardless, Albert's world has changed. He cannot believe in friendly-comment-schema and mean-comment-schema at the same time. He must choose which is his real world.

The facts, however, cannot be understood without reference to a schema for interpreting those facts. Albert's original schema has no room for mean, hurtful insults. Albert interprets the data and "chooses" a schema at the same time. Yet his original schema is being thrown into question and the facts no longer appear so simple. He must decide which schema, which way of treating the facts, is the right way; in order to do so, however, he must already have chosen one way over another. "Trapped in this epistemological circularity the general form of his problem is: 'what is going on here?'" (EC 454). How does one resolve this crisis? "By the construction of a new narrative which enables the agent to understand *both* how he or she could intelligibly have held his or her original beliefs *and* how he or she could have been so drastically misled by them" (EC 455).

Albert must, in this situation, construct a new narrative about his place in the world and in this particular situation. His old narrative saw him as a lovable person with good, lighthearted relatives and friends. His new narrative paints him as a formerly confused and (verbally) abused person. The new narrative suggests that he held on to his old beliefs because they were psychologically easier to bear and because, since relatives were involved, the derogatory comments were with him from birth. Albert, then, must be able to explain why at one time he believed the old narrative. He must also be able to explain how the rival schema was intelligible to him, for if it were not intelligible to him it would not have been a viable rival to his old schema. Here he might note that he finally realized that when people were insulted, they generally took offense, relative or not. Such a realization made him come to see that he should take offense as well.

In this example, we see that Albert makes claims to truth. Making these claims, he must be able to say why one interpretation proves more adequate to reality than another. Truth, as already noted, escapes perspectivism because it entails being able to say why one perspective failed on grounds acceptable to that perspective.

This same process and these same criteria apply to comparisons of traditions or cultures. The following example points out the similarities. Society A has always exploited land and environment technologically. Members of Society A believe that land was given to them to dominate and to use as they desire. Land was made for their use and purposes. It lacks qualities like reason and soul that are essential to deserving respect. Without those qualities, land could legitimately be used solely for the purpose of the members of Society A. Some of their fundamental texts, furthermore, supported this view.

One text, from a religious basis, suggested that God had given human beings dominion over the earth and animals. On this understanding, human beings, especially members of Society A, were made rulers over both earth and animals. A certain hierarchy existed among all things—with God resting at the pinnacle of the hierarchy, human beings toward the top, other animals below human beings, vegetative life below animals, and finally minerals and earth at the bottom. Dominion over the earth and other animals consisted essentially in their being usable for human purposes. Those purposes included glorifying

God and serving Him. Among the edicts, God gave to Society A the edict that they were to show service to Him by being fruitful and multiplying. Members of Society A understood this, in the first instance, to mean increasing the number of human beings. This edict, in turn, required greater and greater uses of resources. Members of Society A also believed that they were commanded to use as much of the earth and its animals as possible. Thus, along with reproducing human beings and tradition, members of Society A thought that they should use human ingenuity to extract as much wealth from the land as possible.

Other texts supported and were informed by the above religious text. These texts defended a view of human beings as competitive and industrious creatures. They suggested that some human beings were superior to others in qualities such as reason. People who were seen to be singularly in control of their lives and surroundings were revered as heroes and ideal types after whom to model oneself. Literature, folk tales, and other cultural artifacts supported a view of the true person, the ideal member of Society A, as strong, independent, and in control. When misfortune struck, such individuals were able, through ingenuity and industriousness, to overcome the forces that dominated all their foes—either other human beings or nature itself.

Society A has lived with and according to these beliefs for centuries. Problems are beginning to arise for Society A, however. Their technology seems to have reached a limit. They have reached a point at which they cannot continue to extract resources from the earth and other animals to serve a heretofore unseen number of human beings. Moreover, their control of the land seems to be backfiring. Various ecological and natural disasters occur that result from their control of the environment. Such disasters include flooding on the plains, extinction of species in record numbers, and the presence of microorganisms that destroy ecological systems. Further, their use of the earth and animals seems to be depleting resources without any clear or possible renewal of such resources. The use of these resources, in turn, has damaged various parts of global nature—from the supply of breathable air to the preserve of various microecosystems.

In light of all of these developments, members of Society A look for solutions. Their dominant ideology dictates that they continue to reap from the earth what they need. One thing they might try to reap from the earth is further solutions to their inability to feed the present, growing population. Moreover, they expect that no end to technological innovation is in sight. That is, they believe that more technology will be invented that will allow them not only to maintain present lifestyles but to improve their lives. The earth is for their use, as are other animals. What is important is learning how better to control it so that it continues to satisfy their needs and wants.

Society A faces both a practical and an epistemological crisis. The crisis is epistemological in that its basic assumptions about the world are called into question. These basic assumptions include that the earth is meant for domination, that an infinite amount of resources are available, and that technology can invent new means for extracting ever more resources from the earth. Its schema for addressing the world has reached its limit for resolving how members of the tradition should understand and act in the world. Just as Albert above, Society A faces problems to which it does not have obvious solutions. It is unable to explain its own failings. These failings, it is important to note, are failings according to its own standards. According to A's schema, it should dominate and extract from the earth and its animals whatever members of Society A need. It is meant to control and dominate the environment and other animals. On their own accounting, however, they are failing to achieve that domination. They cannot control all the aspects of the earth they want; they cannot extract unlimited resources from the earth; they cannot treat the earth as if it were merely meant to serve their purposes—for when they do these things, the earth "fights back." The paradigms for acting in relation to the earth are failing to provide the solutions that they did in the past.

This failure throws members of the tradition into chaos. Various members of Society A may search for answers to their problems. They may question their own premises and paradigms; they may call ancient and revered texts into question; they may even begin to investigate alternative traditions for solutions to their problems, solutions that the tradition of Society A cannot provide. These members of Society A are suffering a crisis—including an epistemological crisis, for their very standards of reasoning and interacting in the world, their whole conception of life, is called into question.

Members of Society A, then, begin to question the truth of their claims. They question the truth of these claims because the claims seem no longer adequate to the way the world actually is. They see that the world seems, in fact, limited in resources rather than, as they believed in their tradition, infinite in resources. This different way of seeing the world shows exactly what MacIntyre meant when he argued that tradition-constituted reason does not lead to relativism of truth. Reason might be constituted by and constitutive of tradition, but truth, as adequacy to the world, proves universal.

Resolution of Epistemological Crises

Epistemological crises need not be the end of a tradition. A tradition can resolve its epistemological crises through creating or unearthing new concepts and developing new kinds of theories. The solution must meet three "highly exacting requirements." First, the new schema must be able to resolve the problems that gave rise to the epistemological crisis systematically and coherently. The solutions cannot be ad hoc if they are to succeed in ending the crisis. Second, the new schema must be able to explain why the tradition went askew in the first place. It must be able to explain why the tradition became "sterile or incoherent or both" prior to acquiring the new concepts. Finally, the new schema must resolve these problems in a way that is fundamentally continuous with the tradition's understanding of itself (*WJWR* 362).

Essential to resolving an epistemological crisis is conceptual innovation. The new schema may not be derivable, in any way, from the old schema. This nonreductionism results from the facts that the new schema is richer than and does not suffer from the same limitations as the old one. The new schema, with its new concepts and theses, is justified just when it resolves the epistemological crisis—that is, success brings justification. Success must entail justification given the way a tradition experiences an epistemological crisis and given the three conditions of success mentioned above. The tradition suffers an epistemological crisis just when it fails to resolve its problematic on its own standards; it overcomes such a crisis when it can systematically solve its old problems according to its own standards—even if these standards themselves have changed. If it can do this, it resolves the crisis. Notice that, in resolving its crisis, the tradition makes a new affirmation of truth. Members assert that they can see where they were wrong and explain both how they were wrong and how the new account supersedes the former account.

Yet, in order to be considered the same tradition, the tradition must be linked to its precrisis form by some basic continuity. One sign of such continuity is that the tradition can explain how it got to be where it was and currently is. It can, in other words, construct a new narrative of its history. This new narrative shows, in ways that demonstrate the tradition's survival and flourishing, how the tradition is continuous with the past; the narrative now also pinpoints a more accurate "structure of justification" that underwrites the claims to truth that members of the tradition make (363).

Of course, a tradition might not resolve its epistemological crisis through conceptual innovation. A tradition might either encounter another tradition that it comes to recognize as superior to itself, or, failing to resolve its epistemological crisis, may cease to be a tradition of inquiry and exist as a desiccated ideology or die out. I want now to clarify how a tradition resolves its epistemological crisis by encountering a tradition it comes to recognize as superior.

Unable to resolve its problematics through new conceptual innovations, a tradition may encounter a rival tradition, whether one it has known for some time or one it has just discovered. What is important is the reaction of the members of the first tradition to its rival. These members might come to know the second tradition in such a way that they not only understand but also recognize the reasonableness behind the beliefs and ways of life of the other tradition or might come to newly appreciate a long-standing rival. The members of the first tradition must accept and live by the standards of reason of the other tradition. If they do not accept and employ those rival standards, they cannot, *ex hypothesi*, find the rival tradition reasonable. To understand a rival tradition via one's own standards of reasons is probably to find the rival tradition, on various accounts, to be lacking, unreasonable.

Now, the members of the first tradition may be "compelled" to recognize that the rival can explain their failures in a way that satisfies the
first tradition's standards of reason. To make this point clearer, let me
put it in the following way: Tradition A is undergoing an epistemological crisis that its members seem unable to resolve. Members of A (A-
ites) come to understand a rival tradition, Tradition B. To understand
Tradition B, the A-ites must learn that tradition as if it were their first
tradition. In doing this, A-ites learn to act and believe according to the
standards of reason they find in B. A-ites are then compelled to examine their first tradition—Tradition A—in light of their adopted tradition. In so doing, the A-ites recognize the possibility of building out of
the concepts and theories specific to the rival tradition solutions they
could not develop from the resources of their own Tradition A. They
discover in Tradition B an explanation of the failure of their own tradition to resolve its crisis that, on their own standards—the standards of
Tradition A—proves sound and illuminating (*WJWR* 364).

A-ites have found, then, in Tradition B what they could not find in
Tradition A—a reasonable explanation for the failure of Tradition A.
This explanation from B is reasonable, according to MacIntyre, from
the standpoint of Tradition A. The A-ites, on this account, judge their
own tradition to have failed, and they understand why it failed according to a new schema. The judgment is made from their own standards
of reason.

Understanding the failure of the original tradition satisfies only
two of the three criteria MacIntyre listed for the resolution of an epistemological crisis. The new schema explains why the crisis happened,
and it does not suffer from the same defects as the old schema. The new
schema, however, is discontinuous with the old. This does not mean
that the new tradition is not superior. It means simply that the original
tradition cannot resolve its own crisis—and must be abandoned.

The epistemological crisis is not resolved, for such resolution requires that the tradition be able to solve its own puzzles. Those puzzles, however, are unraveled by the standards of reason of a different
tradition—a tradition that not only answers the questions of the first
tradition but also explains why the first tradition encountered that
particular epistemological crisis. The first tradition, which was under-

going an epistemological crisis, cannot uphold its legitimacy given that the rival tradition can explain the failure of the first tradition on terms that meet the standards of reason of the tradition in crisis. The tradition in crisis, then, must be abandoned, and it must be abandoned because it cannot resolve its epistemological crisis. The members of the crisis tradition recognize the rival tradition as superior given its explanatory power in light of their failed tradition. The superiority is marked by the way that the new tradition exposes how the original tradition fails to correspond to the world as it is known by the best explanation of the world so far, that is, the one found in the rival.

This "best" explanation is understood as "most successful." As noted above, a theory is considered true insofar as it allows its members to interact with the world in a way that is not liable to disappointment. That is, the mind's expectations for its activities are fulfilled; it is successful in interaction in the natural and social worlds. Such success is afforded by one theory to a degree not afforded by the other. Just as greater success within a tradition allowed that tradition to call its theories true, so the greater success of another tradition, identified through its ability to explain failures of its rivals on their own account, allows the "converted" members of the new tradition to call it true and their original tradition false. (Of course, as MacIntyre notes, that one tradition should be acknowledged as superior in this way does not mean that it is so acknowledged, that is, that everyone will convert.) The new tradition meets greater success because it satisfies the two conditions it meets. On the one hand, it can solve the problems of the old tradition according to the old tradition's standards; it thus has greater problem-resolution capability. On the other hand, it can explain why the old tradition failed, again in a way that satisfies the standards of reason of the old tradition. As such, it meets with greater success than does the old tradition; it has been shown to be reasonably superior. This ability to explain the failure of the crisis tradition and to unravel the riddles of that tradition means that the rival tradition can fulfill its members' expectations better than the tradition in crisis can. It can fulfill those expectations because it has better explanatory power in light of the problems, concerns, and issues of the failed tradition. It is more adequate to the world.

A tradition, then, can undergo reasonable change, and members of a tradition may reasonably convert to another tradition. Some of these transformations prove self-contained, while others involve interactions with rival traditions. All traditions might, at some time, encounter epistemological crises. These crises might be resolved through conceptual innovation or may prove a deathblow to the tradition, through either its ultimate failure to resolve the crisis or its encounter with another tradition that some of its members come to recognize as superior to itself. Because of these changes and the possible reactions to those changes, MacIntyre's tradition-constituted reason and my theory of substantive reason can move beyond relativism and objectivism. They do so by both denying the existence of some permanent, ahistorical ground for reason and by grounding comparisons of reasonable superiority within and between rival (partially) incommensurable traditions in their adequacy in explaining our experience of the world. Truth is a criterion of reason.

This comparison between traditions can ground a critical theory of society because it is not a formal comparison but a substantive comparison. Members of Tradition A find in Tradition B more than just similarities in logic and argumentation. Rather, they find substantive standards of reason as well as substantive theoretical tools which help them resolve the crisis in their own tradition or which explain the crisis in their own tradition in ways that satisfy their own substantive standards of reason. The fact of adequacy to their experience of the world substantiates those theoretical tools as better than what their own tradition had heretofore provided them. That is, it offers a justification for alternative ways of life as better because more reasonable and more true on their own substantive standards of reason

The Task of Reasoning

Although MacIntyre's discussion of epistemological crises sheds light on how intertraditional comparisons are possible, he could make his account of this process clearer. He does not give a clear account of how members of different traditions can begin dialogue. Using

arguments of Charles Taylor, I will now build on the notion of epistemological crises, discovering that other argument forms are available
which further explain the possibility of intertraditional comparison
and debate. Thus I will spell out the ultimate task of reasoning, for that
task relies on the essential function of reason discussed earlier—
evaluation.

Charles Taylor and Ad Hominem Arguments

"The task of reasoning, then, is not to disprove some radically opposed first premise (say, killing people is no problem), but rather to
show how the policy is unconscionable on premises which both sides
accept, and cannot but accept."[35] In arguing this point, Taylor rightly
agrees with much of the impetus of MacIntyre's account of an epistemological crisis. A tradition recognizes another as superior just when
that other surpasses it according to the first tradition's own standards of
reason: the second tradition is shown to be acceptable according to
premises or standards which the first tradition already accepts. Taylor's
point also recognizes what Davidsonian critics require: that rival traditions share some basic beliefs or standards of reason. He goes beyond
MacIntyre's account, however, to bring in more hermeneutical considerations. This hermeneutical account provides a richer understanding
of intercultural comparison.

Rejecting the foundationalist form of argument (which claims that
argument must proceed from firmly established principles according
to strict logical methods), Taylor holds that a new metatheory of scientific and ethical reasoning is needed. According to Taylor, MacIntyre
shows that one theory can be shown to be superior to another when it
can "give a convincing narrative account of the passage from the first
[theory] to the second."[36] Taylor extracts from this claim the idea that
one can "arbitrate between positions by portraying *transitions* as gains
or losses," without referring to ahistorical criteria of progress and
reasonableness. Taylor adduces three forms of argument that, though
rejected and disused in contemporary political philosophy, he finds
usable for such portrayals. Calling these forms of reasoning ad hominem, Taylor begins by stating that such arguments appeal to premises

or ideas that both sides of the argument already accept. In debating eu-thanasia, for instance, proponents might appeal to beliefs that oppo-nents already share, for example, that one ought to relieve the suffering of persons. Proponents attempt to find common ground they share with adversaries in order to begin dialogue and debate. Through such attempts, one can actually make reasonable progress.

According to Taylor, however, such an understanding of ad homi-nem arguments is limited. A more robust understanding recognizes two further aspects of such arguments: ad hominem arguments are (1) directed toward persons and (2) comparative.[37] In trying to argue that X is superior to Y, ad hominem arguments are directed specifically at holders of X and compare X to Y, with the conclusion that whatever might be universally the case, believers in X should abandon belief in X for belief in Y. This form of reasoning fits MacIntyre's resolution of epistemological crises, for an epistemological crisis is resolved when members of one tradition compare their tradition to a rival tradition and find the rival superior.

Ad hominem reasoning occurs when comparative judgments show not only that one theory can account for more facts than can a second but that it can illuminate the history of the other.[38] Theory B can make better sense both of the world and of Theory A's history of attempts at explaining the world than A can. This form of argument is clearly cen-tral to MacIntyre's explanation of reasonable change between tradi-tions. Indeed, Taylor refers to an example provided by MacIntyre, that of the switch from the Aristotelian conception of motion to the Newto-nian conception. Here the question concerns not simply competing theories but competing traditions. For instance, A and B denote two different traditions. As a tradition, A directs its arguments specifically to B and does so in a comparative fashion. Aristotelians, for example, might direct their arguments to utilitarians. Such arguments might compare notions of happiness in making moral judgments. In making these arguments, Aristotelians will appeal to beliefs and standards that they share with utilitarians.

In the case of the Aristotelians and utilitarians, a tradition that is not facing an epistemological crisis engages in reasonable debate with another tradition. There also occur, of course, cases where traditions undergo not only epistemological crises but moral ones. The values and conception of the good of a tradition may come into dispute.

Consider the case of slavery in the United States in the mid-1800s. Members of one and the same tradition disputed what constitutes the good and which value is important—equality or freedom. Opponents of slavery addressed their arguments to the proponents of slavery in such a way as to require comparisons between ways of life, ideas about humanity, or conceptions of the good.

Debate between traditions will occur in similar manner. A Lockean property tradition might be undergoing a moral crisis concerning the moral issue of property ownership and use of land. Members of this tradition might search for solutions in other traditions if they cannot find solutions in their own. Lockeans, as a result, could come to engage Lakota in debates about landownership. Finding shared beliefs and standards between themselves and the Lakota, they could then use these commonalities as the basis for further argument. If they do find a solution to their moral crises within the Lakota tradition, they must then turn around and address other members of their own Lockean tradition, showing how their tradition shares beliefs and standards with the Lakota and how, on the basis of these commonalities, the Lakota tradition provides a way out of the Lockean moral crisis. Of course, the Lockeans might (1) not discover any beliefs or standards they share with the Lakota, (2) discover that, even on the basis of such shared beliefs and standards, the Lakota tradition has nothing to offer the Lockean tradition, or (3) find that on the basis of such standards the Lockean tradition has something to offer the Lakota. Only on this last scenario would a debate then ensue between the Lockeans and Lakota about the comparative moral and epistemological superiority of one tradition over another. In all of these cases, members of the traditions engage in and use ad hominem forms of argument. That is, they address their arguments to members of specific traditions and use comparisons to make their arguments.

A second form of ad hominem argument requires a nonsymmetrical explanation of the successes and failures of both theories: Theory B explains the successes and failures of Theory A better than Theory A explains the successes (and failures) of Theory B. More precisely, "what [pre-Newtonian] science can't explain is the very success of [Newtonian science] *on the latter's own terms*" (emphasis original).[39] Whereas Theory B can assimilate Theory A, Theory A cannot assimilate Theory B. This form of argumentation points to the two requirements that MacIntyre placed on reasonable transitions between traditions. Reasonable transition requires that the new theory be able to appeal to the standards of the old theory and that it be able to explain the failures and successes of its predecessors. Once again, then, Taylor's position converges with MacIntyre's theory of reasonable superiority.

Aristotelians, using this form of argumentation, might argue that, whereas the Aristotelian tradition can explain the successes and failures of the utilitarian tradition, the utilitarian tradition cannot explain the success of the Aristotelian. Aristotelians might even point to Mill's own discussion of a hierarchy of values in their defense. Similarly, the Lakota might argue that, whereas their tradition can explain the successes and failures of the Lockean, the Lockean tradition cannot explain the successes of the Lakota. For example, they might point out that abuse of the land disabled it from continuing to support the human population and that the Lockean tradition continues to ignore the success of the Lakota tradition in providing a comfortable life.

Taylor holds, however, that it may be the case that some traditions differ too much to permit argumentation that relies on or involves comparisons. He introduces, consequently, a third form of ad hominem argument, which shows not that the transition from Theory A to Theory B is reasonable on grounds that A has to acknowledge, but rather that the transition to B is more reasonable because "it can plausibly be described as mediated by some error-reducing move."[40] Such a transition might involve the removal of a contradiction, the overcoming of a confusion, or the recognition of a heretofore ignored factor. Taylor holds that such examples abound in everyday life. For example, one might walk into a room and seem to see something surprising. One rubs one's eyes to get a better look and no longer sees the surprising thing. The second perception is trusted, not because it is necessarily more likely, but because the perceiver has performed an "ameliorating transition."[41] Indeed, Taylor believes that this final form of reasoning is "the commonest form of practical reasoning in our lives, where we propose to our interlocutors transitions mediated by such error-reducing moves, by the identification of contradiction, the dissipation of confusion, or by rescuing from neglect a consideration whose significance they cannot contest." Further, "some of our gains in moral insight prove themselves to us in just this way."[42]

Taylor provides the following example of this third form of argument. Peter was behaving terribly at home because he constantly felt that he was "cheated of his rights." He felt that, since he was the oldest, something was due to him that he was not getting and which he resented not getting. Now he no longer believes that something is owed him. He changed his mind because he realized that his previous behavior had resulted from a principle to which he would never explicitly subscribe—that older children should have more. In other words, he has gone through a moral change; his views of what people owe each other in the family have altered. This change represents growth because it resulted from the dispelling of an unconscious, confused belief.[43]

In the debate between the Lakota and the Lockeans such a transition could arise. The Lockeans claim that people are meant to own land so that they can bring it to greater fruition. The Lakota might point out, however, that the Lockeans are ignoring essential aspects of their largely biblical tradition. The Lakota might point to passages in the Old Testament where the Jewish people are instructed not simply to dominate but to care for and respect the land. The Bible demands that human beings be stewards of the land, not its lords. Such arguments would address not shared understandings but considerations that have been neglected in the tradition. Alternatively, the Lakota might point to a contradiction within the Lockean tradition of ownership or to a confusion. For example, Locke's arguments are based on the belief that the earth contains an inexhaustible amount of resources, and he holds that his arguments are legitimate only on that basis. Thus, the Lakota could point to the declining resources of the earth and the fact that there simply is not an infinite amount of land such that "as much and as good" can be left for others when one appropriates land.

This example does not show what Taylor claims might result from such an error-reducing move, namely, that members of one tradition might find another tradition more palatable. Lockeans may conclude that their recognition of the finiteness of the earth and its resources entangles their tradition in such a crisis that it cannot recover. They might then switch to the Lakota tradition, or at least adopt its beliefs on property and landownership. Of course, the Lockeans might switch not to a Lakota tradition but to a different Western tradition of property ownership. In either case, the move is a reasonable move not because of shared standards but because the Lockeans have come to recognize that their standards are problematic in some way.

Caution, however, is advised in applying this form of argument. Consider again the Azande. The contradiction the Azande seem to get into on Evans-Pritchard's account counts as an error for Evans-Pritchard but does not seem to be one for the Azande. Clearly, one wants to be careful in demanding or expecting that members of a tradition abandon their tradition on the basis of a perceived error. Azande have ways of accounting for the apparent contradiction.[44] It may turn out that these accountings involve their tradition in irreconcilable epistemological or moral crises. Yet this decision cannot be made from the outside.

Taylor holds that arguments of this third sort are useful when traditions are too far apart. One might argue that such is the case vis-à-vis the Lakota and the Lockeans. An even better case would be the issue of rights between Aristotelians and liberals or the issue of the notion of God between Attic Greeks and medieval Christians. Both of these cases suggest limits where reasonable discussion ceases. At the same time, they indicate the sort of cases where, according to Taylor, ad hominem arguments of this third form are the only possible way of making reasonable progress or change.

Taylor addresses only easy cases, but suggests that these same arguments apply to more difficult cases of intertraditional comparison. Such radical cases, for Taylor, are "those dividing people of very different cultures."[45] However, the above discussion already shows how those arguments apply to such radical cases because it illustrated those arguments with radical cases: the case between the Aristotelians and utilitarians and the case between the Lockeans and the Lakota. In so doing, I have effectively extended Taylor's argument. Still, even more radical cases might come to mind. Taylor himself focuses on one: Aztec human sacrifice. Taylor uses this radical case to extend the argument from addressing moral disagreement to explaining the possibilities of hermeneutics for intertraditional comparisons.

In short, Taylor does not hold that cases like Aztec human sacrifice (or, one might add, Zande cannibalism) lie beyond the powers of reasonable argumentation. Reason has resources to deal with even such radically disparate traditions. "There is the effect of working out and developing an insight which is marginally present in all cultures."[46] Although Taylor here suggests that some insights are common to all cultures, he fails to give any specifics. One can imagine, however, that one such insight is that innocents should not be tortured. Taylor suggests, further, again without really spelling out or defending the idea, that such common insights arise through a common universal history: our common human history, for instance, has changed human attitudes about human suffering. More specifically, one might add in defense of this suggestion, this change might reflect common, global experiences, for example, the Jewish Holocaust and continuing instances of genocide, which teach all traditions that nationalism can go too far.

The Fusion of Horizons

Taylor holds that some of the practices of different cultures that modern liberalism challenges "often make sense against the background of a certain cosmology, or of semiarticulate beliefs about the way things have to be. These [cosmologies and semiarticulate beliefs] can be successfully challenged and shown to be inadequate."[47] Again, he makes this claim with an eye toward the tradition of Aztec human sacrifice. He claims that although, on the one hand, we have learned to value ordinary human life, on the other hand, we have also critically undermined the cosmology that justified such human sacrifice. Although this example emerges from the past, Taylor suggests that honest people in the contemporary world can engage in intercultural comparisons if they are sufficiently open-minded to understand other cultures and to recognize that their own culture may just be one of many. This claim allows the introduction of hermeneutics.

Hermeneutics brings to a concept of substantive reason resources that ease intertraditional comparisons. In particular, a discussion of hermeneutics allows the incorporation of Hans-Georg Gadamer's idea of a fusion of horizons, in which Taylor and I are greatly interested. Further, hermeneutics provides a vantage point from which to incorporate biology into an account of intertraditional comparisons.

Taylor holds that the aim of understanding should not be one of escaping one's own point of view in order to "get inside" the other.[48] People can, he says, change their understanding of themselves and their tradition, and encountering foreign cultures can be an important source of such change. Meeting foreign cultures allows one to expand one's understanding by introducing new concepts, ideas, ways of life, and so on. Making a claim that holds equally of MacIntyre's account of intercultural understanding, Taylor says we must expand our horizons in order to escape ethnocentrism. Ethnocentrism errs in insisting that cross-cultural theory must be articulated in either their language or ours. Such articulation, however, would result in a dilemma: "Either accept incorrigibility, or be arrogantly ethnocentric. But as a matter of fact, while challenging their language of self-understanding, we may also be challenging ours." Taylor insists that one cannot challenge the one language of self-understanding without also challenging the other.[49]

Taylor holds, then, that one escapes ethnocentrism by recognizing that understanding need not occur in either one language or another, in the terms of either one tradition or another. Taylor also claims that "the aim is fusion of horizons, not escaping horizons. The ultimate result is always tied to someone's point of view,"[50] and the point of view concerned is not one of those that existed before the fusion of horizons. Encountering other traditions changes a tradition. It cannot remain the same if it attempts truly to understand the other, for such understanding requires that it extend its own boundaries of intelligibility to include beliefs, concepts, and perhaps even standards foreign to it as-it-was-but-no-longer-is. The point of view to which the ultimate result is tied is the extended understanding that remains after the extension.

Taylor articulates the idea of such a fusion through the notion of a language of perspicuous contrast, that is, a contrast that is expressed clearly and understood easily. Such a language is one through which the limits of understanding and conceiving are expanded. Expansion means, moreover, that ways of life, conceptions of the good, and standards of reason from rival traditions can be compared. "This would be a language in which we could formulate both their way of life and ours as alternative possibilities in relation to some human constants at work in both. It would be a language in which the possible human variations would be so formulated that both our form of life and theirs could be perspicuously described as alternative such variations."[51] Taylor thus points to human constants that are at work in both traditions. Later I will show that MacIntyre, too, has pointed to such human constants, for instance in "What Is a Human Body?" and *Dependent Rational Animals*.

First, however, this notion of a language of perspicuous contrast pulls Taylor's position away from MacIntyre's. MacIntyre claims that our understanding of others is always in our own terms. He holds that when someone expands the language of his tradition to include notions from another tradition, he does so in such a way that those notions are always understood within the confines of the original. Cicero, for example, had to expand Latin to include certain Greek notions. But those Greek notions were no longer Greek notions, but Greek-Notions-Understood-from-a-Latin-Point-of-View. Taylor, by contrast, seems much more open to the possibility that one can develop a language that is neither theirs nor ours, but instead a new language that is theirs-and-ours. On both accounts, care must be used to avoid the distortion of the other's reason and self-understanding.

"Suppose a group of Christian and Muslim scholars with great effort and ecumenical understanding elaborated a language in which their differences could be undistortively expressed, to the satisfaction of both sides. This would not be an objective, point-of-view-less language of religion. The effort would have to be started all over again if either wanted to reach an understanding with Buddhists, for instance." On this Gadamerian account, Taylor asserts, one could even imagine an omega point "when all times and cultures of humanity would have been able to exchange and come to an undistortive horizon for all of them."[52] Still, such an omega point could only be a contingent universal, for it is possible that a new alien culture will enter the picture.

While the Taylor/Gadamerian view is appealing, it might face certain problems. The issue concerns exactly what is fused in the expansion of horizons and what results from such fusion. Is the fusion of horizons supposed to include everything in the tradition? Does it include the different traditions' standards of reason? Is agreement supposed to result from the fusion? If not agreement, then what? Is the fusion supposed to be concrete or very abstract? These questions must be answered for understanding the possibilities and limits of intertraditional comparison.

Consider two brief examples. Taylor's example above imagines Muslims and Christians fusing their horizons so that they can engage in undistorted debate. Perhaps such a hope lay behind Pope John Paul II's push toward ecumenical dialogue. Yet John Paul II recognized that such dialogue cannot extend to the point where it undermines the church's position that Catholic Christian scripture and tradition provide an adequate account of the relationship between God and the human person. It seems that the Roman Catholic Church cannot extend its horizon to such an extent that it can engage in fruitful dialogue about the status, for instance, of the nature of Jesus (Christ). The debate between the Lakota and Lockeans provides another such example. Whereas Christianity and Islam do not radically differ in terms of concepts (both groups have similar cosmologies, ideas about the nature of God, and the like), the very notion of *wakan* itself seems to inhibit a fusion of horizons between the Lakota and the Lockeans. Is it possible for Lockeans to include within their symbolic generalizations a notion so alien? These questions are, of course, empirical questions, which admit of testing. Perhaps such dialogue can occur, but it does not seem likely to this author.

Taylor could reply at this point that it would not be Lockeans who would need to incorporate the notion of *wakan* in their cosmology. Rather, it would be Lockeans transformed by a debate with Lakota; they are no longer Lockeans but Lakota-Lockes. Whereas Lockeans may not be able to incorporate the notion of *wakan*, Lakota-Lockes easily can. Whereas one can see the possibility of fusion of Muslims and Roman Catholics beginning (it already has), the notion of *wakan* seems to prevent the beginning of a fusion of Lockeans and Lakota.

On the other hand, even if such a fusion could begin, what is this fusion supposed to bring about? In his example, Taylor notes that such a fused horizon allows the differences between the two traditions to be expressed undistorted. If this is all that results, then wherein does reasonable comparison and debate occur? Perhaps comparison can occur, but what about debate?

When one thinks of debate, one must include in the discussion standards of reason. When thinking of rival standards of reason, the possibility of an omega point seems even less plausible. Consider, for example, that the debates recounted in my argument are debates not simply about beliefs but also about standards of reason. While Christians and Muslims share such standards, Lakota and Lockeans have contrary ones. Can they reasonably debate each other in a way that does not preference one result over another? Again, this question is an empirical one. Yet the possibility of such unlimited intercultural comparisons, the expansion of horizons, and the creation of such a broad perspicuous language puts this project in doubt.

The project of a fusion of horizons seems all the more problematic when considering an earlier discussion. In the discussion of cosmology-laden languages, I argued with MacIntyre that contemporary English is a universal language because it allows translation of a multitude of idioms. Yet that very power of translation undermines reasonable comparison because it eviscerates language of standards of reason. Contemporary English has expanded past a final horizon and, thus, made it reason-less. Americans suffer not from a lack but from an overabundance of standards of reason. These standards tend to conflict with each other. Thus the utilitarian standard conflicts with the Kantian one, which itself conflicts with the Hobbesian. Reasonable debate is not possible for Americans as a whole, but only for this or that group of Americans. Reaganite Republicans can debate among themselves reasonably about the nature of the good and the limits of government. Once Obama-style Democrats enter the picture, reasonable debate is thrown out the window, and not simply because of politics. Or, in a more depressing vein, perhaps Protestant Reaganites cannot even debate with Catholic Reaganites, who are committed to a whole-life ethic. Reasonable debate is forfeited because they do not have common standards between them with which to engage in reasonable debate.

The Taylor/Gadamerian account does not seem to recognize such limits. If traditions differ not only in beliefs but also in terms of standards of reason, at some point the fusion of horizon will hit a wall beyond which it cannot expand, because such expansion would involve the incorporation into one horizon of contrary and possibly contradicting standards of reason. Indeed, that the wall can expand to include contradictory beliefs is not clear to me. Still, some middle ground exists between MacIntyre's position, on the one hand, and the Taylor/Gadamer position, on the other. Both positions recognize the possibility of intertraditional comparisons, and both have accounts for how such comparisons might occur. Whereas MacIntyre seems to suggest that no nondistortive intertraditional debate can occur, Taylor seems to think that it is possible. I imagine that in some cases it is possible while in other cases it is not. Whereas different Christian traditions seem capable of nondistortive dialogue, the Lakota and Lockean traditions do not seem capable of it.

| The conclusion to which this chapter has come points to a conundrum. Throughout the second half of this chapter, I have noted a tension within MacIntyre's own theory and also a tension between the theories of MacIntyre, on the one hand, and those of Taylor and Gadamer, on the other, about the possibility for translation and intercultural understanding and comparison. At times MacIntyre seems to argue, as does Taylor, that encountering other cultures requires that we expand our horizons in order to understand them. We change our understanding of the world when encountering foreign traditions by creating a new language from which the positions of both can be nondistortively compared. At other times, however, MacIntyre seems to suggest that when it comes to standards of reason, at least, such expansion is severely limited or impossible.

I am sympathetic to the Gadamerian notion of a fusion of horizons. Examples from the cultural traditions discussed suggest, however, that such a fusion has limits. How can the Lakota, for instance, expand their horizon to such an extent as to consider the earth as a possible object of ownership or, even more, to accept the standards of reason embedded in the Lockean tradition? Further, how could two opposed religions expand their horizons to such an extent that they embrace two contradictory claims: for example, that Jesus Christ is both the Son of God (Christianity) and not the Son of God (Islam)? These differences seem irreconcilable—at least in terms of admitting different standards of reason within a particular tradition. In fact, given that according to MacIntyre rival traditions are always understood from within a particular tradition, it seems we are left with pluralism. Taylor celebrates the possibility of such pluralism. The pluralism is not a relativism, however, because the pluralism is only for those theories that are unable to fuse horizons and engage in rational comparisons.

One might finally want to ask, what should a Feyerabendian relativist[53] make of the arguments of this chapter? MacIntyre's positions moved beyond what Bernstein identifies as the relativism/objectivism dichotomy. That dichotomy belongs to the Cartesian anxiety arising from a fear that a lack of foundations will lead to chaos. One could imagine a Feyerabendian who rejoices in this chaos. Feyerabend wants to claim that relativism signifies not Cartesian anxiety but progress. How such a person would take the arguments of this chapter seems unclear. The arguments presented here would not seem to knock out the relativist claim. If the Feyerabendian admits that there are standards of reason within traditions and that some traditions can be shown to be reasonably superior to others, then I see no disagreement. If the Feyerabendian does not admit this, then I suppose that I would need to engage in ad hominem arguments of the sort defined by Taylor. Such arguments would begin by finding common grounds of communication and reasoning with the relativist. Beyond that vague sort of gesture, I cannot say what would happen or how to convince the relativist, for such convincing must take place on the concrete level.

Conclusion

Toward a Thomistic-Aristotelian Critical Theory of Society

A group of knights sought a fantastic dream—a Camelot where people were free and equal, justice reigned, and humanity controlled its destiny. These knights put their trust in one artifact, a great sword they believed could slay the dragons of oppression, could be used only for just causes, and would let the people of Camelot live free of fear. That sword was called "Reason!" As the story goes, however, the knights wielded a cursed sword. At the same time that it liberated the people of Camelot from their traditional fears, it unleashed new demons to haunt their grand city. Freed, the people of Camelot were enslaved to their freedom; just, the people of Camelot could no longer see what was good; fearless, they created new fears of imaginary forces to control their lives. Camelot's walls crumbled and the sky above clouded over. The knights knew they had to destroy the great, cursed sword, but feared they would be defenseless and as bad off as before, if not worse off.

The knights represent the modern, particularly Enlightenment, thinkers who sought to free humanity from fear of nature and society through the establishment of rational principles of science, art, politics, and morality. The dragon represents, in some variants, the church or tradition, government, or human beings themselves. Yet even as the knights strove to free themselves of these oppressors, they relied on a rationality that proved instrumental, on the one hand, or formal, on the other. In neither case could this subjective rationality enable agents to question and evaluate the good, the standards of reason, or the powers that oppressed them. It left them simply to satisfy nothing but their own desires, desires that reduced to the simple pursuit of self-preservation.

My argument has shown that these knights need not fear powerlessness. I have uncovered a more robust concept of reason, namely, substantive reason. Each tradition has its own conception of substantive reason and conception of the substantive good. The conception of reason in each tradition is constituted by and constitutive of the conception of the good.

Defending the idea that tradition constitutes reason, that, in fact, reason is not universal and neutral between conceptions of the good, I have admittedly written from within a tradition, both to those inside and those outside of that tradition. Tentatively, one might describe the tradition developed in this book as "MacIntyrean." MacIntyre discourages such talk. He sees himself as continuing the Thomistic-Aristotelian tradition. Over his long and storied career, he embraced Christianity and Marxism, rejected both, and then converted to Catholicism because of his commitments to the Thomistic tradition. In the preface to the third edition of *After Virtue,* he writes that his work really has always been a figuring out of the Thomistic position. Thomism, however, does not exhaust MacIntyre's influences, for Marx was and continues to be essential to MacIntyre's commitments, again something he states in the preface to the third edition of *After Virtue.*

I accept that this work, too, takes place within the Thomistic-Aristotelian tradition. I have, however, strained to get MacIntyre's Thomistic-Aristotelian tradition to speak to the Marxist tradition found in Frankfurt School critical theory. As MacIntyre stated at the "Revolutionary Aristotelian" conference at London Metropolitan University in 2007, getting the Thomists and Marxists speaking to each other is vital. My arguments in this book, then, have engaged with the insiders of both those traditions. It has also engaged with those outside the tradition—the positivists, the Davidsonians, and others. In so doing, I admit both the tradition-constitutive nature of the discussion and the possibility for engaging with members of both the Thomistic-Aristotelian and Frankfurt School traditions, and also with theorists outside those traditions. Fundamentally, however, such discussions will always be contextualized by tradition.

The arguments defended here, importantly, raise possibilities for new research.

The concept of substantive reason I developed here seeks to abet a critical theory of society aimed at establishing a just and emancipated society. So far, however, I have focused on developing a concept of substantive reason. The real task for a critical theory of society, however, lies in social critique, which, we now know, occurs from within a tradition. This fact does not obviate the possibility of the critique. In fact, it provides a foundation for reasonable critique, because reasonable critique must ground itself in tradition.

Bernstein notes that "as Nietzsche, Marx, Freud, Weber, the Frankfurt thinkers, and Foucault have taught us, no intellectual orientation that seeks to illuminate concrete praxis in the contemporary world can be judged adequate if it fails to confront questions concerning the character, dynamics, and tactics of power and domination."[1] These questions must be addressed from an orientation that embraces substantive reason. Horkheimer and Adorno, Marcuse and Benjamin, and, following them, Habermas, were concerned with the domination of human beings, with ideology critique, and with commodity fetishism. Horkheimer and Adorno rightly link the domination of human beings with the domination of nature, an important insight that feminist theorists from Genevieve Lloyd (*The Man of Reason*) to Susan Bordo (*The Flight to Objectivity*), from Seyla Benhabib (*Situating the Self*) to Iris Marion Young (*Throwing like a Girl, and Other Essays*), have developed. Further, Horkheimer and Adorno linked the domination of human beings and nature with the renunciation of the self. Habermas and Axel Honneth (*The Struggle for Recognition*) attempt to address this renunciation of self with their theories of intersubjectivity.

If my argument about substantive reason proves correct, however, if we need to marry Frankfurt School critical theory with MacIntyrean Thomistic-Aristotelianism, then we need to reconsider how we approach these issues. We must first reject the differentiation of rationality spheres that characterizes modernity and which Habermas celebrates. What a tradition-constituted reason shows, first and foremost, is that questions of law and morality, of art, and of science cannot be divorced from each other. A tradition's cosmology and fundamental agreements include an understanding of how these various questions, and others, relate to each other and what role they play in human life. Further, on my theory, intersubjectivity finds its full expression in the development of individual identity in community, a community constituted by tradition. Domination of nature goes hand in hand with the domination of humanity exactly because both emerge out of a tradition's understanding of the universe. Further, given the research of feminists concerning "the reason of man," we should discover that substantive reason undermines misogynistic forms of reason. In fact, a formal rationality—science and technology, positive law, deontology—represents the paradigmatic examples of "the reason of man" and misogynistic reason because it denies the broader understanding of reason as evaluative and embedded in tradition. A philosophical anthropology will highlight not only this fact but the dependence of reason on emotion.

We must, moreover, rethink our approach to ideology critique and to commodity fetishism. I have attempted an example of this ideology critique in "Eucharist and Dragon Fighting." We must, moreover, rethink Habermas's claim examined earlier that ideology critique entails that science, morality, and art "be cleansed of all cosmological, theological and cultural dross."[2] If by "dross" he means only those parts of a tradition that prove inimical to human flourishing, then of course he is correct. If, however, he means that we must rid science, morality, and art of cosmological, theological, and cultural belief, he proposes the impossible.

True, ideologies arise when reason or tradition involves a malformed conception of the human person, one that proves inadequate to experience. Yet they can be combated only within a tradition and only with the resources at the disposal of a substantive reason: the very cosmological, theological, and cultural beliefs that constitute the fundamental agreements of that tradition. Or they must be undermined through the ad hominem arguments proposed by Taylor, arguments which themselves arise from such fundamental agreements. Substantive reason empowers the agent to criticize the deformed beliefs about human nature and the good because it is grounded in tradition. Further, it can unmask the work of the principle of self-preservation within these ideologies. It will be the challenge of future critical theory as I envision it to discover how a substantive reason can undermine such ideologies by opening up tradition to internal and external critique.

This conception of ideology critique, then, leads to a second task, tied to the first: to investigate the possibilities for social critique already latent within Thomistic-Aristotelianism. That critical theory must rest in part on a notion of natural law. MacIntyre has written on natural law, but he has not presented a developed theory that one could find in, say, John Finnis's *Natural Law and Natural Rights*. Given the account of substantive reason developed here, I can develop a theory of natural law that will take the critique of society as its foundation. Martin Luther King Jr. passionately demonstrated in his "Letter from Birmingham Jail" that natural law theory provides a reference point from which to criticize contemporary practices of oppression. A fully developed critical theory of society must explain that possibility. James Daly (*Marx: Justice and Dialectic*) has already undertaken the reconciliation of Marxism with natural law theory. Further work will combine Daly's work with the philosophy of substantive reason that I have argued for here. Such work depends, however, on a developed conception of human nature.

A critical theory of society, then, must lay out a conception of human nature that can not only support but give content to that critical theory. Moreover, a theory of natural law rests on a theory of human nature. The primary, immediate task that emerges from the arguments developed here, then, consists in providing an account of substantive human nature grounded in the marriage of Frankfurt School critical theory and MacIntyrean Thomistic-Aristotelianism. Surprisingly, MacIntyre originally rejected the need for any such account of human nature in the first edition of *After Virtue*. He has since recanted that rejection, most recently in the third edition. Moreover, MacIntyre has presented a basic theory of human nature with respect to reason and the virtues in *Dependent Rational Animals*. This account, however, needs to be broadened. A theory of substantive reason lays the foundation for developing such an account, but it rests on an account of human nature. What are human beings such that tradition constitutes human reason?

A philosophy of human nature must be one that can address the challenges raised against any philosophical anthropology by Axel Honneth and Hans Joas (*Social Action and Human Nature*). That challenge includes addressing human needs from a biological standpoint. This critical philosophical anthropology, moreover, must address the ideologies of evolutionary psychology, on the one hand, and social constructivism, on the other hand, in a way that grounds human needs in real human biology that leads to social life. This challenge includes understanding the drive for self-preservation that underwrites all life and how that drive is transformed by the peculiar nature of *homo sapiens* into a principle of human motivation and behavior. On this understanding, a clearer picture of the development of domination in human society can emerge, leading to a better account of how subjective rationality and objective reason balance each other in the substantive reasons of concrete cultural and philosophical traditions. Further, social life proves, as Aristotle notes, natural to human beings. That is, social life is a biological drive of the human person rooted in human needs and human longing. A critical philosophical anthropology will be both Marxist and Thomistic-Aristotelian and will ground any future critical theory of society—including a critical theory of natural law and morality and a critical theory of politics. The successor to this book will give such an account.

Finally, a philosophy of substantive reason finds its final cause in a critical theory of education. Substantive reason entails that people must be embedded within a tradition in order to reason or to be reasonable. Education, therefore, must aim to pass on to and teach children the tradition of which they are a part. It puts the lie, then, to the concept of a universal or public education free of biases. Such an education is either not possible, because no one is free of tradition, or is contradictory, because one cannot be educated to think without being within a tradition.

One might argue, however, that contemporary public schools do not teach children to think. One might argue, furthermore, that schools ought not teach children values, that values should be taught at home. Since teaching children the standards of reason involves teaching them the conception of the good on which it rests, public schools should not teach children to reason.

On the other hand, one might argue that a philosophy of substantive reason does not aid the purpose of education. If schools taught traditions, then children would miss out on learning about other cultures and times. Education in tradition, furthermore, leads to ethnocentrism and prejudicial thinking.

Both of these complaints arise from a misunderstanding of tradition and of the purpose of education. Learning a tradition, as should be evident from this essay, means learning the conception of the good and the standards of reason in a tradition. People learn to think by learning their tradition. Learning begins not with the question of whether to teach tradition but with the question, which tradition of substantive reason do we teach? Or better, what tradition of substantive reason is being taught by those who profess—and perhaps do not even know they teach—a tradition of substantive reason? I highly respect those who have given their lives to teaching the children of the world, but more serious contemplation must be given to what happens in and through the classroom. The educational philosophies of Maria Montessori and Paulo Freire are necessary components of this contemplation.

Further, learning need not be closed off from other traditions, because all traditions share common experiences. A philosophy of tradition suggests that by learning other traditions one enriches one's understanding of one's own tradition. This richer understanding provides moments for critique and reasoning about one's home tradition.

A philosophy of substantive reason, then, supports a philosophy of education geared toward emancipation. Such a philosophy of education has been defended and outlined by Freire, a Brazilian educator exiled for his attempt to educate the poor. Although this is not the place to discuss his pedagogy of the oppressed, its relation to a philosophy of substantive reason should be pointed out. In fact, Freire holds that education begins by learning one's tradition and beliefs. Such learning instigates a raising of consciousness. That is, such learning allows the learner to become aware of her situation and ways to change it. Education, from the perspective of a philosophy of substantive reason, should be geared toward learning one's tradition in order to allow the educated person opportunities for understanding, criticizing, and changing her tradition. Freire, then, anticipates teaching a substantive reason as critical of existent systems of domination.

We see, then, that the development of a theory of substantive reason is the beginning of the development of a critical theory of society in the Thomistic-Aristotelian tradition, one that leans heavily on the Marxist tradition. It shows how substantive reason works within both philosophical traditions and everyday natural traditions. It shines the light in the closet on the scary monster of relativism to reveal only fear. It promises, instead, the development of a theory of human nature within the Thomistic-Aristotelian tradition—a theory open to our modern scientific and social understanding of human beings—and the development of a critical theory of society based on natural law. Finally, it promises a critical theory of education aimed at critical thought, thought that does not simply reproduce the tradition of which one is a member, but engages it. To these further tasks, critical theorists must now turn.

Notes

Introduction

1. Boss, *Ethics for Life*, 133; Gibbs, "Cause Celeb," 28–30.
2. Stolberg, "New Method Equalizes Stem Cell Debate."
3. BBC News website, "Doctors Defiant on Cloning."
4. Mapplethorpe, "Robert Mapplethorpe: Interview with Janet Kardon," 279.
5. Kant, *Perpetual Peace, and Other Essays*.
6. I am arguing about practical rationality, not logic. Though some might argue that logic itself varies between cultures, I do not need to and will not make that claim in this book.
7. Warnock, "Reason," 84.
8. Baier, *The Rational and the Moral Order*, 28.
9. *Oxford English Dictionary*, 211–14.
10. Lewis, *A Latin Dictionary for Schools*, 868–69.
11. Liddell and Scott, *A Greek-English Lexicon*, 1057–59.
12. See Knight, "Revolutionary Aristotelianism," 1998.

1. The Frankfurt School Critique of Reason

1. Schmidt, "Language, Mythology, and Enlightenment," 821.
2. See Gray, *Enlightenment's Wake*, 145–57.
3. See Wiggershaus, *Frankfurt School*, 9.
4. Jay, *Dialectical Imagination*, 256.
5. Cf. Cohen, *Self-Ownership, Freedom, and Equality*.
6. Brunkhorst, "Paradigm-Core and Theory-Dynamics," 71.
7. Ibid., 88.
8. Jay, *The Dialectical Imagination*, 259–60.

9. Wiggershaus, *Frankfurt School,* 334.

10. Kellner, *Critical Theory,* 86.

11. Wiggershaus, *Frankfurt School,* 334–35.

12. Schmidt, "Language, Mythology, and Enlightenment," 821.

13. It should be clear that this critique is the one Hegel makes of Kant, one that is accepted and drawn upon by Horkheimer and Adorno in the *DOE.* It should also be clear that I accept this criticism of Kant, though that is a discussion for a different day. The argument I would make would be similar to the one against Habermas in the following chapter.

14. Importantly, Horkheimer provides a truncated history of moral philosophy in the modern period. He does not discuss the "intellectualist" or natural law tradition that developed during this period from Suárez through Grotius to Kant. This intellectualist tradition contended against rationality with an objective order in the universe. Despite this tradition, I think Horkheimer's analysis proves right. While this tradition did exist, it proved less important and influential than the moralities of the dominant form of subjective rationality.

15. For more on this see my "Eucharist and Dragon Fighting as Resistance."

16. See Wiggershaus, *Frankfurt School,* on this issue.

17. *Eclipse,* 70, quoting from Hook, "The New Failure of Nerve."

2. Habermas's Communicative Rationality

1. Habermas, "Entwinement of Myth and Enlightenment," 106.

2. Ibid., 112.

3. Cooke, *Language and Reason,* 5.

4. Ibid., 3.

5. Ibid., xi–xii.

6. Ibid., 34.

7. Ibid., 41.

8. Ibid., 38.

9. Ibid., 39.

10. Thanks to Chris Zurn for clarifying this confusion.

11. Habermas, *Philosophical Discourse of Modernity,* 115.

12. Taylor, "Language and Society," 30.

13. Ibid.

14. Ibid., 31.

15. Ibid.

16. Ibid., 32.

17. Ibid.

18. Ibid.
19. Habermas, *Postmetaphysical Thinking,* 145–46.
20. Rehg, *Insight and Solidarity,* see esp. chap. 5.
21. Taylor, "Language and Society," 32–33.
22. Ibid.
23. Ibid., Taylor's emphasis.
24. Ibid.
25. Ibid.
26. Habermas, "A Reply," 219.
27. Ibid.
28. Ibid., 220.
29. Ibid.
30. Ibid.

3. MacIntyre's Tradition-Constituted Reason

1. Again, as I shall argue throughout, reason is both constitutive of and constituted by tradition. I will not write that each time, however, and will presume that the reader keeps that in mind.

2. This question was posed to me in a different discussion about the nature of reason by Gerald Twaddell, whom I thank for putting the matter so clearly.

3. I thank an anonymous reader for pointing this out.

4. Locke, *Second Treatise,* 277.

5. Cf. Lakoff and Johnson, *Metaphors,* particularly chap. 24.

6. Evans-Pritchard, *Witchcraft;* cf. Wilson, *Rationality,* and Hollis and Lukes, *Rationality and Relativism.*

7. Kuhn, *Structure,* 181.

8. MacIntyre actually claims that it is only with reference to a neutral rationality that such possibility arises. That aspect of the claim is ignored in the above discussion because he later, in the same work, suggests that what is needed is not a neutral rationality but a tradition sufficiently open to examine multiple conceptions of the good within a particular tradition-constituted reason. See "Relativism, Power, and Philosophy," 406.

4. A Substantive Reason

1. In this book, all discussion of the Lakota in relation to Lockeans or English settlers comes from Hoffman, "Moving beyond Dualism," 447–61, and Holly, "The Persons of Nature," 13–31. Holly's article was particularly helpful

and influential. Further, one should note that the terms "Lockean" and "English Protestant settler" are used interchangeably.

2. Holly, "Persons of Nature," 17.

3. Evans-Pritchard, *Witchcraft*, 67–68.

4. One might want to say "depended" rather than "depends" here given the status of nomadic tribes at the moment. However, two notes will justify my use of the present tense. First, Native American nations are beginning to take up once more a limited nomadism in the West, particularly where Caucasians are abandoning the plains because they are not as amenable to farming as once thought (and as the U.S. government propagandized them to be when it was bent on imperial expansion and the elimination of the Native American). Second, the nomadic life lives on as a dream and in memory. So while it is not actively practiced, it remains alive.

5. Cf. Gilson, *God and Philosophy*; also Sokolowski, *God of Faith and Reason*: "In Greek and Roman religions, and in Greek and Roman Philosophies, god or the gods are appreciated as the most powerful, most independent and self-sufficient, most unchanging beings in the world, but they are accepted within the context of being. Although god or the gods are conceived as the steadiest and most complete beings, the possibility that they could be even though everything that is not divine were not, is not a possibility that occurs to anyone. The being of pagan gods is to be part, though the most important part, of what is; no matter how independent they are, the pagan gods must be with things that are not divine" (12).

6. Holly, "Persons of Nature," 19.

7. Kuhn, *Structure*, 176.

8. Gilson, *God and Philosophy*; Sokolowski, *God of Faith and Reason*.

9. See Nicholas, "Rights, Individualism, Community."

10. I may have an interpretive disagreement here with MacIntyre, who considers Aristotle a continuation of the Platonic tradition. If so, the disagreement is minor.

11. Cf. Aquinas, *Summa contra gentiles*, book 3, chap. 37.

12. Kant, *Critique of Practical Reason*, 110.

13. Kant, *Grounding for the Metaphysics of Morals*, 393.

14. Ibid., 395.

15. Ibid.

16. Hume, *Treatise*, 457, 458.

17. Ibid., 479.

18. Bentham, *Introduction to the Principles of Morals and Legislation*, 18 (ch. 1, §3).

19. Cf. Saran, "Interrelation of Social Organization," 73–84; Evens, "Witchcraft and Selfcraft," 23–47.

20. Saran, "Interrelation of Social Organization," 74.

21. Evans-Pritchard, *Witchcraft*, 130.
22. Saran, "Interrelation of Social Organization," 74.
23. Evans-Pritchard, *Witchcraft*, 388.
24. Ibid., 389.
25. Ibid., 391.
26. Kuhn, *Structure*, 184–87.
27. Bernstein, *Beyond Objectivism and Relativism*, 61.

5. Beyond Relativism

1. See *Why We Fight*, a 2005 documentary.
2. See *Food Inc.*, an excellent documentary on food production in the United States.
3. Alasdair MacIntyre, letter to the author, July 18, 2002.
4. Krausz and Meiland, "Introduction to 'On the Very Idea,'" 62.
5. Davidson, "On The Very Idea of a Conceptual Scheme," 67.
6. Bernstein, *Beyond Relativism and Objectivism*, 75.
7. Krausz and Meiland, "Introduction to 'On the Very Idea,'" 62–63.
8. Davidson, "On the Very Idea of a Conceptual Scheme," 67.
9. Ibid.
10. Ibid., 77–78.
11. Ibid., 78.
12. Ibid., 79.
13. Ibid., 82.
14. Haldane, "MacIntyre's Thomist Revival," 95.
15. Kelly, "MacIntyre's Critique of Utilitarianism," 137.
16. Haldane, "MacIntyre's Thomist Revival," 95; Kelly, "MacIntyre's Critique of Utilitarianism," 137.
17. See MacIntyre, "A Partial Response," 296; MacIntyre, "Incommensurability, Truth, and Conversation," 113–15.
18. MacIntyre, "A Partial Response," 296.
19. Krausz, "Introduction," 6–7.
20. Haldane, "MacIntyre's Thomist Revivial," 95.
21. Davidson, "On the Very Idea of a Conceptual Scheme," 67.
22. Lynch, "Three Models of Conceptual Schemes," 415.
23. Davidson, "On the Very Idea of a Conceptual Scheme," 67.
24. *Wakan* is difficult to explain. It refers to something like Aristotelian soul or St. Thomas's *anima*. The Lakota find all nature imbued with *wakan*. Interestingly, it is not really the European concept of soul, for individual human beings do not have *wakan*. *Wakan* is found in lakes, bears, human beings, but not in individuals. *Wakan* is similar to Iroquois *orenda*. Of that, Holly

writes: "An *orenda* is sacred, not entirely predicable to humans, and mysterious. . . . Each creature or entity is conceived of and experienced as a Thou, in the terminology of Martin Buber." Holly, "The Persons of Nature versus the Power Pyramid," 16.

25. MacIntyre, "A Partial Response," 295.

26. Cf. Lynch, "Three Models of Conceptual Schemes."

27. Rice, "Combating Ethical Relativism," 61.

28. Bernstein, *Beyond Objectivism and Relativism*, 18.

29. Ibid.

30. MacIntyre, "What Is a Human Body?," 147. Thanks to Christopher Lutz for pointing out this passage.

31. MacIntyre, "Moral Relativism, Truth, and Justification," 8.

32. Ibid., 11.

33. Ibid., 19.

34. Ibid., 21.

35. Taylor, "Explanation and Practical Reason," 36.

36. Ibid., 42.

37. Ibid., 53–54.

38. Ibid., 43.

39. Ibid., 47.

40. Ibid., 51.

41. Ibid., 52.

42. Ibid.

43. Ibid.

44. See, for instance, Evens, "Witchcraft and Selfcraft," 32–34.

45. Taylor, "Explanation and Practical Reason," 52.

46. Ibid., 56.

47. Ibid., 56.

48. Taylor, "Comparison, History, and Truth," 148.

49. Taylor, "Understanding and Ethnocentricity," 125.

50. Taylor, "Comparison, History, and Truth," 151.

51. Taylor, "Understanding and Ethnocentricity," 125.

52. Ibid.

53. See Feyerabend, *Against Method* and *Farewell to Reason*.

Conclusion

1. Bernstein, *Beyond Objectivism and Relativism*, 156.

2. Habermas, *Philosophical Discourse of Modernity*, 115.

Bibliography

Apel, Karl-Otto. "Normative Ethics and Strategical Rationality: The Philosophical Problem of a Political Ethics." *Graduate Faculty of Philosophy* 9
(Winter 1982): 81–107.

———. "Normatively Grounding 'Critical Theory' through Recourse to the
Lifeworlds? A Transcendental-Pragmatic Attempt to Think with Habermas against Habermas." In Honneth et al., *Philosophical Interventions*,
125–70.

Aristotle. *The Basic Works of Aristotle.* Edited by Richard McKeon. New York:
Random House, 1941.

———. *Nicomachean Ethics.* Translated by Terrence Irwin. Indianapolis: Hackett, 1985.

———. *Politics.* Translated by Ernest Barker. New York: Oxford University
Press, 1995.

Bacon, Francis. *"Advancement of Learning" and "Novum Organum."* Rev. ed.
Special introduction by James Edward Creighton. New York: P. F. Collier
& Son, 1900.

Baier, Kurt. *The Rational and the Moral Order: The Social Roots of Reason and
Morality.* Chicago: Open Court, 1995.

Baynes, Kenneth, James Bohman, and Thomas McCarthy, eds. *After Philosophy: End or Transformation?* Cambridge, MA: MIT Press, 1987.

BBC News website. "Doctors Defiant on Cloning." March 9, 2001. http://news
.bbc.co.uk/hi/english/sci/tech/newsid_1209000/1209716.stm.

Benhabib, Seyla. *Situating the Self: Gender, Community, and Postmodernism in
Contemporary Ethics.* New York: Routledge, 1992.

Benjamin, Walter. "On the Concept of History." 1940. Translated in 2001 by
Dennis Redmond from *Gesammelten Schriften.* Frankfurt am Main: Suhr-
kamp Verlag, 1974. http://www.efn.org/~dredmond/ThesesonHistory
.html.

Bentham, Jeremy. *An Introduction to the Principles of Morals and Legislation.*
In *The Utilitarians.* Garden City, NY: Dolphin Books, 1961.

Bernstein, Richard. *Beyond Objectivism and Relativism: Science, Hermeneutics, and Praxis.* Oxford: Blackwell, 1983.

Billy Jack. Action/Drama. Written by Tom Laughlin and Dolores Taylor. Directed by Tom Laughlin. Warner Bros., 1971. DVD.

Bordo, Susan. *The Flight to Objectivity: Essays on Cartesianism and Culture.* New York: SUNY Press, 1987.

Borland, Hal. *When the Legends Die.* New York: Bantam Books, 1982.

Boss, Judith. *Ethics for Life: A Text with Reading.* 2nd ed.. Mountain View, CA: Mayfield Publishing, 2001.

Brunkhorst, Hauke, and Peter Krockenberger. "Paradigm-Core and Theory-Dynamics in Critical Social Theory: People and Programs." *Philosophy and Social Criticism* 24, no. 6 (1998): 67–110.

Capitalism: A Love Story. Documentary. Edited and produced by Michael Moore. Overture Films, October 2009. DVD.

Cohen, G. A. *Self-Ownership, Freedom, and Equality.* New York: Cambridge University Press, 1995.

Cooke, Maeve. *Language and Reason: A Study of Habermas's Pragmatics.* Cambridge, MA: MIT Press, 1997.

Creighton, James Edward. Introduction to *Advancement of Learning and Novum Organum,* by Francis Bacon, iii–ix. Rev. ed. New York: P. F. Collier & Son, 1900.

Dallmayr, Fred R. *Critical Encounters: Between Philosophy and Ethics.* Notre Dame, IN: University of Notre Dame Press, 1987.

Daly, James. *Marx: Justice and Dialectic.* London: Greenwich Exchange, 1996.

Davidson, Donald. "On the Very Idea of a Conceptual Scheme." In Krausz and Meiland, *Relativism: Cognitive and Moral,* 66–80.

d'Entrèves, Maurizio Passerin, and Seyla Benhabib, eds. *Habermas and the Unfinished Project of Modernity: Critical Essays on the "Philosophical Discourse of Modernity."* Cambridge, MA: MIT Press, 1997.

Descartes, René. *Descartes Selections.* Edited by Ralph M. Eaton. New York: Charles Scribner's Sons, 1955.

Evans-Pritchard, E. E. *Witchcraft, Oracles, and Magic among the Azande.* Oxford: Clarendon Press, 1958.

Evens, Terrence M. S. "Witchcraft and Selfcraft." *Archives européennes de sociologie* 37, no. 1 (1996): 23–47.

Feyerabend, Paul. *Against Method.* Third edition. New York: Verso, 1993.

———. *Farewell to Reason.* New York: Verso, 1987.

Finnis, John. *Natural Law and Natural Rights.* Oxford: Clarendon Press, 2001.

Food, Inc. Documentary. Robert Kenner. Magnolia Pictures, 2008.

Freire, Paulo. *Pedagogy of the Oppressed.* New rev. 20th anniversary ed. New York: Continuum, 1993.

Gadamer, Hans-Georg. *Reason in the Age of Science.* Translated by Frederick G. Lawrence. Cambridge, MA: MIT Press, 1981.

Gellner, Ernest. *Reason and Culture: The Historic Role of Rationality and Rationalism.* Cambridge, MA: Blackwell, 1994.

Gibbs, Nancy. "Cause Celeb." *Time,* June 17, 1996, 28–30.

Gilson, Étienne. *God and Philosophy.* New Haven: Yale University Press, 1969.

Graham, Gordon. "MacIntyre's Fusion of History and Philosophy." In Horton and Mendus, *After MacIntyre,* 611–76.

Gray, John. *Enlightenment's Wake: Politics and Culture at the Close of the Modern Age.* London: Routledge, 1995.

Habermas, Jürgen. *Between Facts and Norms: Contributions to a Discourse Theory of Law and Democracy.* Translated by William Rehg. Cambridge, MA: MIT Press, 1996.

———. *Communication and the Evolution of Society.* Translated by Thomas McCarthy. New York: Beacon Press, 1979.

———. "The Entwinement of Myth and Enlightenment: Max Horkheimer and Theodor Adorno." In *The Philosophical Discourse of Modernity,* 106–30.

———. "Modernity: An Unfinished Project." In d'Entrèves and Benhabib, *Habermas and the Unfinished Project of Modernity,* 38–58.

———. *The Philosophical Discourse of Modernity: Twelve Lectures.* Translated by Frederick G. Lawrence. Cambridge, MA: MIT Press, 1993.

———. *Postmetaphysical Thinking: Philosophical Essays.* Studies in Contemporary German Social Thought. Translated by William Mark Hohengarten. Cambridge, MA: MIT Press, 1992.

———. "A Reply." In Honneth and Joas, *Communicative Action,* 214–64.

———. *The Theory of Communicative Action.* Vol. 1, *Reason and the Rationalization of Society.* Translated by Thomas McCarthy. Boston: Beacon Press, 1984.

———. *The Theory of Communicative Action.* Vol. 2, *Lifeworld and System: A Critique of Functionalist Reason.* Translated by Thomas McCarthy. Boston: Beacon Press, 1987.

Haldane, John. "MacIntyre's Thomist Revival: What Next?" In Horton and Mendus, *After MacIntyre,* 91–107.

Halton, Eugene. *Bereft of Reason: On the Decline of Social Thought and the Prospects for Its Renewal.* Chicago: The University of Chicago Press, 1995.

Hobbes, Thomas. *Leviathan.* Edited by Richard Tuck. Cambridge: Cambridge University Press, 1991.

Hoffman, Thomas J. "Moving beyond Dualism: A Dialogue with Western European and American Indian Views of Spirituality, Nature and Science." *Social Science Journal* 34, no. 4 (October 1997): 447–61.

Hollis, Martin, and Steven Lukes, eds. *Rationality and Relativism.* Cambridge, MA: MIT Press, 1997.

Holly, Marilyn. "The Persons of Nature versus the Power Pyramid: Locke, Land, and American Indians." *International Studies in Philosophy* 26, no. 1 (1994): 13–31.

Honneth, Axel. *The Struggle for Recognition: The Moral Grammar of Social Conflicts*. Studies in Contemporary German Thought. Translated by Joel Anderson. Cambridge, MA: MIT Press, 1996.

Honneth, Axel, and Hans Joas. *Social Action and Human Nature*. Translated by Raymond Mayer. Cambridge: Cambridge University Press, 1989.

Honneth, Axel, and Hans Joas, eds. *Communicative Action: Essays on Jürgen Habermas' "The Theory of Communicative Action."* Translated by Jeremy Gaines and Doris L. Jones. Cambridge, MA: MIT Press, 1991.

Honneth, Axel, Thomas McCarthy, Claus Offe, and Albrecht Wellmer, eds. *Philosophical Interventions in the Unfinished Project of Enlightenment*. Cambridge, MA: MIT Press, 1992.

Hook, Sidney. "The New Failure of Nerve." *Partisan Review* 10, no. 1 (January–February 1943): 2–57.

Horkheimer, Max. *Eclipse of Reason*. New York: Continuum, 1974.

———. "The Rationalism Debate in Contemporary Philosophy." In *Between Philosophy and Social Science*. Translated by G. Frederick Hunter, Matthew S. Kramer, and John Torpey, 217–64. Cambridge, MA: MIT Press, 1995.

Horkheimer, Max, and Theodor Adorno. *Dialectic of Enlightenment*. Translated by John Cumming. New York: Continuum, 1994.

Horowitz, Asher, and Terry Maley, eds. *The Barbarism of Reason*. Toronto: University of Toronto Press, 1994.

Horton, John, and Susan Mendus, eds. *After MacIntyre: Critical Perspectives on the Work of Alasdair MacIntyre*. Notre Dame, IN: University of Notre Dame Press, 1994.

Hoy, David Couzens, and Thomas McCarthy. *Critical Theory*. Cambridge, MA: Blackwell, 1995.

Hume, David. *A Treatise of Human Nature*. 2nd, rev. ed. New York: Oxford University Press, 1992.

Ingram, David. *Habermas and the Dialectic of Reason*. New Haven: Yale University Press, 1987.

———. *Reason, History and Politics: The Communitarian Grounds of Legitimation in the Modern Age*. Albany, NY: SUNY Press, 1995.

Jay, Martin. *The Dialectical Imagination: A History of the Frankfurt School and the Institute of Social Research, 1923–1950*. Berkeley: University of California Press, 1996.

Johnston, Araminta Stone. "Theory, Rationality, and Relativism." *Tradition and Discovery* 20, no. 3 (1994): 16–28.

Kant, Immanuel. *Critique of Practical Reason*. Translated by Lewis White Beck. 3rd ed. New York: Macmillan, 1993.

———. *"Grounding for the Metaphysics of Morals" and "On a Supposed Right to Lie."* Translated by James W. Ellington. Indianapolis: Hackett, 1981.

———. *Perpetual Peace and Other Essays on Politics, History, and Morals.* Translated by Ted Humphrey. Indianapolis: Hackett, 1983.

Kellner, Douglas. *Critical Theory, Marxism and Modernity.* Baltimore: Johns Hopkins University Press, 1992.

Kelly, Paul. "MacIntyre's Critique of Utilitarianism." In Horton and Mendus, *After MacIntyre,* 127–46.

King, Martin Luther, Jr. "Letter from Birmingham Jail." 1963. http://abacus. bates.edu/admin/offices/dos/mlk/letter.html.

Knight, Kelvin. *Aristotelian Philosophy: Ethics and Politics from Aristotle to MacIntyre.* Cambridge: Polity, 2007.

———. "Revolutionary Aristotelianism." In *Contemporary Political Studies,* vol. 2, edited by I. Hampsher-Monk and J. Stanyer, 885–96. West Sussex, U.K.: Political Studies Association of the United Kingdom, 1996.

Krausz, Michael. "Introduction." In *Relativism: Interpretation and Confrontation,* edited by Michael Krausz, 1–11. Notre Dame, IN: University of Notre Dame Press, 1989.

Krausz, Michael, and Jack W. Meiland. "Introduction to 'On the Very Idea of a Conceptual Scheme.'" In Krausz and Meiland, *Relativism: Cognitive and Moral,* 62–65.

Krausz, Michael, and Jack W. Meiland, eds. *Relativism: Cognitive and Moral.* With introductions. Notre Dame, IN: University of Notre Dame Press, 1982.

Kuhn, Thomas. *The Structure of Scientific Revolutions.* 2nd ed. Foundations of the Unity of Science 1 and 2. Chicago: University of Chicago Press, 1970.

Lakoff, George, and Mark Johnson. *Metaphors We Live By.* Chicago: University of Chicago Press, 1980.

Lewis, Charlton T. *A Latin Dictionary for Schools.* New York: American Book Co., 1916.

Liddell, Henry George, and Robert Scott. *A Greek-English Lexicon.* Revised by Henry Stuart Jones and Roderick McKenzie. Vol. 7. Oxford: Clarendon Press, 1948.

Lloyd, Genevieve. *The Man of Reason: Male and Female in Western Philosophy.* Minneapolis: University of Minnesota Press, 1993.

Locke, John. *The Second Treatise of Government.* In *Political Writings of John Locke,* edited with introduction by David Wootton, 261–387. New York: Mentor Books, 1993.

Lukács, Gyorgy. *History and Class Consciousness.* Cambridge, MA: MIT Press, 1971.

Lukes, Steven. "Some Problems about Rationality." In *Essays in Social Theory,* 194–213. New York: Columbia University Press, 1977.

Lynch, Michael P. "Three Models of Conceptual Schemes." *Inquiry* 40, no. 4 (December 1997): 407–26.

Lyotard, Jean-François. *The Differend: Phrases in Dispute.* Translated by Georges Van Den Abbeele. Minneapolis: University of Minnesota Press, 1988.

———. *The Postmodern Condition: A Report on Knowledge.* Translated by Geoff Bennington and Brian Massumi. Minneapolis: University of Minnesota Press, 1984.

MacIntyre, Alasdair. *After Virtue: A Study in Moral Theory.* 2nd ed. Notre Dame, IN: University of Notre Dame Press, 1984.

———. *Alasdair MacIntyre's Engagement with Marxism: Selected Writings, 1953-1974.* Historical Materialism Book Series. Edited by Paul Blackledge and Neil Davidson. Chicago: Haymarket Books, 2009.

———. *Dependent Rational Animals.* New York: Open Court, 1990.

———. "Epistemological Crises, Dramatic Narrative, and the Philosophy of Science." *The Monist* 60, no. 4 (October 1997): 453-72.

———. "Incommensurability, Truth, and the Conversation between Confucians and Aristotelians about the Virtues." In *Culture and Modernity: East-West Philosophic Perspectives,* edited by Eliot Deutsch, 85-123. Honolulu: University of Hawaii Press, 1991.

———. *Marcuse: An Exposition and a Polemic.* Modern Series Masters. London: Fontana Press, 1970.

———. "Moral Relativism, Truth, and Justification." In *Moral Truth and Moral Tradition: Essays in Honour of Peter Geach and Elizabeth Anscombe,* edited by Luke Gormally, 6-24. Dublin: Four Courts Press, 1994.

———. "A Partial Response to My Critics." In Horton and Mendus, *After MacIntyre,* 283-304.

———. "Relativism, Power, and Philosophy." *Proceedings of the American Philosophical Association* 59, no. 1 (December 1985): 5-22. Reprinted in *After Philosophy: End or Transformation?,* edited by Kenneth Baynes, James Bohman, and Thomas McCarthy, 385-411. Cambridge, MA: MIT Press, 1996.

———. "Reply to Roque." *Philosophy and Phenomenological Research* 51, no. 3 (September 1991): 619-20.

———. *Three Rival Versions of Moral Enquiry: Encyclopedia, Genealogy, and Tradition.* Notre Dame, IN: University of Notre Dame Press, 1990.

———. "What Is a Human Body?" In vol. 1 of *The Tasks of Philosophy: Selected Essays,* 6-104. New York: Cambridge University Press, 2006.

———. *Whose Justice? Which Rationality?* Notre Dame, IN: University of Notre Dame Press, 1988.

Mandelbaum, Maurice. *History, Man, and Reason: A Study in Nineteenth-Century Thought.* Baltimore: Johns Hopkins University Press, 1971.

Mapplethorpe, Robert. "Robert Mapplethorpe: Interview with Janet Kardon." In *Theories and Documents of Contemporary Art: A Sourcebook of Artists'*

Writings, edited by Kristine Stiles and Peter Howard Selz, 274–80. Berkeley: University of California Press, 1996.

Marcuse, Herbert. *Eros and Civilization: A Philosophical Enquiry into Freud.* New York: Routledge, 1987.

———. *One-Dimensional Man: Studies in the Ideology of Advanced Industrial Society.* Boston: Beacon Press, 1991.

———. *Reason and Revolution: Hegel and the Rise of Social Theory.* 2nd ed. Atlantic Highlands, NJ: Humanities Press International, 1995.

Midgley, Mary. *Beast and Man: The Roots of Human Nature.* London: Routledge, 1995.

Moreau, Marc. "Storied Reason: Beyond Hume, Kant, and Williams." *American Catholic Philosophical Quarterly* 69, no. 4 (Autumn 1995): 585–604.

Nicholas, Jeffery L. "Eucharist and Dragon Fighting as Resistance." *Philosophy and Management* 7, no. 1 (2008): 93–106.

———. "Rights, Individualism, Community: Aristotle and the Communitarian-Liberalism Debate." *Review Journal of Political Philosophy* 1, no. 1–2 (2003): 223–49.

Nietzsche, Friedrich Wilhelm. *On the Genealogy of Morals.* In *Basic Writings of Nietzsche.* Translated and edited by Walter Kaufman. New York: Modern Library, 1992.

Oxford English Dictionary: A New English Dictionary on Historical Principles. The Philological Society. vol. 8: Poy–Ry. Oxford: Clarendon Press, 1961.

Plato. *The Republic.* Translated by Benjamin Jowett. Buffalo: Prometheus Books, 1986.

Putnam, Hilary. *Reason, Truth and History.* New York: Cambridge University Press, 1993.

Rehg, William. *Insight and Solidarity: The Discourse Ethics of Jürgen Habermas.* Philosophy, Social Theory, and the Rule of Law. Berkeley: University of California Press, 1997.

Rice, Eugene. "Combating Ethical Relativism: MacIntyre's Use of Coherence and Progress." *American Catholic Philosophical Quarterly* 75, no. 1 (Winter 2001): 61.

Roque, Alicia Juarrero. "Language-Competence and Tradition-Constituted Rationality." *Philosophy and Phenomenological Research* 51, no. 3 (September 1991): 611–18.

Rorty, Richard. *Contingency, Irony, and Solidarity.* Cambridge: Cambridge University Press, 1993.

Saran, A. B. "The Inter-Relation of Social Organization, Ethos, and Ethics among the Azande." *Eastern Anthropologist* 17, no. 2 (May–August 1964): 73–84.

Schmidt, James. "Language, Mythology, and Enlightenment: Historical Notes on Horkheimer and Adorno's *Dialectic of Enlightenment.*" *Social Research* 65, no. 4 (1998): 807–38.

———, ed. *What Is Enlightenment? Eighteenth-Century Answers and Twentieth-Century Questions.* Berkeley: University of California Press, 1996.

Schrag, Calvin O. *The Resources of Rationality: A Response to the Postmodern Challenge.* Indianapolis: Indiana University Press, 1992.

Sokolowski, Robert. *The God of Faith and Reason: Foundations of Christian Theology.* Notre Dame: University of Notre Dame Press, 1982.

Stolberg, Sheryl Gay. "New Method Equalizes Stem Cell Debate." *New York Times,* November 21, 2007.

Taylor, Charles. "Comparison, History, and Truth." In *Philosophical Arguments,* 146–64.

———. "Explanation and Practical Reason." In *Philosophical Arguments,* 34–60.

———. "Language and Society." In Honneth and Joas, *Communicative Action,* 24–35.

———. *Multiculturalism: Examining the Politics of Recognition.* Edited by Amy Gutman, Princeton: Princeton University Press, 1994.

———. "Overcoming Epistemology." In *After Philosophy: End or Transformation?,* edited by Kenneth Baynes, James Bohman, and Thomas McCarthy, 464–88. Cambridge, MA: MIT Press, 1987.

———. *Philosophical Arguments.* Cambridge, MA: Harvard University Press, 1995.

———. "Rationality." In Hollis and Lukes, *Rationality and Relativism,* 87–105.

———. "Understanding and Ethnocentricity." In *Philosophy and the Human Sciences,* 116–33. Vol. 2 of *Philosophical Papers.* Cambridge: Cambridge University Press, 1985.

Thomas Aquinas. *Selected Political Writings.* Edited by A. P. D'Entrèves. Translated by J. G. Dawson. Oxford: Blackwell, 1948.

Toulmin, Stephen. *The Place of Reason in Ethics.* London: Cambridge University Press, 1950.

Turner, Stephen, and Regis A. Factor. *Max Weber and the Dispute over Reason and Value: A Study in Philosophy, Ethics, and Politics.* London: Routledge and Kegan Paul, 1984.

Voltaire. "The Story of a Good Brahmin." In *The Portable Voltaire,* edited by Ben Ray Redman, 436–38. New York: Penguin, 1979.

Warnock, G. J. "Reason." In *Encyclopedia of Philosophy,* edited by Paul Edwards. New York: Macmillan/Free Press, 1967.

Weber, Max. *Max Weber: Essays in Sociology.* Edited by C. Wright Mills. Translated by Hans H. Gerth. Oxford: Oxford University Press, 1958.

White, Stephen, ed. *The Cambridge Companion to Habermas.* New York: Cambridge University Press, 1995.

Why We Fight. Documentary. Written and directed by Eugene Jarecki. Arte, 2005. DVD.

Wiggershaus, Rolf. *The Frankfurt School: Its History, Theories, and Political Significance*. Translated by Michael Robertson. Cambridge, MA: MIT Press, 1994.

Williams, Bernard. *Ethics and the Limits of Philosophy*. Cambridge, MA: Harvard University Press, 1985.

Wilson, Bryan R., ed. *Rationality*. Oxford: Blackwell, 1974.

Winch, Peter. "Nature and Convention." *Proceedings of the Aristotelian Society* 60 (1960): 231–52.

———. "Understanding a Primitive Society." In *Understanding and Social Inquiry*, edited by Fred R. Dallmayr and Thomas McCarthy, 159–88. Notre Dame, IN: University of Notre Dame Press, 1977.

Young, Iris Marion. *Justice and Politics of Difference*. Princeton: Princeton University Press, 1990.

———. *Throwing like a Girl, and Other Essays in Feminist Philosophy and Social Theory*. Bloomington: Indiana University Press, 1990.

Index

Jeffery Nicholas is assistant professor of philosophy and Catholic social thought at Providence College. He is cofounder and executive secretary of the International Society of MacIntyrean Enquiry.